EDUCATION AS ADVENTURE

Lessons from the Second Grade

EDUCATION AS ADVENTURE,

Lessons from the Second Grade

John G. Nicholls, 1940 -
Susan P. Hazzard

Teachers College, Columbia University
New York and London

Published by Teachers College Press, 1234 Amsterdam Avenue
New York, NY 10027

Library of Congress Cataloging-in-Publication Data
Nicholls, John G., 1940–
    Education as adventure : lessons from the second grade / John G.
Nicholls, Susan P. Hazzard.
        p.   cm.
    Includes bibliographical references and index.
    ISBN 0-8077-3240-0 (alk. paper). — ISBN 0-8077-3239-7 (alk. paper:
pbk.)
    1. Education, Elementary—United States—Aims and objectives.
    2. Education, Elementary—United States—Curricula.   3. Motivation
in education.   4. Second grade (Education)—United States.
    I. Hazzard, Susan P.   II. Title.
LA219.N53   1993
372.24'1—dc20   92-36030

ISBN 0-8077-3239-7 (pbk.)
ISBN 0-8077-3240-0

Printed on acid-free paper
Manufactured in the United States of America

99 98 97 96 95 94 93   7 6 5 4 3 2 1

There is, I think, no point in the philosophy of progressive education which is sounder than its emphasis
upon the importance of the participation of the learner
in the formation of the purposes which direct his [or
her] activities in the learning process.

John Dewey

Contents

Preface

Our story began by chance, but it could not have been better designed. I, John Nicholls, was standing in front of a class of undergraduate elementary education majors, wondering whom to chat with before starting class. Karen Smith caught my eye. She wanted to talk about a teacher, Susan Hazzard, in whose second-grade class she was working. Sue was very good at motivating her students to write. Perhaps, Karen suggested, I might invite Sue to talk to this class about motivation.

Though I hadn't gained a sharp picture of the way Sue taught, I invited her. She turned out to be a delight. She supplied rich details as well as a larger vision. The students were obviously grateful, and I tried to make my own gratitude obvious as well.

Though I found the genre of the college textbook on education unsatisfactory, I had been playing with the idea of writing something like a text on motivating students. Sue, however, knew much of what I would want to put in that book and, no doubt, more. The same year, I had conducted a study of teachers' beliefs about student motivation. The results likewise indicated that teachers already knew much of what academic researchers had been trying to tell them. If I had any case for writing something like a text, it was eroding.

At the same time, I was becoming interested in students' conceptions of knowledge and the idea that they should be taken seriously as critics of schooling. Scant attention has been paid to students' beliefs about the nature of knowledge and their analyses of the aims and methods of education. The idea that I might observe in Sue's class for about five months gradually became more attractive. I might learn by watching her in action and by talking with her. I might also learn about students' understandings of the nature and purpose of their schoolwork by observing and interviewing them.

Perhaps the information gained in these interviews would help Sue adapt her teaching and would guide both of us to additional questions and insights.

Teachers have reason to be wary of researchers. As one put it, "Given the opportunity, [teachers] would like to talk about the difficulties that face the children. Yet such conversations rarely happen as a part of the research process because to enter such a conversation is to undermine one's own authority with little hope that the risk will pay off in terms of improved classroom conditions" (Newman, Griffin, & Cole, 1989, p. 145). Another teacher wrote, "I was suspicious of research. It seemed so alien to classrooms and children" (Calkins, 1983, p. 5).

To commit myself to the idea that this would be a collaboration and to make this intent clear to Sue, I proposed that, if our project warranted a book, it should be jointly authored. We had different concerns and competencies, and a collaboration that is unresponsive to such differences is hardly a collaboration. As Sue was not addicted to writing, I would have prime responsibility for that. Sue would see everything I wrote and make whatever suggestions and additions she saw fit. She would, conversely, have responsibility for the class, and I would be able to advise there. Fortunately for me, Sue accepted this wide-open contract.

As time went on, we each made plenty of suggestions. Each affected the story recorded here in ways that were as fruitful as they were impossible to unravel fully. Once the project was under way, we talked about what was happening almost continuously, but kept no track of most of those conversations. This is not primarily the story of the collaboration of Hazzard and Nicholls. On the other hand, we do not try to hide our concerns or our interdependence by presenting the story as if it were being narrated by a fly on the wall. It is our negotiated story of the negotiated development of a class of second-grade students.[1]

Our sense of what we were doing—of how the class might evolve and what might be written—changed as the year proceeded. Because the class and what might be written about it both got steadily more interesting, I stayed all year rather than the five or so months I had anticipated. We start the account with one of many incidents that helped define our evolving purposes—an incident wherein three students unknowingly helped clarify where the class and this story would go.

Our story might seem not to be a real story (it certainly provides no textbookish lessons), but maybe the prevailing sense of story (and of lesson) is ill-fitted to the task of exploring the experience of learning and teaching. Gail Martin (1987), writing of her work with Arapaho students in Wyoming, recounts: "When I asked Pius Moss why Arapaho stories never seem to have an 'ending,' he answered that there is no ending to life, and stories are about Arapaho life, so there is no need for a conclusion" (p. 167). If we have any conclusions, they are but brief resting places in the never-to-be-concluded cultural conversation about what knowledge is worthwhile and what schools are for.

Our sense of whom the emerging book might be for fluctuated. I wanted to learn more about student motivation from Sue and the students and to communicate that knowledge to teachers and researchers. But we both believed that motivation could not be sharply separated from learning, from specific aspects of the curriculum, or from the social life of the school. This feeling strengthened during the year. So we thought of a broader audience, one not focused on motivation alone. Sue had helped many student teachers and hoped to speak to them. I was with her in this as I had found it very difficult to find descriptions of classrooms that gave student teachers a compelling sense of the hard-to-define difficulties as well as the amazing potentials of life on the front line of education. As the year developed, it became clearer that the second-grade students had much to say that might surprise and interest their parents. Perhaps, if we were lucky, we might leaven the public debate on education by providing an antidote for abstract talk about competencies, academic disciplines, test scores, school choice, and competitiveness in education.

One of the livelier second graders, Vicki, said, "When adults are around you have to listen and be good. . . . Nobody listens to children anyhow." In the end, we think the book is for anyone who suspects there might be reason to listen to children.

We are indebted to Karen Smith for suggesting that I invite Sue Hazzard to talk to my undergraduate class.

John Parente helped greatly by encouraging us from the beginning and by maintaining a school where our story could unfold. Teachers and researchers are not often so fortunate. The second graders pay "Mr. Parente" their own tribute in Chapter 6.

We changed the students' names and some of their identifying features. Although we cannot thank them by name, we hope our debt to them is obvious.

For invaluable comments on early versions of this work, we thank Bill Ayers, David Hansen, Ann Lopez Schubert, and Theresa Thorkildsen. By suggesting the right book or article at the right time, friends can open new vistas in familiar territory. For timely suggestions, we thank Eleanor Binstock, Paul Cobb, Vicki Hare, Peter H. Johnston, Alfie Kohn, Ron Nelson, Michael O'Loughlin, Christine Pappas, and Bill Schubert.

The events described took place when I was at Purdue University, and most of the writing was done at the University of Illinois at Chicago. Thanks to all concerned at these institutions for words and deeds that helped keep the project moving.

PART I

Where Are We Going?

CHAPTER 1

Possible Rebels, Possible Causes

[September 20] School has been in session for a month. Yong Kim, Carlos, and Paul are sitting at a round table at the back of their second-grade classroom alphabetizing columns of words on worksheets. Sue is working with a reading group at the front of the class. The three boys are quiet and industrious. As Carlos finishes the first column, he stops and sits up, looking proudly at his accomplishment.

"I'm on 2!" He looks across and is stunned to see Yong Kim working on the third and last column. "Whew! Look where Yong Kim is."

Paul, who has done slightly less than Carlos, looks up and is also startled. He tries to distract Yong Kim.

"Yong Kim! Look!" He points behind Yong Kim, who turns, sees nothing, and looks perplexed. Carlos's eyes glint. As Yong Kim returns to his assignment, Paul varies his strategy.

"Look! Look! A spider." Paul again points behind Yong Kim and giggles as his trick takes effect. He repeats it until he is ignored. Then Carlos joins in.

"Yong Kim! Yong Kim! Look at the spider over there. Look! Look!" He and Paul laugh together as Yong Kim is again confused and distracted. When Yong Kim goes back to his paper, Paul improvises further.

"Yong Kim! Look! Your mother. There's your mother." Yong Kim's mother came into the class a few days earlier—an unusual event. Eyes popping, Yong Kim looks for his mother in the doorway. Carlos is delighted with Paul's ingenuity. Carlos and Paul's glee reaches its zenith. When their trick no longer succeeds, the evildoers horse about, giggling together. Yong Kim finally ignores them. Head down, he finishes the assignment, then returns to his regular seat.

With a delinquent gleam in their eyes, Carlos and Paul continue entertaining each other. They create a moment of collaborative adventure. Schoolwork is almost completely forgotten. Solid plodding is replaced with almost manic excitement. Occasionally they return to the worksheet, but each time they are overcome with lassitude. Carlos momentarily bats a wad of paper around the table with his pencil; then they are back to talking and giggling.

Tall, slim Wole, invariably industrious, quick to finish his school-work, and often absorbed in reading, comes by. He is outraged.

"Hey! You guys are just playing. I'm going to tell." He doesn't tell and, for Paul and Carlos, his observation seems to confirm that their mission is to "play."

Joan brings her assignment over. She sits down as if to work, but talks about where she lives, where Paul lives, and when she has seen him after school.

"Did you see me and Alice play outside last night?" She poses flirtatiously as she assails the two with questions and information. They are awkward in the face of her assurance and sophistication. Losing interest, she notices how little work they have done and stands up haughtily. "I'm higher than all you guys. I'm on [the more advanced reader] *Towers.*" Tossing her head, she struts away.

Carlos and Paul are labeled deviant by one of their classmates and incompetent by another, but they create a moment of common purpose. The task they abandoned was solitary, cut and dried. It allowed no possibility of adventure and made obvious their poor standing compared to Yong Kim. They created an activity involving ingenuity, initiative, humor, and social solidarity. It united them in the attempt to slow Yong Kim down, but it also became a quest for excitement.

This second-grade initiative also excites me, and I move close to observe them and scribble down their words. Sue notices my inter-est and, though she could easily have stopped the little insurrection, allows it to take its course. This incident helps crystallize one of the themes of this classroom and this book: the challenge of enlisting in the service of education the initiative, humor, and collaborative verve of Carlos and Paul's little rebellion.

Can schooling become a collaborative quest for excitement and meaning? When the imagination is captured, people will undertake arduous preparations and risk all in strenuous but exciting journeys. In the land of the free and the home of the brave, is it too much to hope that students might be encouraged to seize more of the initia-tive for reaping and renewing the cultural riches of this world? Might schooling become an adventure, with attendant risks and difficulties, wherein the participants negotiate the nature, direction, and details of the ongoing journey?

*   *   *

Ironically, among the most compelling accounts of robust inge-nuity and vigor in schools are descriptions of students who are opposed to their school's ethos: individuals who reject the title "stu-dent." Consider Paul Willis's (1977) description of a group of British high school boys who call themselves "the lads." Their lives in school are devoted to outwitting their teachers and schooling themselves in delinquency. They spell out their scorn for those who would learn the lessons teachers try to teach with the epithet "ear 'ole." To be a diligent student is, for the lads, to be a passive ear hole absorbing irrelevant information. These rebels are no mere name-callers. They embody the camaraderie and élan of the romantic stories of Allied officers escaping from Nazi prisoner-of-war camps. After capturing one of these lads in a drunken escapade, his principal wrote to the boy's parents, "He seemed bent on justifying his behavior and went as far as describing the school as being like Colditz"—one of the more fabled of the World War II prisoner-of-war camps where British officers were interned (p. 21).

Even if their teachers try to be humane, these lads resist. Their constantly evolving adventures and insurrections give substance to their claim that the educational ideal they reject is a pale and wizened thing. They might have hard times, but they are comradely adven-turers, swashbuckling entrepreneurs, creators of freedom and excite-ment in a world of passive, dull conformity.

Looking back at high school, Joey, one of these rebellious lads, says, "I thought we were the artists of the school, because of the things we did; I thought we definitely had our own sort of art form, the things we used to get up to. And we were definitely the leaders of the school . . . and placed amongst . . . if we were all separated and placed amongst groups of the ear 'oles we could have been leaders in our own right. . . . something should have been done with us, I mean there was so much talent there that it was all fucking wasted" (Willis, 1977, p. 195).[1]

They will not know it, but these rebels have distinguished intel-lectual company. Both popular and less easily accessible books echo their claim that schools waste the ingenuity, initiative, and collabo-rative spirit of students. In such accounts, school is rarely an intellectual adventure. If it is difficult, it will not present a meaningful challenge. If it seems important, it will seem more solemn than serious. If it is a struggle, it will be a struggle to keep plodding on the assigned path—not a struggle to make sense of life's complexities. It will be an exercise in endurance, waiting, and remembering—not a journey of discovery or an artistic production.[2]

✳   ✳   ✳

Carlos and Paul are not articulate about the reasons for their fledgling insurrection, but one is tempted to see it as starting with their recognition of their relative incompetence. Antischool ideologies cannot all be explained this way, however.

Among the lads Paul Willis describes are some of obvious ingenuity who had been "successful" students before their change of heart. Joey, who bemoaned the waste of his and his friends' talents, was described by his principal as "a young man of intelligence and ability who could have done well at most subjects, but decided that he did not want to work . . . his qualities of leadership were misplaced." Of Joey's collaborator, Spansky, this principal wrote that in the first three years he had been "a most cooperative and active member of school. He took part in the school council, school play and school choir in this period and represented the school at cricket, football and cross-country events. Unfortunately, this good start did not last" (Willis, 1977, p. 62).

In Sue's class, Joan is clearly above the class average in academic performance, and her haughty claim of superiority over Carlos and Paul reveals her desire to stay on top. Yet she surely has potential to rebel. In first grade, she was at odds with her teacher and hated school. She overcomes her apprehension of the second grade in the first week, but, during the second and third weeks of school, she often combs her long hair or shuffles the contents of her desk while everyone else is attending to the topic of the moment. Joan does these things in a way that is as close to challenging Sue's authority as she can come without open defiance. From the beginning, she wants Sue's approval and is eager to help with chores. Nevertheless, she also acts as if she were the only one with an inalienable right to speak. She demands her right to an audience, but rarely accords Sue or her classmates the attention she expects from them.

When Joan sets her jaw and attacks someone she believes has wronged her, she is a sword tempered in the fire of divine justice. Her fists and words are strong and fast. Parents and teachers may subdue her, but her will is not to be captured easily. During a class discussion of families, she asks, "Why do I try to think of ways to annoy my mother? I do! I lie in bed thinking how to drive her crazy." It is easy to believe that her mother might be near to insanity. Early in the year, Joan's slim body has a tense, assertive bearing. She is a bossy snob, but she is more. Her tight stance says she is tough and ready to defend her rights in a hostile world—ready to lead a rebellion or struggle alone for freedom and fairness.

Peter soon reveals his ability to complete assignments rapidly and accurately. He is equally exceptional in his disposition to challenge authority and to initiate exploits that interfere with his and others' progress in schoolwork. In the first week he extracts from Yong Kim Korean swear words. He teases others with them. He darts across the room to pass a note with one written on it. As much as anyone, he is likely to make it hard for Sue to continue with lessons, and to distract and annoy those sitting beside him.

His sheer intellectual energy makes him a potential threat to the typical classroom order. So too does his determination that life should make sense. Sue begins each day with the pledge of allegiance. This ritual is led by the children. One holds the flag. Another asks the class to stand and, when all are quiet, leads the recitation of the pledge. Two more stand on the flanks as color guards. These are just some of the roles Sue creates to give everyone some responsibility each day. The children accept this brief ritual and most enjoy it. It marks the beginning of each day and helps accustom the shyer ones to confronting the whole class.

One day as the little ceremony begins, Peter's hand shoots up. "Why do we have to have a color guard?" This is no request for information. He sweeps his hand passionately from the direction of the door to the tableau at the front. "No one's going to burst into the room and take the flag. We don't need that." Like Joan, he can become outraged if adults dictate practices that do not make sense to him.

In their own ways, Carlos, Paul, Joan, and Peter are poised to provide dramatic stories of student disaffection and rebellion. Each might become the student who teachers wish could be transferred to another room. Can the energy, critical consciousness, and sense of fairness of these small people and their peers be engaged in education? Might we create classrooms where social solidarity and moral responsibility coexist with intellectual excitement and adventure?

The second graders do not appear as authors of this volume, but Sue told them my purpose at the beginning of the year, and we sought to take seriously any lessons they might teach. Psychologists who study student motivation have paid scant attention to students' critiques of schooling or to their views about the meaningfulness of what is taught in school and the fairness of the practices they live with. Other researchers call for the voices of teachers to be heard among those of researchers and planners. Few, however, contemplate students as collaborators in the formation of the means and ends of education. The recent cries for reform in education have been dominated by the voices of people closeted far from the worlds of second-grade teachers and students. Yet, if we want initiative, imagination, and excitement in education, is not the classroom the place to start?

Whether or not we acknowledge it, students are curriculum theorists and critics of schooling. If they are drawn into the conversation about the purposes and practices of education, we may all learn useful lessons. Children can change our priorities and shape our stories in unexpected and interesting ways. Education can become an adventure in which teachers, researchers, and children together learn new questions as well as answers, so that their lessons are never complete.

CHAPTER 2

Early Days

When the school year begins, the themes of conversation, adventure, and students as collaborators in curriculum construction are not as obvious to us as they will become. Before seeing the other's work in detail, neither of us is sure we can even work together. Anything from boredom to incompatibility is possible. A year later, Sue reflected:

> I had taught for twenty years and felt I had been successful. I had been able to foster the motivation of my young students. I was accustomed to succeeding with talks to professors' classes, and John seemed impressed when I spoke to his students. I was flattered by his invitation to start this new project, but also a bit confused. I couldn't fathom what I could offer. After all, he had been doing research for about as long as I had been teaching. He was an expert on theories of education and motivation. He had studied the work of other experts and spoken with them at conferences. I had been attending university classes for years but was still "just" an elementary school teacher. I was uncertain what use could I be to a researcher.
>
> I had sought diverse courses on teaching, but not on ways of doing research. The occasional research projects assigned in courses did little for me. Research, as my courses seemed to suggest it should be conducted, was not something I was eager to become committed to. This project might be a little different, but it was hard to be sure.
>
> As the new year approached and the fact that this project was actually going to happen sank in, I gradually became more apprehensive. Normally I ignore rumors about the students in my incoming classes. Now I was bothered by clues that some students might prove difficult enough to disrupt progress. What

if I had given John a false impression? After all, we had only met when I spoke to his classes and when he proposed the project. Now he was going to be observing me for months. What had I agreed to? Would I measure up? This was serious. Had I been foolish?

Even if I had not been there, Sue would have faced uncertainty on the first day of school. Each student is a unique puzzle, a life evolving in unknown directions. Before the year begins, scraps of these puzzles appear, one in the form of a memo from Sue's principal.

"I had a conference with Mr. Norton with regard to [his son] Dan's classroom behavior last year. He is most concerned that Dan operate with structure and discipline. At home they have him on a strict program that relegates him to isolation if he misbehaves. Dan . . . worked with counselors or psychologists and worked in group settings on getting along with others. He has improved some. . . . Dan does like attention, be it good or bad. . . . Using a positive approach, I believe that we can help him to have a good year." A possible rebel?

The principal also receives a letter and phone calls from Jodie's mother, who expresses doubts about Sue's competence and reliability and wants her daughter placed in another class. He relates the information to Sue but does not take it as valid. Sue ruminates about the possible source of the mother's unease. In each case, however, her information is inadequate for specific planning.

The term begins on the afternoon of Monday, August 22. When Sue reaches the top of the stairs to the second floor, with me following, a small group of children and adults is waiting outside the shut but unlocked classroom door. Sue distributes smiles, "hellos," and "welcomes" and sweeps everyone in. A grandmother hangs back as her granddaughter, son, and daughter-in-law enter with the others. Sue gathers her in. Looking anxiously at her grandchild, who we will learn is called Vicki, the woman clearly feels out of place.

Most of Sue's energy goes to greeting children and recognizing something unique about each of them. "How are you? I like that shirt. Get your name tag from the desk at the front. You can choose any desk you like—any desk that isn't being used." This message is also printed at the front of the room above a collection of name tags.

"Hi, sweetie. So you're Joan. Before you got here, I tried to guess what face went with your name, and now I know. Do you know any of the other girls?"

"Yes."

Joan's mother hovers in the background. Apprehension shows in child and parent. Later Sue will learn how stressful first grade was for Joan. Now others press for attention.

A father asks if the ruler he has purchased for his daughter will do—it is not the type they were asked to purchase. Sue puts a pencil through the hole in the ruler and spins it like a helicopter blade. "The reason we don't like holes," she grins, "is that children do this all day." From the beginning she gives reasons for school practices. Students and parents alike receive this treatment.

A child, looking lost, stands by the door. Sue, a juggler poised to field balls as they materialize in the air, is beside him quickly.

"Is this the second grade?" he manages to wheeze. His expression says the second grade is a bullet with his name on it. The reality of five second-grade classrooms is as remote as the far side of the moon. Second graders stand little above an adult's belt. Sue bends toward the small human.

"What's your name, honey?"

He mutters incomprehensibly. English is almost as foreign as the location of his class. Sue leads him to her desk and gets him to write his name. This he can do. From among the parents and second graders, one of Sue's former students, relaxed and confident, now in the third grade, appears to say hello.

"George! How good to see you. Come here. You can be a big help. Will you take Ramon and look for his name on the lists outside the other second-grade classes so he gets to his room?"

When they have chosen their desks, children unpack their equipment and put it in order. This new material must be lined up. Tim, slight, pale, with dark hair, has a large packet of pencils.

"Look how many I've got," he says to his neighbor. He takes them to Sue.

"Do you want to sharpen some?" She steers him to the sharpener and, barely taking a breath, greets a new arrival with a diffidently hovering mother.

"Honey bun! Who's your teacher this year?" The honey bun peers up, uncertain about how solemn the occasion should be, and points at Sue, who erupts with a big laughing self-depreciating "Ohh!" and engulfs the girl in a hug. The mother slips out, smiling back at Sue and a more relaxed daughter.

Tim is unable to control the pencil sharpener. Sue takes over, but the lead breaks. "Oh, this pencil sharpener wants to eat it up. Do you think it is the machine or the person who is going wrong?"

"The machine."

"I don't know, sometimes this person doesn't do such a good job." This is the first instance of a pervasive theme: The teacher isn't always right or competent, no one has to be perfect, there's no need to panic if things don't always work. The mundane task of sharpening pencils is an occasion for defining the nature of life in this class.

New children keep drifting in. "Hi, sweetie. Get a name tag and look and see where you'd like to sit."

Three girls want help with putting their names on their new rulers. Sue asks them to spell their names and marks the rulers.

George reappears proudly to report completion of his mission of finding Ramon's classroom. He leaves with Sue's thanks.

Children who aren't arranging things in their desks sit and look around at the room. Their names are all above the blackboard at the front. They scan the pictures and messages (including "Welcome to second grade") on the walls. Most have used safety pins to pin name tags to their clothes. Vicki, whose parents and grandmother brought her to the room, stands up at her desk at the front, holding her name tag with its pin and looking uncertainly at the other students. She seems to be trying to discover what she is supposed to do with her tag. So far, she has talked to no other students.

Calm descends when everyone finds a seat. They wait expectantly. Sue comments, "All the rumors I heard about good students are true. Look at how you're sitting ready to work. I'm excited about this class already. I think we are going to have a good year. Your first-grade teachers told me what fine students you are. Well, we need to see who we are and what buses we all go on. We need to make sure the right people wait for the right bus. OK, anyone know Christie?" She checks her list. "Wait a minute, I'm not as organized as I thought. I need to check the list [of names] outside the door." Again, the teacher can be less than perfect. The children sit quietly. Some point out things on the walls to others. "Thank you for waiting," says Sue as she returns. This is no trivial gesture of politeness. Partly intended to encourage orderliness, the words also carry an easy but substantial respect for the small students.

"Jill, what bus are you on?"

"F."

"Good. That's what my records show." The teacher is not simply exercising power. There is a list, and the list itself is up for scrutiny—the two sources of information need to agree. How much of this children read from this specific comment, we cannot tell. If they miss it this time, the theme will keep coming up. Things need to make sense to everyone. Anyone might have relevant information. People will check their information against that of others.

"Paul Guarez—how do you say it? Did I get it right?"

"No."

"So what is it?" He pronounces it. "OK, that's good. Now what is your bus?"

"C."

"You remember well," and so on until everyone is identified and the pronunciation of their names is cleared up.

"Well, now." Sue moves to the front of the room. "What is second grade all about?"

"Learning."

"Learning what?"

"Cursive writing."

"Yes."

"Math."

"Yes. Is there anything you learn in the second grade you didn't learn in first grade? Anything you haven't learned you want to learn?"

"Cursive writing."

"Spelling."

"Why spelling?"

"'Cause people will not know what words you wrote if you can't spell."

"Times."

"Division."

"Right. We'll get on to that too. Why are you here at school?"

"To learn."

"Why?"

"You don't know any words if you don't. You don't even know anyone's name."

"'Cause when you grow up you won't know anything."

"What do you need to know when you grow up?"

"How to drive a car. You need to read to learn it."

"Do chores. Work with my dad in his shop."

"Mathematics."

"What about mathematics?"

"You should learn some."

"Why?"

"So you'll know a lot of numbers—up to 1,000."

"Well, I think you are all right. You are here at school to learn some things you don't know."

If their words and expressions mean anything, the children are here to learn. They are not here to drive the teacher crazy. At least one child noted the significance of spelling for communication. Much of what they will learn and hope to learn involves acquiring the skills that will help them join the conversation that is adult society. Cursive writing seems to symbolize participation in this conversation. Mathematics seems harder for them to justify explicitly. This is hardly surprising. Mathematics teachers are often inarticulate about the purpose of their discipline. But the subject is certainly on the list. If words count—and now (a few moments after the beginning of the year) they seem to—then teacher and students have a common purpose.

"But what is my job?" asks Sue. "What should I do about this?"

"Teach."

"Give advice."

"Help us."

"Right! And to teach you new things, I have to find out what you know. How can I do that?"

"Ask us things."

"Ask us to write papers."

"Is there anything wrong with not knowing something?"

"No!"

"If you know everything, I don't have a job."

"No one knows everything."

"Yes. When I'm spelling, I often need to look in the dictionary."

"No one knows all the words there are."

The message keeps coming: You don't have to be perfect. This is about learning, not about being perfect. And the students themselves are helping construct the message.

Evelyn sounds a different note. "My parents want me to get all A's." This is no surprise to Sue. It is part of the reason for this discussion and for her emphasis on learning rather than grades and tests. We will come to see Evelyn's comment as revealing her slightly cowed desire to please adults, a desire that is not matched by a belief that their demands will make sense.

"Now there's another thing about the second grade. We are going to become a family. You will be able to count on everyone to be your friend. Look at all the different faces. Every one of you is special. And every one of you can be friends to each other. Look at this poster. What does it say?"

"'If you want a friend, be a friend.'"

"What does it mean?"

"Be nice to people and they'll like you and be your friend."

"What happens when someone doesn't want to be your friend?"

"You can find another one."

"Find something to do by yourself."

"If someone doesn't want to be your friend, should you cry?"
"No!"

Unpredictably, the conversation moves to people who yell at you. This too is made relevant to the developing ethos of the class.

"Why do they do that?"

"They think a thing is your fault."

"What can you do?"

"They forget it in the night."

"When my parents have a problem, they yell at me," says Joan.

"It's good your mind knows they're not really mad at you, and it's something else upsetting them. Sometimes your mother and father yell at you because they're afraid that you'll get hurt if you don't listen to them."

"They still love you."

"Yes," says Sue coming back to her topic. "And what would you do if your teacher yelled at you and it wasn't your fault? What would you do?"

"I could say it wasn't me."

"Good. So, if I make a mistake you tell me." There is no doubt who is in front of the class. There is only one teacher here. But the messages keep coming. Respect and consideration is the order of the day. The teacher can be corrected. Things can be negotiated. The rules are not arbitrary.

"There shouldn't be any yelling anyhow. I won't yell at you. I don't like that, and I know that with you sitting and listening and thinking like you are, there won't be any yelling. I think we will be a real family and help each other learn."

A trip to the music room for half an hour intervenes. On the way back, Sue stops the class as they rumble up the stairwell. She waits quietly and confidently for them to calm down and explains softly, "The sound in here where the stairs are gets extra loud. It echoes in here so we have to remember to be extra quiet on the stairs. Everyone get ready to keep going quietly like you are now. Let's go."

Such little incidents are standard for the beginning of the year. Potentially disruptive actions are checked quickly—well before there is any real disorder. They are treated as occasions for calmly explaining or re-explaining the reason for the approved practice rather than as insurrections that must be put down.

When the class is back in the room, they are asked to get out scissors and glue in preparation for a form of bingo, using paper squares they will cut out and on which they will write the initials of class members. A few children spin their scissors on the desk tops.

"Let me tell you about our desks, everyone. We have brand-new desks. Our class and Mrs. Stone's are the only ones that have these desks. See how nice and smooth the tops are. That's really nice for writing on. What happens if we spin things like scissors on them?"

"They get scratched."

"When you put paper on your desk and write, what happens if it has scratches?"

"It's hard to do good work."

"That's true. So let's be careful and not scratch with scissors or anything else." Again the children understand and contribute to the justification of classroom practice.

As Sue proceeds, a hand waves.

"We need pencils."

"Right. Get out your pencils. I'm glad I have you around. You can't write with your nose." Another chance to send casually the message that students' ideas make sense. Most children get busy writing and cutting. Some finish before others have made much progress.

"Yong Kim. Do you want help?" He doesn't acknowledge his obvious need—he has not begun. "Who will help Yong Kim and Paul?" Hands go up. George is selected to help Yong Kim. He simply takes over while Yong Kim watches. Jack helps Paul by cutting squares. Paul pastes these while Jack quizzes him.

"Are you right- or left-handed? Which hand do you use?" He gets no answer.

As they work, Jack, Dan, and Paul discover a common interest in the Chicago Cubs baseball team.

"They've been winning."

"Especially with André Dawson."

"He's been whacking it out of the ballpark." They exchange information with an authoritative air—men of the world discussing men's games. Others who have finished wait or talk quietly.

I ask Jill if she is glad to be back in school after the holidays. Her "no" is immediate and from the soul. I ask why not, but she is passive. When asked what she thought about on the way to school, she again gives no answer. She looks beyond anxiety, very tired, and close to depression. Dark rings show under her eyes. Her blond hair and fair skin seem very faintly dirty.

James's expression as he sits next to her, listening, fluctuates from a wide, easy, toothy smile to relaxed thoughtfulness. His red hair shines and his freckles are sharp on his translucent skin. He is almost delicate, like fine porcelain. His clothes are clean and pressed. Did he want to come to school?

"Yes, and I went to the barber to get a haircut. And my sister started kindergarten. She got up at 6 o'clock and got dressed to come to school. She really wanted to come. I didn't get dressed that soon." He chatters easily about the details of coming to school. James and Jill give but a hint of the individual differences that will soon become more obvious.

When a student's name is called in the bingo game, that person stands and says his or her name and something they like to do. Among the boys, soccer is the overwhelmingly favorite choice. They soon give substance to their declarations. On the next day and in subsequent months, soccer is the game most choose at recess.

Alan likes helping his father make things.

"I like baseball and once I hit a grand slam," Jack announces solemnly. "Another time we were hitting, and I hit it over the corner of a two-story house. That's how good I am." He is the only one who explicitly refers to his competence. He will return to the topic many times.

The girls have a more diverse range of interests: swimming, swinging, reading, playing hide-and-seek, baseball, and hugging the teacher.

From time to time, Sue asks for quiet, each time explaining why. "Girls, this isn't going to work if you talk while I do." And "Listen now, everyone. If you listen carefully, you'll find some friends who like to do the same things as you do."

The practice of raising hands for permission to speak is also explained. "If we are both talking, people won't hear either of us very well, so put your hand up if you want to talk."

When the game is finished, Sue says, "Boys and girls, I'm very proud of your behavior. The game took a long time and you had to wait at times, but you did well." The activity was not as effective as Sue had hoped. She will modify or drop it next year. Nevertheless, it served to let children introduce themselves and to introduce some work without threatening anyone's sense of competence.

School is ending for the first day. Procedures for hanging up bags, finding buses, and buying lunches are checked.

Tim wants to know, "What if we lose our lunch money?"

"I know where the lunch menus are," offers Jack and explains in detail.

"What do we do with our name tags?" asks Paul.

"I'm glad you asked," says Sue.

"When do we have gym?"

"Oh, Evelyn! I wish my brain worked as fast as yours. You need to know when to bring your gym gear, don't you."

As the children leave, Sue relaxes and the strain of the first afternoon shows. First impressions in teaching are important. If the first few days go poorly, it is hard to recover. Much of the strain comes from trying to understand the 20 small strangers suddenly thrown together with her. Sue cannot establish an ethos of mutual respect or a commitment to collaborative learning if she does not herself listen and convey respect. This means quickly discerning diverse hopes, fears, and quirks of temperament. All the criminals, misfits, and maniacs as well as the saints of the nation pass through second-grade classes. Sue must discover what she faces. She does not want fear, but she must establish some ground rules. These must make sense to the children, so Sue must hear their voices without permitting a Babel.

Human communication is ever fraught with ambiguity. When the children leave, the strain of giving and receiving clear messages shows. It is too early to say how things will turn out, but so far, so good.[1]

Things are shaping up for the adults in the room, too. Sue recalls:

> In the first session, I am completely absorbed: observing students, making everyone comfortable. Only when I sense the students are relaxing do I notice John at the back of the room, scribbling furiously. "Oh, no! Is this what he needs for the research?" His face tells me nothing, so I press ahead. When the children leave, I feel I must critique my work and justify it. But he compliments me. He details what he liked and asks for information. He really sees me as the expert! What a delightful change. But I am exhausted and still uncertain.

At this point I wish I could be a fly on the wall so as to let Sue get under way without having to worry about me. But even before the first school bell rang my hopes were raised. Sue's treatment of Tim when he had trouble with the pencil sharpener was intriguing because it was relevant to attribution theory, an influential research perspective on student motivation that focuses on teachers' and students' interpretations of events (Weiner, 1979). I realize that I have never seen or heard any researcher (whether inclined to or against attribution theory) suggest that teachers might, by attributing incompetence to themselves, allay anxiety about incompetence. So my hope that this might be a place where I can learn is quickly strengthened.

＊   ＊   ＊

[August 23] James and I are the first to arrive in the classroom on day 2. James talks easily about playing soccer, which he declared as an interest the previous day. Joan arrives next and, with no preamble, solemnly announces to James, "I'm starting on *Moonbeams*." This is a graded reader. These books have not been touched yet, nor will they be until two weeks from now, when Sue will feel she has assessed the level of each student. But snobbish Joan already has her mind on the question of reading competence, symbolized by the levels of the readers.

"You don't know, you might skip," responds James.

"Last year, Christine skipped *Bears*, but not any other people skipped."

"Albert skipped books, I know. He was the smartest kid in our class last year."

Other children come in and hang up their bags in the closets that were pointed out at the end of the previous day—one for girls and one for boys. Yong Kim is uncertain about which closet to choose. He looks very slowly from one to the other three times and moves tentatively toward the girls' closet. He stops and looks at me. I point at the other one. Silently he changes course.

As soon as Sue appears, children clamor to show her things, tell her things, and ask questions. Away from her desk, the theme of social comparison comes up again. Jack, who yesterday announced his prowess at baseball, makes an inventory of the many small possessions in his desk.

"I bet you don't have one of these," he says to Dan, showing an animal-shaped eraser.

"Yes, I do."

"One of these?" Another eraser.

"No."

"You probably don't have one of these." Yet another eraser.

"Yes, I do."

This parade of objects goes on with short silences for four minutes.

"Do you know what this [pencil sharpener] is?"

"Yes."

"Do you have one exactly like this?"

"No."

"Do you have a ruler like this?"

"I have one but it's not exactly the same."

Jack keeps initiating these comparisons. Dan answers without reciprocating Jack's egotism. At most, toward the end, he reveals a hint of boredom with the barrage.

After the brief announcements over the intercom signal the beginning of the school day, Sue asks, "I need some help. Would someone take this [attendance list] to the office for me? Dan, your hand went up fast."

The boy who has been in the charge of psychological experts, whose parents have him on "a strict program that relegates him to isolation if he misbehaves," has his hand up before the others have digested Sue's question. Remembering the note Dan's father sent the principal, Sue is pleased to give him this small responsibility. He bustles off, brisk and happy, with no hint that he ever was or might become a problem.

As Sue moves to the front of the class, Tim raises his hand. "Will we do some work today?" More than most, Tim wants to tell the teacher (and later me) his concerns. He is serious and emotional, and his wide, dark eyes and pale face convey a sensitivity and complexity of emotions that overwhelm his vocabulary. His expression now says he wants work. Perhaps he feels that yesterday there wasn't much real work. Does he retain the first grader's expectation that he should suddenly acquire new skills on the first day of school? Sue soon learns that his parents make it very clear to him that he must work hard and "do well" in school. In any event, Sue reassures him that work will be done.

Wole, sitting by Tim, his friend from the first grade, has an urgent message. "Yesterday, I forgot to say that I like to read as well as play soccer." As the weeks go on, he distinguishes himself by spending any spare time reading. If these two are any guide, the children went home thinking about what happened on day 1 and expecting their thoughts and afterthoughts to be taken seriously. Their expectation continues to prove justified.

Sue recalls yesterday's discussion of the purposes of school. Learning, writing cursive, reading, and math come up again. Sue's job is recalled—helping, teaching, giving advice. Then:

"For us to work and learn, what do we need to do?"

"Have a clean room?"

"Yes. What else can we do to make it easy for us to learn?"

"If you don't know something, start with something easy and work up to harder things." Joan offers this tentatively.

"Now that's a good idea," says Sue. Joan visibly begins to relax. After today, "tentative" is never the word to describe her.

"Turn on the fan."

"Yes. We have to be comfortable." It is 87 ° F and humid, and there is no air conditioning in the school.

"Keep the room quiet."

"Some people work better when it is quiet. How many of you are like that?" Hands go up.

"You don't listen to your mind when someone else is talking," says Joan.

"Yes. That can happen," says Sue. "What can we do if someone makes it noisy?"

"Ask them to be quiet."

"What if they don't listen and keep making noise?"

"Punish them."

"What's a good punishment?" Sue asks.

"Stand in the corner for a whole day."

"A whole day? Is that what you did in kindergarten?"

"No."

"Put their name on the board."

"Make them miss recess."

Young children freely suggest draconian treatment of evildoers. If acted on, their own proposals would leave them disturbed. They do not always know "what is good for them," and Sue has no intention of handing punishment over to them. But neither will she impose her way without consulting them.

"What's a way to make someone remember that their behavior upset the class?"

"Keep them away from recess."

"Talk to them."

"That's a good idea. Everyone is coming up with good ideas."

"Make them work hard."

"Is that going to make them be good in the classroom?"

"Put their names on the board."

"That's if someone is loud. What if someone is dangerous? What things are dangerous?"

"Fooling with scissors."

"Yes. How about tipping chairs?"

Children contribute stories about people who hurt their heads. Evelyn tells how she chewed a pencil and cut her mouth on the metal.

Joan gives a long, halting digression on the dangers of eating paper. Her desire to talk is stronger than the coherence of her message. Elizabeth tells of someone who ate paper and got sick. Each story is acknowledged, but eventually Sue ends the discussion.

"Let's get back to school things. Tomorrow, if I put up a name on the board, it's probably because you might hurt someone or stop us learning. Is that fair?"

"Yes."

"Sometimes I might make a mistake. You will tell me if I do something that's not fair, won't you?" There are murmurs of agreement.

Someone raises the sin of copying. What is copying in one class might be helping in another. Here is another opportunity to define the meaning of life in the classroom.

"Usually people copy if they are worried they can't do their work or aren't good at it. It doesn't matter to me who is best. What matters is that you are learning things. If you can't get your work done, we'll talk about it. I'll want to know if it's because you were not working or because it was too hard. Maybe I gave you too much work. You can talk to me if I do that. Don't sit and worry—come and tell me. We're here to learn, not to worry."

"Our first-grade teacher threw all our papers away 'cause no one got one right," says Jodie.

"That's right. I might make a mistake and give you things that are too hard and some that are too easy. I'll keep trying to find the right work for you."

"If it's very hard, don't give up," says Joan.

"It's best to get your work done right than to get it done fast," says Vicki.

"This girl in our class [last year] got D's and F's in her work, and she got upset and threw her work away. . . ."

"Well, if I do my job, no one will get D's and F's."

"Maybe the teacher didn't know the girl couldn't do it because the student didn't tell her."

"That's right. And another thing—if you find a friend who is good at something, you can ask the friend to help—if it doesn't stop other people from learning. Our job is to be friends and to help each other learn."

*   *   *

On day 3, responsibilities are assigned. Students' input is again requested and again they are all pillars of the emerging community.

"We could do more learning if you could help me do my job. Would you do that?"

"Yes." "Yes." Hands wave. Suggestions abound.

"How could you help?"

"Keep the calendar."

"Pass out books."

"Erase the board."

"When you come in, get to work right away."

"Put chairs down when you come in."

"Pick up trash."

"Help other kids."

"Push chairs in under the desks if someone forgets."

There is no shortage of suggestions. Sue explains that she has written the names of these jobs and some other ones on small disks. Included are the roles of color guard, pledge-leader, calendar-keeper, and roll-taker. A lottery ensues, with Sue picking jobs out of a bowl. These are to be reassigned weekly. At first, as responsibilities come up they are sometimes forgotten. But there is enthusiasm for them. Students often spontaneously adopt others' overlooked assignments. When the person assigned to push chairs in as the class leaves the room forgets, Joan or someone else invariably rushes around pushing them in.

When quiet, serious Claire begins her duty of handing out papers, the increasingly assertive Joan bids to take charge.

"I'll be your friend all day long, and you can play with my toys, if you let me pass the papers out." But Claire does not waver from her duty. Children sometimes forget their roles, but, like Claire, they see them as privileges, freely accepted obligations. The class begins to fall into routines for dealing with everyday necessities. The children look more relaxed, as if they belong here, are part of whatever is evolving.

It is easy to overlook the complexity of the task of teaching young children. I regularly give elementary education students accounts to read of different styles of teaching. One is of a teacher who simply tells students what she wants done, dictates to them what they have to know, and expects them to understand and set about it. This teacher's students learn poorly and are unmotivated and often unhappy. Yet there are always a few students who, though they do not like the atmosphere in that class, aspire to teach in essentially the same way and expect their students to thrive. They presume that if they kindly and firmly tell their students what to do, their students will love them, be motivated, and learn well.[2] Would they appreciate the subtlety and complexity of what Sue does, the extent to which her actions derive from the children's particular concerns and competencies as she works to establish agreement that this is a place where everyone wants to learn and where everyone has something to offer, where we all listen to one another in negotiation of priorities and strategies?

"The teacher's authority ... must be won and maintained on moral, not coercive grounds. There must be consent from the taught" (Willis, 1977, p. 65).[3] Rousseau (1762/1911) proposed that the teacher "let [the child] always think he is master while you are really master. There is no subjection so complete as that which preserves the forms of freedom; it is thus that the will itself is taken captive. ... No doubt he ought only to do what he wants, but he ought to want to do nothing but what you want him to" (p. 84). Even if they want such control, teachers lack the omniscience, omnipresence, and omnipotence to achieve it. They must find, foster, or conjure up in students needs that they can arrange to satisfy. They must make or discover some contract, implicit or explicit, that students see as fair or at least better than the apparent options.

Sue's children arrive expecting to learn. If school is to be seen as fair, this expectation must be fulfilled. But there are many things to learn and many ways to learn them, and mandated testing must somehow fit into the agenda. Some children arrive hoping to learn more than their peers and get "all A's." Others fear being revealed as stupid. The future of this class is waiting to be constituted out of the hopes and fears of the students and their parents, out of the possibilities and constraints of assigned texts, library books, collective visions of what children might become, and state and local requirements. A community of adventurous scholars will not spring spontaneously from this soil.

PART II

A Course Amid Shoals

CHAPTER 3

Concerns About Competence

[**August 24**] On morning 3, Sue reads a short story about families. Initially, there is some inattention. Sue quietly gathers in strays well before anything approaching disorder develops. "Girls, I feel you aren't listening and that makes me sad." The discussion soon has students offering all manner of information about families. This leads to drawing and writing.

"What I want you to do is to tell something special about your family. I'd like you to tell me these things in two ways. Tell me with pictures and with words. This way I can find out about you and your families when I have more time."

"Claire, you are the supply monitor. These are big pieces of paper." Sue implies it's OK if Claire has trouble handing them out, and that if she can do it, that will be impressive.

Sue demonstrates how she wants children to write their names on the paper, then introduces a task for those who finish early, "to see if you can follow directions without help. That's except for Paul, Carlos, and Yong Kim, because they are learning English. People may help them." She demonstrates the spelling of "family" on the board and, to avert anxiety, says, "Other words don't matter. You write them the way they sound to you. I want to see the story, not the spelling."

As they start, Sue takes a small group aside for diagnostic reading. To them she repeats one of the themes of day 2. "If you can't get it, don't worry—try. I need to know what you know so I can help you and give you work that will be right for you."

One of the artists sings as she works.

"That's a beautiful voice, but we don't need it right now. That's a bit much noise."

I sit beside Jodie to observe her progress. As time passes she reveals a view of life as a rich, ironic soap opera. Now she points (with her sharp, delicate, ironic flair) to a surplus man, with beard and glasses, in her family group and says, "That's you."[1]

Sue finishes with the small group and walks around the room. "That's great." "I like your picture." "Very pretty writing." "Oh, you are going to be a writer, George. You say things very well." For Vicki, who was very uncertain on day 1, "I didn't notice the back of your shirt—turn around again. Wow, you should have had that the day we did art." Vicki warms a little. Sue is working at making everyone feel recognized and adequate.

This is not easily accomplished. The competence of these large drawings is more public than that of most schoolwork. Paul does a somewhat unusual but expressive and relatively competent drawing of a man. He erases it and forlornly goes to tell Sue he can't draw. She encourages him to try again. James, pleased to be back at school and generally smiling, is acutely embarrassed by his stick-figure drawings, which are less sophisticated than most.

Two days later, Sue says, "I read your stories last night and looked at the pictures. I thought they were interesting. In fact, they were so interesting I thought we should share them. Who would like to go first?" Tim is the first eager volunteer. He has trouble reading his story about a trip with his family to Niagara Falls. He goes over to Sue, who helps him translate his script and quizzes him gently.

"Did you like Niagara Falls? . . . How many people in your family?"

"My family is weird and my little sister is very weird," announces Peter when he takes his turn. A lively, mischievous grin reveals delight in weirdness.

"Why is she weird?"

"She goes around making weird noises." He demonstrates. "The neighbors say, 'What is she doing?' She's trying to get attention. She's trying to show off."

Others volunteer to share and, when necessary, Sue helps and encourages. When the supply of volunteers dries up, 8 of the 20 children have not participated.

"Paul?" asks Sue. He shakes his head.

"May I read it?" asks Sue. He shakes his head again. "I'm glad you did [your picture] again," she says. "You should be proud of it."

Jodie had, on her own initiative, talked to me about her picture, but she too declines the public display.

Yong Kim nods "OK" when Sue asks if she can show his picture. He has not been in the United States long and is hesitant with English. His drawing shows a large Old Glory waving over a cluster of diminutive figures. He answers Sue's questions about this tableau by shaking or nodding his head. Sue cannot find a way to discern the significance of the flag—one of the multitude of details that must be passed by.

Tired-looking Jill agrees to bring her work up for Sue to read. She stands coyly as Sue comments. "This is a paper to be proud of . . . I can see you gave it a lot of thought . . . It has not just people but a lot of background." Jill returns contented to her seat.

James doesn't want his stick people displayed. Sue discusses how she used to draw stick figures and slowly figured out how to put clothes and flesh on them. Elizabeth opts out. Finally George lets Sue discuss his.

Those who volunteer to display their work include some like Peter, who is robustly confident of his competence. He is more able than most at reading, writing, and speaking. He seems to know this and relishes telling his story to the class. Tim is also falling over himself to communicate his experience, but he is no Peter. He is relatively incompetent at reading and writing. For now, however, the question of his competence does not occur to him. He is not put off by the fact that he needs Sue's help to tell his story while some others do not. He is preoccupied with his narration and gives no thought to his standing in the hierarchy of competence. More than most, he has the childlike absorption in the work of discovering and communicating that evokes, in adults, romantic notions about early childhood. Several times later this year he will face hard times, become self-conscious, and lose confidence. Sue will seek to prevent this, but when that is not wholly possible, the classroom ethos will help him to name and face his concerns.

Concerns about competence are more evident during this session than they have been since day 1. Why will children go to Sue to express dissatisfaction with their work, but not want the work displayed to their classmates? Are they more ready to trust a teacher not to denigrate them? Is it harder to reveal one's competencies in front of a sizable audience?

Perhaps the answer does not matter. What is clear is that peers are respected, even feared, as evaluators of competence. If Sue's task were merely to persuade each individual that she would not denigrate them if they fell behind the others, it would already be accomplished. She has to do more—she has to create a community committed to learning from and with others. Encouragement to speak and to perform in front of the group will continue. If peers are seen as a source of ideas and constructive suggestions, incompetence will no longer be a threat, and Sue's reassurances will be superfluous.

*   *   *

Beginning and even experienced teachers are commonly more concerned about maintaining control in the class than about any other aspect of teaching. This is as understandable as a fear of falling among mountain climbers. Even if one can survive the experience, a loss of discipline is, like a fall on a mountain, harrowing enough to cast a long shadow. One cannot teach—or climb mountains—with verve while thinking of disaster. A route worth climbing demands full attention. Yet teachers can become more preoccupied with averting chaos and maintaining order than with the adventure of human development.

Sue does not expect to fall, but her strategy for forging ahead assumes that many of her children will be looking down, fearing serious injury. Her mission is to allay these fears, to help the children come to terms with the fact that everyone can't be above average, and, above all, to help keep them looking up, focused on the tasks ahead, discussing where they are going instead of their standing in the class, the state, or the nation. This is not primarily a matter of raising self-esteem, of making them confident, though there is some of that. Rather, Sue is encouraging cooperation, so that superior ability means an opportunity to help others rather than an opportunity to gloat. She is fostering the desire to know what makes sense and to find ways to make sense. These qualities are not to be confused with confidence that one is abler than others at cut-and-dried tasks.

*   *   *

In some accounts of classroom life, concerns about competence play no significant role. Other writers see much student and teacher energy bound up in attempts to manage displays of competence and avoid displays of incompetence.[2] In this class, children's concerns about competence were evident from day 1.

By second grade most children construe their competence in terms of their rank among their peers. This understanding, the concerns of parents, school tests, graded readers, and the many opportunities for comparison of competencies that formal schooling allows mean that children can become preoccupied with their competence.

Standing in the hierarchy of competence can become the basis of a class pecking order—the organizing framework for social relations on the playground as well as in the class.[3]

Concerns about standing come up early in Room 7, especially in the context of reading groups. It is possible to teach without reading groups, but they are nearly ubiquitous in American classrooms and, for children, they provide an obvious index of competence. Before Sue could make a move, children were (like Joan and James on day 2) assessing their standing.

* * *

[September 5] Arriving at school in the third week, the day before reading groups are formed, Jack announces to Dan, "I'm in *Towers* [the most advanced reader, which will identify the most advanced reading group], I bet you a million bucks."

Next day, the most advanced reading group assembles with Sue for the first time. As Jack predicted, he is included. Dan, who is not, had no expectation of being there. He knew last year that he had been diagnosed as needing "special" help.

As Sue begins with this group, one of them announces, "We are the best!"

"I don't think it means that," says Sue. "It just means you are going up and up in your work." Discouraging egotism without diminishing the egotists is a perennial challenge.

[September 26] Jodie asks me to help her with a workbook exercise. Her neighbor Vera watches, so I suggest, "Maybe Vera can help you figure these out."

"Oh, she's in *Moonbeams* [a lower reading group]," says Jodie, dismissing the idea.

"But that doesn't mean she can't figure things out, does it?" Vera edges her seat closer and helps by sounding out a word. Jodie accepts Vera's intermittent participation.

As his (most advanced) reading group forms, Peter declares, "I can't wait to finish this book."

Later, I ask why he wants to finish.

"So I can get to the next one."

"What will you do then?"

"I'll finish reading."

"Why's that good?"

"When I go to college, I won't have to read these books. Like Yong Kim [who is one of the slowest readers], when he's in junior high school, he'll only be on *Towers* [which Peter is now read-ing]."

Peter is always ready to voice his dislikes, but does not complain about the reading group. Nevertheless, getting done with books and being ahead of others is one of his preoccupations. He is bright enough to have his way in this. Wole is equally competent at read-ing but almost never makes such comparisons. Wole invariably has a book he is reading; Peter rarely does. More than reading, being at the top is Peter's desire.

[October 10] When his reading group has finished working with Sue, Peter, as he walks to the back of the room, stops to tell Yong Kim, "We're going to be on another reader soon—on another whole book." Peter regards Yong Kim as a friend though not an equal—perhaps a strange creature, capable of teaching him interesting tricks like origami. In a half hour, when both have finished their assign-ments, Peter has his arm around Yong Kim's shoulder as they sit on the carpet looking at a book.

Reading groups provide an obvious basis for judging competence relative to others. Assignments and tests where everyone starts together on the same work and where there is but one acceptable answer to each question also make comparison easy. Carlos soon learns that he compares unfavorably.

[September 26] During a spelling pretest, Carlos makes an attempt at each word when Sue calls it. He writes the first one, two, or three letters of each word and then usually stalls. Next he looks over at Jill's paper and copies what she has written. He sits at the back of the room, facing the side wall, looking away from Sue. As it happens, he has the best place in the room for cheating. He does it well, avoiding head movements that would make his mission obvi-ous. He looks across at Jill's paper only when the others at his table are busy. He monitors Sue's position as she moves back and forth.

[September 28] To fill out a worksheet requiring identification of the numbers of syllables in words, Carlos copies from George on his right. George completes his paper and takes it up before Carlos has finished. Carlos then copies from Alan, who sits on his left. On a second sheet, involving alphabetization, he apparently feels confi-dent. He works accurately and as quickly as most others, without a glance at his neighbors' work.

[October 2] Sitting beside George and across from Jill during a spelling test, Carlos no longer attempts to spell any of the words himself. He does not even begin the first letter or two of each word. He waits for one of the others to finish each word, then copies it. When George inadvertently moves to block his view, Carlos turns to Jill's paper.

[October 10] The desks have been relocated, and Carlos sits at the back, between Jack and Wole, facing the front of the room. The new arrangement requires a modified technique. A student teacher, less vigilant than Sue, stands at the front, administering the weekly spelling pretest. Carlos leans his head on his left hand, shading his eyes as he copies from Wole on his right. He waits for Wole to write each answer. This means he occasionally is one of those who put their hands up to signal that they are not ready for the next word. He does this without giving a hint of why he needs extra time. At the end, the students check one another's work. Unaware that he is scoring a transcript of his own work, Wole records a perfect score for Carlos.

When they go on to selecting the 10 words they want to learn for their next assignment, these two horse around. Wole attends intermittently to spelling and makes several unsuccessful attempts to get Carlos to follow suit.

Turning around, Carlos presents me, sitting close behind him (where I have been throughout the session), with a dilemma by holding up his test paper and saying, "Look what I did."

"Yes, I saw how you did it" drops out of my mouth.

"How?"

"Well, we both know. You know how you did it."

"With my brain?"

"Sort of. Your brain and your eyes." I try to stick to the facts without conveying an accusation.

Carlos turns back, does a little work, then talks and giggles with Wole. This is an occasion for Sue to suggest quietly to the student teacher that he be moved away from Wole. By now he has written two spelling words, and Wole has done nine. I decide that after class I, the fly already off the wall and deep in the soup, must tell Sue about Carlos's skill at concealing his lack of skill.

Carlos took extreme measures, but he was not the only one concerned about ability during this session. After students had checked one another's pretests, Paul turned around to Jack, sitting on Carlos's left.

"I just got three wrong."

"I got none wrong. I never get anything wrong," says the invincible Jack, setting his solid jaw firmly.

"Even your shoes? Don't you ever get your shoes wrong?"

"I wouldn't do that. I'm too smart. I'm too intelligent."

Paul has an artist's sensibility but generally keeps his face impassive. He turns back to his desk looking more puzzled than hurt. Carlos, engaged with Wole, who was wondering what it would be like being as small as a mouse, does not hear this.

Jack, however, is no unidimensional egotist. During this test he quietly helped and encouraged his other neighbor, Yong Kim. He sounded out some words in a whisper without actually spelling them. He sounded out the end of a word that Yong Kim had started. Occasionally he was more directive: "Hill has two *l*'s." Yong Kim does not score as well as Carlos, but he probably learned more. Normally highly moralistic about maintaining classroom procedures, Jack presumably thinks he is helping Yong Kim learn rather than helping him cheat—a distinction that is not always clear to second graders.[4]

[October 17] As Sue begins administering a spelling pretest, she reminds the class, "It's OK on the pretest if you don't know how to spell it." The message is stated generally, but intended for Carlos. Sue repeats it as the session proceeds. Carlos, now sitting facing Sue near the front of the class, begins to take a furtive peek at Elizabeth's work. But this is the alcoholic's farewell to liquor—he opts to do his own work. He often has to raise his hand to ask Sue to wait while he finishes a word. Slowly he sounds them out, showing every sign of giving his best effort. Sue's message must have reached him. He manages 5 correct answers out of 10, which is low, but not the lowest in the class. A week ago he got all 10 correct but made no attempt to sound any out. Neither of us sees him try to cheat again.

[January 18] "I didn't get any wrong," Joan announces loudly after a spelling test.

Sue immediately asks the class, "How many did as well as they thought they would? How many got more than they expected? OK. That's the important thing, isn't it? Are you learning what you can?"

This sort of "course correction" is routine in the attempt to keep the children focused on doing their best and making sense.[5]

❋   ❋   ❋

After appearing happy for the first two weeks of school, Tim is anxious and slightly depressed. He forlornly follows Evelyn around the room. She complains to Sue, "Where I go, Tim goes."

"Maybe he thinks you know something," suggests Sue. "Or maybe he likes you."

Tim goes back to his seat, but a minute later approaches Sue. "I'm allergic to the flag." Old Glory hangs about 12 feet from Tim's desk. Sue is puzzled, but suggests that Tim might prefer working at the back of the room. Is he feeling foreign in the country where he has lived but a year?

Peter is amused, confused, and fascinated. "Tim is allergic to the flag?" He repeats this, shaking his head and looking over to Tim's new location. He quickly finishes his work and goes to interrogate Tim.

"Why would you be allergic to a flag? If you are allergic to a flag you'd be allergic to your clothes." Peter repeats his question, crouching down to look up into Tim's downturned, unresponsive face. Eventually Tim strikes back.

"I'm allergic to you." This puzzles Peter. Tim then distracts Peter and ends the interaction by pointing to the plant behind Peter. "There's a spiderweb." Peter goes to inspect this and leaves Tim alone.

I wait a moment and ask, "How are you feeling today, Tim?"

"I'm tired."

"Why's that?"

"I had not enough sleep 'cause of all my homework." He sighs heavily. "It's hard being a second grader."

His usual seat is between Peter and Wole, who are both considerably abler, faster workers on most assignments. They are much more men of the world than the childlike, sensitive, poetic Tim. Peter at times upsets Tim with his almost manic energy. In a few days, Sue moves Peter to a new seat.

*   *   *

[September 9] Evelyn has been out of the class for special tutoring. When she returns she says to Sue, "I'm scared I won't get my [math] work done." She looks thoroughly unhappy.

"Well, since you were [out of the class] with Mrs. Gustafson, let's say you don't have to do these ones." Sue indicates a block of the work. Evelyn is clearly relieved.

Later, when she has almost finished, I ask how her work is going. She points at the work she has been excused from and says emphatically and scornfully, "I don't intend to finish that." She has time to work on some of it, but will not respond to my question about this prospect.

"Are you worried about this work?" I ask.

"You are worried," she parries.

"Do I worry?"

"All the time."

"What do I worry about?"

"That I'm going to keep your pencil," which she grabs. She is a volatile combination of insecurity and manipulativeness and would rather avoid the whole business of schoolwork. She does not want the embarrassment of failing to keep up with others, but she finds no intrinsic value in the work. If she can find an excuse, she will not do it.

*   *   *

Where some children see exciting puzzles, others see only the prospect of being left behind.

[October 2] "I'm going to present a puzzle for you to think about," says Sue. "Everyone get out your crayons [to use for counting]. I'm going to put a numeral on the board and I want you to select that number of crayons." The number 14 goes up on the board. "This number represents a sum—the sum of two numbers. I'm going to put up a list of numbers, and you decide which two added together will give me this [14]." She writes; 3, 6, 4, 8, 9. "Let's see. Will 3 and 4 give us 14?"

"No." "No."

Other combinations are considered. Most children figure out the answer quickly. A similar problem is presented and solved using 17 and the sequence 8, 9, 3. When 8 + 9 is suggested as an answer, Sue asks, "How did you figure it out?"

"You say 9 + 7 = 16, and 9 + 8 is 1 more."

"Are there any other ways?" There is much enthusiasm to offer other ways: "You use the trick of the 9's—9 + 9 = 18 and 9 + 8 is 1 less."

"8 + 3 and 9 + 3 are both too small [so it must be 9 + 8]."

"Good thinking. You all had different ways of figuring it out." What could be a cut-and-dried task with one standard method to be memorized becomes, with a little encouragement, an occasion for invention and diverse approaches.

"Here's a slightly different sort of puzzle: 9, 0, 8, 1, and . . . Can we find two of these numbers that add up to give one of the others? What can we put here to show that? Does 9 + 8 = 1 work?"

"No! No!" They figure out 8 + 1 = 9 and go on to 11, 3, 13, 8.

Alan comes up to the board and writes: 11 + 3 = 13.

"What is 10 + 3?" Sue asks.

"14," he says, then realizes he is wrong. Alan returns to his seat puzzled but unabashed. No one has made a derogatory sound, and he remains engrossed in the problem. This is what Sue aims for: the orientation that makes opportunities out of mistakes. At the back of the room Alan sits peering at the board, still puzzled. In the middle of someone else's eager attempt he bounces up on his seat, waving his arm. "Oh! Oh! I see! I see!"

When the students start work on two pages of similar problems, they all appear busy and involved. Walking around, Sue observes their progress. "Look at these whiz kids! They're just like computers solving these problems." Most are merrily moving along, finishing this assignment, and going on to others. Most work alone. A few discuss the problems briefly.

Martha is mousy and nervous, without Evelyn's leavening of assertiveness. She is often beset with difficulties. She cannot get enough sleep and is occasionally distressed by her life at home. She cannot keep possession of a toothbrush. After Sue buys one for her to keep at school, her first act on arriving each day is to clean her teeth, which seems to increase her sense of well-being. For Martha, difficulties in math do not occasion thinking about math. Furtively looking at Evelyn's work, she seeks answers, not insights. She follows two to three lines behind and thus is lost when Evelyn turns a page.

When Evelyn finishes, Martha's source of answers dries up. She goes to Sue, who helps her through a problem, explaining without actually working it for her. But explanations are not what Martha is listening for. She returns to her seat and, having gained no insight, is back at Sue's desk almost immediately. She wants a savior, not a Socrates. Sue questions, revealing that Martha is perfectly able to do the problems, and teases, "Why are you coming to me? You know how to get those answers." But, unlike Alan, Martha still does not focus on the mathematical task and learns nothing from the reasoning Sue elicits from her.

"They are going faster than me," she whines.

"Why worry if they are ahead of you? Do you understand what you just did?"

"Yes," Martha says, though the question of understanding seems not to have arisen for her.

"Well, that's what matters, isn't it?"

Martha goes to her seat, but almost immediately returns to Sue.

"Are you going to show me how much your brain knows again?" challenges Sue gently but firmly. Again Martha is helped and returns to her seat. I ask her to show me how she is trying the next problem, which involves the sequence 18, 8, 16, 8. She quickly chooses 8 + 8. Her method is to write down 8 strokes, then to mark 8 more to get 16. This laborious process ends with her exclamation, "It's 16!" She is surprised and annoyed. She incorrectly assumes the answer must be 18—the first number in the line. She counts again. "It's still that." Exasperated, she starts toward Sue. I stop her, urging her to think of it a different way, hoping she will see that 18 is not the only acceptable answer. She writes 16 + 8, counts 8 more than 16 and is frustrated. "It's too big."

"Can you think of another thing to try?"

She counts 8 + 8 and again gets 16. This defeats her. With some reason, she turns to another problem, writes in a wrong answer quickly, then returns to the previous and only remaining problem of the set.

Vicki, sitting across from her, asks, "8 + 8 is what?"

"16! It's 16!" Martha is annoyed with this apparently pointless question.

"That's it!" says Vicki. Martha is still annoyed and does not see the point. Vicki persists more loudly. "8 + 8 is 16." She repeats this insistently until Martha writes: 8 + 8 = 16. There is no hint of insight. She does not see that she defined the task in a way that made it impossible. She shows only relief at being done. Understanding was neither her goal nor her accomplishment. Her concern about being behind, about being stupid, has left her unenlightened, though enlightenment was within her reach.

*   *   *

If youngsters and teacher do not heighten concerns about competence, parents can and often do step up to do so.

[September 28] When Sue explains the information students are to take home about upcoming parent conferences, Dan asks, "Are we doing bad?" The boy who has been making business for counselors and psychologists doesn't want to "do bad" at schoolwork. He probably speaks for many of the students. Sue reassures him and the class.

During the conferences, Sue again finds herself calming people down. Conferences seem as threatening to parents as to children. Parents have no clear sense of how their children behave and perform in school, and fear bad news. They often come away feeling more included in their child's education, with a clearer sense of the child's interests and strengths and of things they can do to help.

The day after conferences, many children are visibly livelier and more relaxed. They had not been obviously tense before, but the contrast is palpable. The air is brighter and sharper.

[October 12] At the beginning of the day, Tim looks sick. Sue twice tries to persuade him to see the school nurse. He reluctantly admits feeling unwell but will not leave the room. His father, he says, said he must come to school and "stay and get a good education." He resists Sue's persuasion, worrying that the nurse will call his parents. A little later, when he does not improve, Sue insists he see the nurse, who reports that his temperature is 103.6 °F. Tim's parents do not fulfill his fears. They arrive quickly to take care of him.

[February 1] In the context of a discussion of report cards Peter confides, "I was really smart in kindergarten, and I could read and everything. So my Mom and Dad told everyone I'm a genius. They keep buying hard toys and games. They bought me this chemistry set for Christmas and I don't know what to do with it. It's so hard. I'd just like some cars or a soccer ball."

Peter is not as obviously disturbed as others by parental pressure. Though he now complains about it, he often shares their preoccupation with being gifted, with being ahead, and his classmates recognize his propensity to dominate.

[March 13] Parent conferences come up first thing in the morning.

"They talk about us," Dan declares.

"They talk about the bad things," says Tim.

Anxious murmurs buzz around. Despite the fact that everyone was happy after the first round of parent conferences, these concerns will not go away.

"Just a minute now," Sue calls. "I'd tell you if there were anything bad. Do I hide things from you? Anyway, conferences are when I get to brag about how far you've all come and how well you are doing."

"That's different," says Peter. "Some teachers just say what you need to do."

"Well, sometimes, like on your reading books, I might say what you are working on. But I also say what you've already done well. That's about all it is."

"I wonder how third-grade teachers will be? They're all different," says Dan.

"It's nothing to be scared about," says Alan.

"I hope not," says Sue.

CHAPTER 4

Measuring Ability or Fostering Learning?

[August 26] When Sue announces the first test of the year, her tone changes. She is quite formal.

"Now we're having a spelling test. This is our first one. Some words will be hard for all of you. If you can't get a word, put down the letters you *can* remember. Don't look at other people's papers, because I need to see what you remember. I need to find out what you know so I can tell what to teach you. When I give a test there will be no talking. No one can go for a drink or go to the bathroom. We all need to be very quiet so your mind can do its best thinking."

This introduction echoes a theme from day 1—to teach, the teacher has to know what people know, and no one knows everything. The rules about looking at others' work, silence, and trips to the bathroom help define this situation as differing from learning contexts where helping is not cheating, where work-related talk and trips to the bathroom are normal.

Even first graders understand that tests have different purposes than do situations where learning is the goal. When tests and learning contexts become dominated by interpersonal competition, children see them as unfair and as ineffective for achieving their purposes. Yet they see interpersonal competition as fair in contests such as spelling bees.[1] Sue need not be conscious of the research on testing for her introduction to appeal to the students' sense of the purpose of tests, which is—as she reminds them—to find out what they know. This is calculated to make the test seem reasonable and to reduce the fear of looking "dumb," which would be heightened if the occasion were construed as a contest to see who is ablest and who is least able.

[September 12] The school district, like many, requires administration of a standardized test. This test takes a large part of each day of one week to administer. Later in the year a similar test must be administered at the command of the state legislature. The educational "reform" movement spurred by William Bennett and the 1983 Commission on Excellence in Education has wished more of these time-consuming sessions on teachers and children. Apparently the sessions are intended to promote learning, but it is hard to watch them and discern any way in which they promote intelligent thought about school experience or any desire to learn.[2] Sue has already spent time seeking to avert the panic these tests can precipitate.

"We already talked about the Iowa Test. As I said before, this is a pretest." This is barely a half truth, but Sue has her reasons. One experiment indicates that calling a test a pretest will help prevent those who doubt their competence or are anxious about tests from losing their grip on their own knowledge.[3] Probably, few researchers are aware of this particular experiment. It is certainly cited infrequently. Though she assumes what it showed to be true, Sue has not heard of the experiment. Yet her modification of the test introduction will help ensure that potentially anxious students are not paralyzed.

Sue's innovation, however, involves a small deviation from the standard instructions under which the designers of the test would have it given. If teachers vary the way tests are introduced and their handling of other details, this can, argue purists, lead to misleading scores. On the other hand, there are researchers, concerned about test anxiety, who argue for modifying test administration procedures as Sue has done. The apparently simple business of giving an achievement test is fraught with moral dilemmas. When, as now, there is much pressure on teachers to produce high scores, teachers do not stick exactly to the recommended practices. In extreme cases, the pressure will induce some teachers to cheat.[4]

"It's to tell me how I can give you the most help. Like on your spelling tests, you'll all do your best work."

This is not the whole truth either, because Sue would rather not use this test at all, even though her classes have always looked good when the results come in. For all the labor and psychometric sophistication that goes into instruments of this kind, they provide very crude information about student knowledge. Sue needs more specific information to guide the complex, unpredictable business of daily teaching. Do the students have a sense of the point of the topic at hand? Do they have conceptions of what they are about that guide their attempts to make meaning and polish their skills? What intrigues students, what confuses them, what words or symbols are strange to them, what might they best learn next?

These tests cannot help teachers discern what a child understands about addition of two-digit numbers, the nature of sentences, the source of rain, how to tell how long it will be until lunchtime, or any of the other myriad topics that will come up in the next few days. Each topic has many aspects that can be understood at many levels and in many ways. Children's knowledge changes rapidly. Even if these behemoth tests could provide information at the level of detail a responsive teacher could use, by the time the results came back from scoring, the information would be dated. Even if it were not dated, the collation on paper of so much detailed information by the teacher would leave little time and energy for the process of education. This psychometric enterprise has nothing to do with the delicate, idiosyncratic, evolving, forward-looking, creative process of teaching. The common response of legislators and deans of schools of education to teachers' negative attitudes toward tests is that teachers should learn more about existing tests and how to use them, that they should accept these tests as useful.[5] But down here in the second grade, the show must go on, so Sue tries to cast a positive light.

"Now this test has some third-grade work in it. You'll know when you come to that. You'll be able to see that some of it is third-grade work. So, if you come to one that you can see is a third-grade one, don't just look at it and dry up. Give it a try. Put down an answer. Make the best guess you can and go on. Don't sit there saying, 'I don't know this. I don't like this.' There have to be some things you can't do if I'm to find what you don't know so I can teach you."

"Is there first-grade stuff?"

"Yes." Cheers of relief go up.

"There's first-grade, second-grade, and third- [groans and murmurs] grade stuff. Because it is a pretest, I have to know exactly what you know, so we'll have no talking. If you have questions, what do you do?"

"Put up your hand."

"Right. Dan? Is there a question?"

"No copying?"

"Right. That would make me give you wrong work, so if you do your own work, we can see what is best for you." The no copying rule helps distinguish this one from regular learning activities, where helping is encouraged.

The test instructions require separation of desks and a check that everyone's pencil is a number two. Those who want a drink or a trip to the bathroom are then released. These things also separate the test from the usual activities and undermine Sue's attempts to relax the class.

Postures and expressions show that the children are not happy. As Sue introduces the first item, Tim's hand goes up.

"I think I might do bad. My father said you are his friend and that if I don't do good you'll tell him." His parents could not hope for a more dutiful son. Do they know how dutiful? Right now he looks paralyzed. The way he reveals his fears to Sue indicates that they are caused by the test and his parents, not by Sue.

"Tim!" Sue looks at him calmly and waits for him to look her in the eye. "Am I *your* friend?" He is not yet calmed. "Tim, you are a good student already and I'm glad you're in our class. Everything will be all right." She maintains eye contact. "OK, Tim?" He is relieved enough to nod.

Two items into the test, Paul puts his hand up. "On top of my mouth, here," he points. "It's hurting."

"I don't understand this one," bleats Jodie, probably defining Paul's problem.

"That's OK. Some of these are made so you won't understand them. Just put an answer and get ready for the next one."

By item 16 Paul, who will not score very highly, has recovered ·his balance. He puts up his hand. "Do you know why I'm good?"

"Why are you good, Paul?"

"'Cause in first grade I did the pretest too."

Within five minutes Jodie announces that she is sick.

"I know how you feel, Jodie dear, but I think we'd better tough it out until lunchtime." Everyone toughs it out, today and for the next four days.

[September 20] The first new day that will not be dominated by the Iowa Tests of Basic Skills is here. Above the hum of morning reunions, baseball card trading, and discussions of schoolwork before the bell that starts the day, Joan calls across the room, "I'm glad we're done with the Iowa Test."

"Now we can get down to real work," answers Sue.

In the teacher education program I went through it was often repeated that "testing is not teaching." This simple truth seems endangered in the schools of today. The rationale that "To teach you, I have to find out what you know" is probably the best justification a teacher can come up with for these tests. But these tests do nothing to increase the likelihood that students will play an active role in letting the teacher know what does and what does not puzzle them. They do not help students develop the power to evaluate their own knowledge. They undermine the atmosphere of mutual trust and joint commitment to construction of meaning that makes it possible to monitor student knowledge in the very act of fostering the development of that knowledge. Assessment in this more constructive sense is no more separable from teaching than the attempt at mutual understanding is separable from an ongoing conversation among friends. Such conversation will not survive long if the preoccupations with testing and with how able students are predominate over a shared interest in ideas.[6]

*   *   *

Second graders have no trouble telling that a standardized test session is not the same as the rest of school. They are, nevertheless, still working to comprehend the nature of these and everyday classroom tests. Students' doubts about the adequacy of their abilities flourish during these different tests. But the nature of tests is, even for children not worried about their competence, something that takes years to figure out. The purpose of a test is to assess current abilities. Children's conceptions of the nature of abilities, and thus their conceptions of tests, continue to develop over the elementary school years (Thorkildsen, 1991). The related question of when a situation is a test and when it has some other purpose can also present intellectual and moral puzzles. Sue's second graders occasionally seem to define tests as learning situations: They will help others and collaborate during tests. Occasionally, they define what could be learning situations as tests and resist helping others. The identities of the variety of situations that are defined in school are not immediately obvious to them. Here are, for children, significant questions: questions about the different functions school encompasses and when these diverse functions should be served.[7]

[September 30] Peter has chosen to help Yong Kim with alphabetizing. "Do you know what you're supposed to do?"

"Know what?" Yong Kim surfaces from a daydream.

"Turn the page to 28, then do the words in A-B-C order. Take all the 'A' words and write them first. Take all the 'B' words . . . B—baby."

"I'm not a baby."

"I know. I'm just joking." This is not the first or last time Peter plays with Yong Kim while helping him.

While this helping is going on, Wole appeals. "Mrs. Hazzard! Tim [who is doing the same task as Yong Kim] was copying me."

On this occasion, Sue confirms Wole's interpretation of the situation: "Tim, I'd like *you* to do that page, 'cause you can do that yourself. It's not a difficult page at all." Three yards away, Peter goes on helping Yong Kim.

[October 6] As they begin, in pairs, to test each other on their personal spelling lists, which they are supposed to have learned, Vicki asks her partner, "It doesn't matter if you get them wrong 'cause we're just learning—right?" Vicki must be working on convincing herself of this, because two weeks later others caught her copying when they worked with her. They objected and did not want to do this testing with her.

On the other side of the room, Paul dictates one of Yong Kim's spelling words. "Orange." When Yong Kim hesitates, Paul prompts, "Or—ange," and hovers solicitously as Yong Kim attempts it. "You got it wrong." Paul is full of concern. "Try harder. Try again."

Peter, who has finished his list, comes to help translate Paul's Latino accent for Yong Kim. He announces the next one. "Black cat."

"Black cat," repeats Paul.

"Tell me," Yong Kim appeals to Peter, who stands with a hand over Yong Kim's shoulder, ruffling his hair with the other hand.

"Yong Kim! He can't tell you. It's a spelling test." The informality of the whole occasion is, for Paul, getting out of hand. Peter too draws the line at "telling," and Yong Kim has to take his best shot.

[October 17] At the end of a spelling pretest, Carlos has failed to hear one of the words he should have tried to spell. Elizabeth, sitting by him, is one of the more diligent students in class. A full member of the "top" reading group, as sensitive and committed to words as she is to people, an unobtrusive but solid pillar of the little community, she has quietly repeated the word for struggling Carlos. He starts trying to spell it when, because the test is over, Sue asks, "What are you writing?" Her tone is firm and formal but not explicitly accusing. Carlos, who has just given up cheating in spelling, is startled to find himself in the spotlight. Straight arrow Elizabeth also stiffens. Knowing she shares some responsibility here, she immediately takes over for openmouthed Carlos.

"He didn't know what a word was and I was telling him. He missed it."

Sue nods her acceptance, correctly assuming that, this time, telling "what a word was" means telling the question, not telling the answer. Elizabeth's faith in the reasonableness and the humanity of the regime is confirmed along with her interpretation of the rules of tests. Even during tests there are legitimate forms of helping.

To say that tests are distinguished from occasions for learning by a rule about copying or helping conceals the complexity of the difference. The definitions of the different types of classroom situations are negotiated and renegotiated as Sue and the children try to decide what this classroom is for.

*   *   *

[January 19] As the year progresses, more and more topics become grist for the mill of classroom discussion. During a discussion of the point of learning to read, the question of copying arises.

"Is it fair to copy?" asks Sue.

"Not when you're grown up."

"The only way babies learn to talk is to copy. The only way 4- and 5-year-olds learn to write words is to copy."

"My little brother copies."

"When you get older and copy, like on the ISTEP [a State-mandated standardized achievement test], it's wrong."

"What if you get the wrong answer by copying?" asks Sue.

"They are both wrong 'cause if they both don't know it they are both wrong."

"What if you get it right by copying?" asks Sue.

"No! 'Cause in an exam it's what you know," says George, like Elizabeth a solid, competent, quiet but thoughtful pillar of the community.

"So," adds Sue, "if you copy, the teacher will get the wrong idea and might give you the wrong work?"

"You don't learn from copying. If you did that for a long time you wouldn't learn anything."

"It's like lying. It's a hard thing to get out of."

"Is there any reason to copy?" Sue asks.

"Like if you're from a different country you have to copy to learn words."

"On a test it's not good to copy," says George, restating his theme.

"It's bad to copy," declares Wole, who has been mumbling disagreement whenever people suggest occasions when copying might be legitimate. He looks as if someone had proposed that stealing should be allowed in class.

"Have you ever let anyone copy your work?"

"Not really."

"In first grade did you help anyone?"

"He helped me with something," volunteers his loyal friend Tim, "and I got it. I didn't know a word."

Wole is inarticulate but glowers his discontent with the tenor of the discussion.

"So are you saying there's never a time in class when it's OK to copy?" Sue encourages him to clarify.

"I don't know."

Others take over.

"It's OK when the teacher says to copy."

"Copying words in your spelling dictionary is all right."

"It's OK when you copy words into your spelling dictionary," Wole concedes. This is not copying from a peer's work. He remains tense with his sense that injustice is being brazenly promoted.

"OK," says Sue. "I think copying is taking on two meanings." Before she can clarify, children clamor to add their insights. The various themes already raised are reasserted by other players. Sue again seeks to sum up.

"OK, I think I hear two things coming out here. Is this what I'm hearing? First of all, you can copy to learn."

A chorus of "Yes!" is her answer. "But when you have to show what you have learned, you should not copy." The chorus again signals assent. Only Wole still looks uncomfortable. What is the basis of his unique reaction?

A month earlier, after finishing their work, Tim and Wole play checkers. Tim is unfamiliar with the rules that Wole demonstrates for him patiently and skillfully.

"This is harder than chess," says Tim. "In chess you just jump any way you want." Wole knows better but does not challenge him. During the checkers game, he keeps suggesting to Tim moves better than those Tim tries. How easily he does this, with no hint that Tim's first choices might be inadvisable. He helps competently and gladly, without flaunting his own superiority. This is no sacrifice. It is exactly what he wants to do.

The friendship between these two formed in the first grade despite Wole's clear superiority in academic as well as physical skills. In the second grade, they sit together at the outset and their friendship lasts all year despite a separation created by an early change in seating.

Wole could not be called an egoist. The students readily accuse Peter and, occasionally, others of bragging and of attempts to dominate. But the question does not arise with Wole. Yet it seems he sees much of school as a test. In tests you don't help one another. In tests that is cheating. In other contexts Wole is a tactful and patient guide to the less able, but in schoolwork he is sure this is wrong. Wole is determined to do well in school. This, however, does not mean he sets out to best others. It means that he must do his own work and, if school-that-is-a-test is to be fair, so must his peers. He therefore objects and appeals to Sue when Tim seeks his help with alphabetizing.

For much of the year Wole has difficulty getting started during imaginative writing sessions. These sessions are difficult to consider as tests. The criteria of correctness are too ambiguous. On the tests Wole has encountered, everyone must answer the same explicit questions, and the answers are unambiguously right or wrong. Right answers, it seems, are all he expects to produce in school. When he must decide what to write a story on and how to write it, Wole's aptitudes seem to desert him. He becomes lost and incompetent. He even occasionally fools about in a rather tentative, incompetent fashion. The awkwardness of his attempts to "goof off" on these occasions indicates how out of character they are for this solemn, hardworker. Like helping Tim with a worksheet, imaginative writing is inconsistent with what he takes to be school-as-a-test.

*   *   *

In this class, Wole is extreme. His classmates, nevertheless, sometimes resemble him, objecting to helping and copying.

[February 16] Jill and Vicki come to the round table at the back of the room at which I am sitting. Both are uncertain about the nature of their assignment and seek my advice. As they start writing, Vicki glances in passing at Jill's work. Jill abruptly covers it up, saying, "She's looking at my work."

Vicki is instantly offended. Scowling at Jill, she grabs four large hardcover books and builds a wall around her work.

"There! Don't look!" she snaps. After a few minutes, they give up scowling and adjusting their screens and become absorbed in their work.

[March 13] After finishing reading a play together, Yong Kim and Carlos begin workbook assignments. Carlos has somehow gained the notion that Yong Kim did page 33 yesterday, and, even though the page has not been assigned, he is determined to do it to "catch up." Yong Kim tries to point out that Carlos is in error. Carlos checks with me, but, not getting the answer he wants, persists in announcing maniacally his intent to catch up. Only after consulting Sue does he forsake his quest.

Starting on the day's assignment, he encounters a problem, and brings it to me. Yong Kim leaps up to follow. "Don't tell him answers," he urges. On returning to the table they are sharing, Yong Kim hides his work behind a book. Carlos works for a few moments.

"I can do this work," he declares, pleased and relieved.

"But I'm faster than you," claims Yong Kim. They work quietly for 10 minutes until the bell for recess rings.

[March 17] Vicki and Joan are sitting together writing out spelling lists. Joan glances in the direction of Vicki's work with no apparent intention to read it—she immediately looks away again and shows no sign of having registered anything from the paper. Vicki, however, rearranges her position so Joan cannot see her paper.

In the preceding cases it was sometimes hard to tell whether the children were dominated by concerns about others' catching up or getting ahead of them or were defining what might have been occasions for collaborative learning as tests where copying was wrong. There seemed to be elements of both. Classroom discussions, however, make it clear that the ethics of cheating and collaboration is still being worked out well into the year.

[March 13] Sue introduces a worksheet that requires completion of six riddles about the sun. At the bottom of the page is printed, "Choose your answers from these [six] words: flares, the Sun . . ."

Peter's hand is up. "That's like cheating."

"No," says George. "You have to choose."

"You might not get them all right," adds Paul. "And, also, if we didn't remember the answers, how would we get the right answers?"

"He's a good student." Dan is referring to Peter. "It's like cheating for him but helping for me."

"So do you want something more challenging, Peter?" Sue reads one of the questions to illustrate a possibility. "We could cut off the answers here to make it harder."

"No!"

"Why not, Jodie?"

"'Cause of the spelling." Jodie demonstrates how she would have probably have spelled *flares* wrong if it had not been printed there.

After a little more discussion they are happy to see the sheets as an opportunity for learning. The consensus that Sue sums up is that, on this assignment, if you are learning something, you aren't cheating.

[April 24] During assignments that require each child to search for information on a different dinosaur, a number have trouble deciding where to search. Peter helps, but tends to take over and do the search himself.

"Peter. Don't help everyone. They have to do it on their own."
Out of context Sue's intervention sounds like a prohibition of all collaboration. It is, however, taken as intended—as discouragement of
Peter's tendency to simply take over. Children continue seeking
information and advice and showing their discoveries to one another.
The distinction between taking a free ride and gaining assistance or
sharing knowledge seems in place.

Evelyn's approach to the last section of the assignment—drawing a picture of a dinosaur—indicates that the definition of cheating
may remain a puzzle. She traces a picture, saying to no one in particular, "I'm cheating. I don't care if I'm cheating." She looks around,
pouting slightly, tossing her abundant curls. "So what. I don't care."

*   *   *

Moral education has generally been taken to refer to the promotion of the moral values and knowledge of individual students. In
moral education programs, such as those inspired by Lawrence Kohlberg,
who saw his efforts as continuous with those of John Dewey, there is
also a democratic emphasis on student responsibility for the ethos
of the school community. Discussion, inquiry, and action are concerned with creating and sustaining a just community, not merely
with developing moral individuals. Yet these moral development
programs and schools stop short of fostering active negotiation of
the rules that govern the conduct of the school's intellectual work.
It hardly needs to be pointed out that few schools promote discussion of such matters. When open discussion of ethical issues does
occur in schools, it is likely to focus on other topics such as stealing, property damage, drug use, and disruptive behavior. The real stuff
of citizenship in a democracy—the question of how we should conduct our daily work—is left out.[8]

Here is an interesting parallel with adult society. Adults can take
part in discussions of foreign policy, school board policy, national
and local economic regulations, and much more. It is, however, a
rare worker who expects and receives the opportunity to contribute
to and live with the consequences of collaborative decisions about
how his or her daily work is conducted. Most workers have to choose
between doing things their boss's way and seeking other employment.
The world of adult work offers few opportunities for democratic life.
It is often so in schools as well.[9]

This need not be so. Though they are not generally asked to think
about the fairness of teaching and testing practices, children have no

difficulty articulating views on these questions. When, for example, they are presented with the problem of adapting teaching to individual differences in rate of learning, they generally favor having those who learn faster assist those who are slower. This is true even for students who have not experienced this practice in school. It is true also for highly able students who might be giving more than they received if this practice were implemented.[10]

Combine this with the evidence that students who seek understanding also see collaboration as an effective way to succeed in school, and it is not hard to see the compatibility of the collaborative pursuit of knowledge with the pursuit of social justice. The preoccupation with superiority and the tendency to see much of school as a test both work against this, but the students' ability to address these issues in open discussions is a source of hope. In Sue's class, these discussions move in the direction of constructive conceptions of the nature and role of helping. But the importance of these discussions does not reside only in the conclusions that emerge from them. It is in the quality of these discussions that the spirit of democracy is most clearly evident and most soundly defended.

Democracy, wrote John Dewey (1940), is not something that takes place "mainly at Washington and Albany—or some other state capital" (p. 222).[11] Nor is its primary defense in

> legal guarantees of the civil liberties of free belief, free expression, free assembly. [These] are of little avail if in daily life freedom of communication, the give and take of ideas, facts, experiences is choked by mutual suspicion, by abuse, by fear and hatred. These things destroy the essential condition of the democratic way of living. . . . The heart and final guarantee of democracy is in free gatherings of neighbors . . . to discuss back and forth . . . and in gatherings of friends . . . to converse freely with one another. (p. 225)
>
> Democracy is a way of life controlled by a working faith in the possibilities of human nature . . . by faith in the capacity of human beings for intelligent judgment and action if proper conditions are furnished. (p. 223)

The citizens of Sue's class seem to have found these conditions, beginning to exemplify "a genuinely democratic faith in . . . the possibility of conducting disputes, controversies, and conflicts as cooperative undertakings in which both parties learn by giving the other a chance to express itself" (p. 226).

Sue did not characterize the condition emerging in Room 7 as democracy. Mutual respect seemed more apt, and respect is the word that kept occurring to me in the first week as I sat trying to capture Sue's evolving relationship with the children. But mutual respect and the making of different perspectives into intellectual and social challenge, even adventure, are, as Dewey hoped to persuade us, the essence of democratic education and democratic life.

Here is Susan Hazzard, with 20 young students, promoting this spirit in a time when scores on the Iowa Tests of Basic Skills seem to be the only thing that matters in Washington and the state capitals, a time when legislators regularly appear on television, lengthening the school year, shortening the time for teaching by announcing new tests, declaring standards for graduation from each grade, withdrawing benefits from families of students who do not attend regularly, berating the schools, and ignoring the complex, recalcitrant details of daily life in classrooms. Democracy may not be something that takes place in state capitals, but the seeds of its destruction may be growing there.

The committees and legislators who wish more testing on the nation's students are like those who would evaluate farmers only by their immediate yields of corn. It is as if the daily work of the nation's farmers were governed by people whose vision of farming was gained from the window of a trans-continental airline flight. A remote and elevated viewpoint provides certain satisfactions and makes some patterns more easily detectable, but the daily challenges faced by those who work the soil are invisible from up there. Without the people on the ground, there would be no farms to look at, and the people on the ground, not the vistas from 20,000 feet, are the point.

CHAPTER 5

Law, Order, and Mutual Respect

As they come in on the third day of the school year, most children get to work coloring patterns or solving puzzles in a work packet they received the day before. James announces to Sue that he's going to return two books to the school library.

"Thanks for telling me," says Sue as he darts off.

Others are at Sue's desk asking for clarification of directions on the packet. Their difficulties are never attributed to them; rather, "The directions got messed a bit in the machine," or "These are all squiggled up, aren't they?" comments Sue.

Peter bounces into the room with a huge grin. He kneels on his seat at the front of the room as if sitting would be too confining. His attention is captured by the rules, based on the previous day's discussion, that are now posted at the front:

Classroom Rules

1. Follow directions the first time they are given.
2. Speak only when given permission.
3. Keep hands, feet, and objects to yourself.
4. Complete assignments on time.
5. Promptly line up when told to.

Rewards

1. Verbal praise from the teacher.
2. Positive note from the teacher.
3. Stickers.
4. Class points for additional fine arts activities.

Consequences

1. Warning.	Name goes on board.
2. Miss 10 minutes of recess.	Check beside name.
3. Miss entire recess.	Second check beside name.
4. Parent(s) notified *and* miss recess.	Third check.
5. Student goes to office.	Fourth check.

6. Go to office immediately; parent called; conference with parent, teacher, and principal.

Peter reads quickly down the list and interprets it for his neighbor Tim. "If you don't line up properly you go to the office. If you do all these things you go to the principal's office." He is excited and shakes Tim's shoulder to get his attention. Tim did not notice the list of rules. Puzzled and annoyed by Peter's excitement, he attempts to keep reading his book. Peter remains transfixed and keeps trying to draw Tim's attention to the ultimate punishment. Is this an accident of location? He sits by the rules. As it turns out, during weeks 1 and 2 Peter is as big a threat to order as anyone.

When class starts, Sue recalls the previous day's discussion.

"Yesterday, you really used your heads. We came up with some good ideas to help us learn. Your brains were on super-power so I wrote down some rules that will help the room be the way we want. Here they are.

"Number one, *Follow directions the first time.* Is that fair?"

"Yes."

"Yes. It will help me and I think it will help you all, too.

"Two. *Speak only when given permission.* Why do we have this rule?"

"So people won't interrupt class."

"Does this mean you can't talk?"

"No."

"That's right. Many times you can talk—when you are helping each other and other times."

"What does permission mean?"

"You are allowed to do a thing."

"How do you get permission?"

"Be nice."

"Ask."

"OK, and what's the best way to ask?"

"Raise your hand."

"Yes, and then everyone can hear and everyone can have a turn."

"Number three. *Keep hands, feet, and objects to yourself.* Here's one no one mentioned, but it's sometimes a problem." Sue explains that this rule is hers—not one that came up in their discussion. If mutual trust is important, honesty in such matters is essential. The students seem happy with the addition.

"Number four. *Complete assignments on time.* This just means do your best. Remember, Joan [who has her desk lid up and her head under it], what did I say to do if you can't finish?"

"Go to the teacher and tell her," says Joan as she surfaces.

"Yes. We're a team. If you do your best and can't finish, maybe I gave you work that is too hard. You can tell me and we can think of what to do."

"Do we have to go to the office if we don't finish our work or don't try hard?" asks Peter, whose preoccupation with the ultimate punishment has not been accompanied by careful reading of or reflection about the discipline plan.

"No."

The rest of the rules and the rewards and consequences are explained with continuous input from students. Sue emphasizes that she is sure no one will ever get many checks beside their name. She also plays down the possibility that anyone would ever face the ultimate consequence.

* * *

The commercially prepared form on which Sue wrote the class rules was copyrighted by Lee Canter and Associates. The Canter (1989) Assertive Discipline program is widely used in the nation's schools. Like the Bible, it is interpreted in diverse ways, some of which must embarrass its prophets.[1] But, as with the Bible, its appeal and impact cannot be denied. Many school faculty lounges around the nation display a glossy poster advertising a course in Assertive Discipline for three graduate credits. Various universities and colleges are listed as collaborating in the presentation of the course. From a photograph on the poster, Lee Canter in a dark suit, hands on hips, looks directly out in a way that must be intended to be assertive. Alongside are his words.

"I want to say something very clearly. You are not paid to put up with behavior problems. You are not paid to put up with kids talking back. And it's not only bad for you, it is bad for the children. We want to create a positive environment in the classroom and you are not going to be able to create that positive environment unless you are the boss . . ."

Those spreading the doctrine that teachers are "paid to put up with behavior problems" are not identified. Presumably, the purpose of implying that they are, like the devil in The Book of Job, going to and fro on the earth, is to sustain the implication that teachers must choose between putting up with behavior problems and being the big boss and stamping them out.

Sue had taken the three-credit Assertive Discipline course the year before, and many teachers in her school use the system. Though she has taught for 20 years without using it, now she feels obliged to give it a try.

The previous year, Sue described to my classes of elementary education students her approach to motivation and discipline. Instead of recipes, formulae, or abstract principles, she offered strategies illustrated with rich examples of the things she does, the difficulties she faces, and the experience of teaching. Her stories about specific student behavior problems showed her sensitivity to the uniqueness of every case. She conveyed respect for children and ingenuity in appealing to their potential reasonableness and their desire to learn. The student teachers, many fearing to lose control and contemplating taking the old advice to not smile until Christmas, were heartened and excited by Sue's message. It eventually led me to propose the collaboration that produced this book.

Sue's brief and half-hearted mention of Assertive Discipline at the end of her presentation was, for me, inexplicably inconsistent with the subtlety of the rest of the session: A virtuoso exposition of the complexity of teaching, of the need for a unique response to the unique features of each problem was concluded with a reference to a recipe book. It was as if medical school were to end with the suggestion that illness can be cured with aspirin and that if one aspirin does not work, more should be used.[2]

Sue has her worries, but maintenance of order is not a big one. If she wants to, she can, with a combination of playfulness, reason, and firmness, have all five classes of second graders hanging on her words, waiting for her instructions. When these five classes are excited and chaotic after a film session and tumble boisterously into the corridor, pushing and shoving, Sue is easily able to calm them. With a joking modification of "Simon says," she has them hanging delightedly on her every word. Back to their classrooms they go, relaxed, eager, and amused.

A display such as this is not, for Sue, the point of teaching. It does, however, exercise her ingenuity, humor, and goodwill. Assertive Discipline exercises none of these. It requires an accountant's mentality, which Sue lacks, and, when she reflects on the matter, does not want.

Sue often forgets to apply the Assertive Discipline consequences. When problems occur, she normally takes as long as necessary to deal with them at the moment they surface. When they are dealt with, she looks ahead and forges on with whatever was interrupted. Assertive discipline requires the teacher to bear a grudge until recess. The grudge might be borne coolly on the blackboard, but borne it is nevertheless. When recess comes, there is always something worthier of the teacher's attention than the ledger of checks on the board. For a teacher focusing on what may happen, on opportunities for teaching, preoccupation with past sins is a step backward.

Sue cannot keep it up. When Vicki has accumulated two checks beside her name and recess arrives, Sue has forgotten. Vicki reminds Sue that she must lose 10 minutes of recess. Others are less conscientious and occasionally get forgotten.

The Assertive Discipline program emphasizes simple consistency in treatment of infractions like talking inappropriately. But, when Peter talks excitedly to a neighbor, disrupting the class while they are grouped together watching a filmstrip, Sue does not ask him to put his name up on the board. Her tone is businesslike but matter-of-fact. "Peter. Would you move over there." Without a word he moves away from his friend and is quiet. The lesson proceeds without faltering and the incident is forgotten. Later, I point out this deviation from the "official" discipline plan. Sue is surprised, having been on automatic pilot. Peter, however, showed none of the bad humor he will show if asked to put his name on the board.

Peter's name goes up more than most over the first few weeks, and he often resents it. In the last week of the school year, Sue asks what she might do differently with next year's second graders. Peter is first with the announcement that "I got kind of mad when a lot of us were making noise, and you put my name up." He is "kind of mad" quite often over the first weeks and, at times, Sue feels the same way about him.

[August 29] Sue means it when she says "Peter! I'm running out of patience. Soon I'll be an angry person. I don't want you to distract others." Peter says nothing but glowers in his seat. Sue's flexibility, wit, and ingenuity have, for the moment, gone. Peter is the only one to regularly make her tense.

It is easy, when teaching, to find oneself doing things one had no intention of doing—things that make one feel ridiculous, less than adult. Teachers can become as silly as 7-year-olds battling to sit by the window in the family car. Everyone in such situations becomes less than themselves. Observing a teacher in this dilemma is akin to sitting through dinner with a couple who are so determined to belittle each other that all decency flies out the window. Disagreements are inevitable, but some methods of dealing with them diminish all parties. So it is with the early battle of wills between Sue and Peter. I find it embarrassing to watch. I avert my eyes and only later realize I failed to record details.

[September 9] Peter is especially annoying to Sue this morning. He cannot stay put or stop talking. When he goes across the room to talk to Paul, she stops him. He tries to justify himself. Sue takes this as a challenge and will hear nothing. He is excited and distracted and cannot settle down to his work. Because she shuts him up abruptly each time he begins to speak, Sue does not discover that he is trying to find a new and especially valued addition to his baseball card collection that he has lost. His collection is dear to him. Before school, he trades cards avidly and chatters about them to anyone who will listen. He is genuinely worried about the new card. Standing in line ready to leave for recess, he explains his dilemma to me. He cannot think of a way to get Sue to hear his problem. He thinks Paul might have the card but he can't find out. As they walk out, he cannot restrain himself from trying to find out who might have his card.

After recess, during a lesson, Peter asks, "Can I go and get my card?" It has come to him that it might be in his bag in the closet at the rear of the room. Sue has figured out that his lost card is his problem, but her heart does not melt.

"No! Your card will wait, but your behavior will change."

Peter is quiet but distracted until lunchtime. Most of the time he looks into space, playing with his mouth. When the children are released for lunch, he dashes to the closet and reappears as his spunky self with his recovered card.

There does not seem to be any identifiable turning point, but gradually the relationship between Sue and Peter becomes based on mutual respect and humor. This arrangement does not follow the Assertive Discipline formula, but it is what Peter respects. It also comes more easily to Sue. Sue uses the Assertive Discipline consequences less and less and when, after two months, the list of rules and consequences comes unstuck and falls on the floor, it is put behind a cabinet.

[September 30] "Would you like to get out your green math books," says Sue as the class completes an assignment. Peter springs upright in his seat like a terrier leaping to look over long grass for his quarry. He seeks the meaning of Sue's request.

"Do we have to? You said, 'Do we want to?'"

Sue grins with a wry twinkle. "Well, I guess I just meant to ask you nicely to get out your books." She pauses, then, nodding to Peter but addressing the class, says, "Would you *please* get out your green books and get ready."

The terrier nods sharply and readies his book.

[October 18] Returning from the corridor after quieting a group of children from another class, Sue quips, "They must think I'm the Wicked Witch of the West."

"Oh no," says Peter. "You don't know how many people have gone up to my mother and said how you turned their kids around. You don't know how many kids were in trouble that you made OK."

Peter is no sycophant. He is ever ready to question. However, as the year progresses he increasingly becomes the most determined articulator of the view that discipline must be based on joint consideration of the reasons for action. Sue can rely on him, more than anyone else, to provoke students with more authoritarian views to reconsider their positions.

*   *   *

When the Assertive Discipline system requires an automatic punishment, it thereby conveys an automatic judgment by Sue that the behavior at issue is wrong. There are times when no discussion is needed, when children readily acknowledge they behaved wrongly. At other times, however, the automatic judgment precludes the joint examination of the ethics of playground or classroom conduct. When significant discipline problems do occur, they can be transformed into intellectual challenges that make every child a legislator—a moral philosopher. Instead of exercises in the control of behavior, there are adventures in ethics.

[January 18] When the class returns from recess, Sue is confronted with a clamor for justice from people who claim to have been wronged. "Vicki pushed me," claims Tim.

"Why, Vicki? Why do that?" Sue queries.

"He was slow."

This and another problem are easily dealt with.

Dan presents a more substantial difficulty. He defends his

reported aggression on the grounds that someone wanted him to do it. He is unusually tense, very defensive, and not about to back down.

"Do you do things just because someone says to?" asks Sue. He scowls, sulks, and says nothing. He will not look at Sue. "What if someone said, 'Take these drugs'? Would you just do it?" He will not look at her or answer. The others sense his tension. "What if someone said, 'Take this gun and shoot that boy.' Would you?"

"Yes, I would, if my grandfather told me to." He is hurt but defiant.

"Would you really? That really surprises me." Sue is truly startled, and with good reason. Dan would not normally take this position. Children regard gratuitous killing as invariably wrong—as something not even God could declare legitimate.[3] If Dan's expression had not already told Sue that she is facing more than a playground disagreement, this stand would have.

Something has clearly gone wrong for Dan. Though Sue was warned that he could be difficult, he has been no trouble. When, on the fourth day of school, Sue recalled earlier discussion of rules and mentioned the need to be sure they all made sense so there wouldn't be any problems, Dan chimed in quietly, "Never will be." Until now there have not been.

Back then he was one of the first to spontaneously hug Sue who, while being embraced, exchanged a grin with me as if to say, "This is our troublemaker?"

At the end of the second week, he appeared before school with five different brightly colored threads, which he industriously plaited, with James's help, into a wristband—a friendship bracelet. He proudly presented it to Sue and insisted on tying it on her wrist.

It is, however, easy to see that he could become "behavior disordered" or "delinquent" in some classes. Short for his age, he is all energy and motion. Much of the time his problem is to keep himself entertained. In the first week, when Sue asks the class to stand up, several times Dan goes down. His timing is excellent. He drops to the floor exactly at the peak of the rumble of rising classmates and is invisible behind his desk at the back of the room. Sue sees this about half the time and chooses to ignore it. He is silent, distracting no one, and shows no intent to annoy Sue. He is obviously already devoted to her. He cannot, however, easily march in step. Today the spark has gone out of him.

"Dan, I can see you don't want to listen. Are you tuning me out?" Today, he certainly is. Sue does not press.

"Well, I'll check with someone else."

"My mother says not to listen to my brother when he says to be silly," Jack volunteers.

Ann tells a rambling story, the moral of which is, "do as your parents say."

"Why should children do what their parents say?" asks Sue.

"They [children] don't have the money and things."

"So, if the child had the money, should the child tell the parents what to do?"

"No."

"No."

"Well, why should children do as their parents say?"

"They are older."

"You can't boss adults," says Paul.

"Why?"

"'Cause they are bigger and you have to listen."

"You listen to them 'cause they've already gone through what you've gone through. Like my mom," declares Evelyn, who generally finds reasons to obey authorities, at least to their face.

"What Paul said," calls out Joan, who now revels in Sue's Socratic challenges. "Ann is bigger than Claire, so why can't Ann boss Claire?"

"That's not right."

"I think he means older [people can boss you]."

"What if there was a giant that was big but still a baby?" argues Peter, the counterpunching philosopher. "We wouldn't have to listen to him."

"So size isn't it?" asks Sue. They seem to agree. "Now . . . Ah, someone else said you should do what older people say."

"I'm older than her so I could tell her?"

"Jodie is older than Jack," Sue notes. "Should he do what she tells him?"

"No."

"Why?" They are momentarily stumped. Again Sue asks, "Why?"

"'Cause you have to . . . I don't know."

"Younger people don't know the same things as they [older people]."

"Jodie is older than Jack, but he is taller." Sue recalls the emphasis on size.

"They're grown-ups [so you should obey]."

"What if you meet a grown-up you don't know on the street, and he tells you to do something?"

"No."

"He's not your mother or father or even your friend and he can't tell you."

"What about a policeman? You wouldn't know him, but if he tells you to cross the street, do you do that?"

"No, 'cause cars might be going along."

"But isn't the policeman the law?"

"So you look both ways."

"You can run across."

"The government is there to help you and the policeman wants to help you," says Evelyn.

"So do you mean," asks Sue, leading gently, "that you can trust lawmakers and law enforcers? We learned to trust parents because we know they want to help you and make you healthy. So you know you can believe what they tell you?"

There are no objections so she asks, "What about a classmate?"

There are lots of "no's," which is not surprising as Dan appears just to have done violence at a friend's insistence.

"Someone mentioned experience," Sue recalls. "People want to stop you from making mistakes they made."

"So when they say don't slug someone, they know why," adds Peter.

"OK, it's lunchtime now. We can talk more later, but in the meantime, I don't want anyone hitting."

Dan has not participated. He has become steadily more relaxed but still burns. Only now making eye contact with Sue, he calls out, "I'm not the only one!" He concedes what he wouldn't earlier—that he did wrong.

"That's right, and I don't mean to single you out. I know you weren't the only one, and I didn't want to make it sound like that either."

At the beginning of the session Dan was alienated from all of humanity except his grandfather. Difficulties remain, but he is once more a member of the class. He can talk with his teacher and classmates.

Many teachers hold that class time should not be wasted on matters of discipline. This is a theme of Assertive Discipline. If, however, schools are to produce citizens whose actions are based on consideration of their consequences for others and who are ready to insist that authority must have more than power on its side, then reasoned dialogue about discipline is no waste of time. With Sue keeping the discussion focused, the children provoke one another to clarify and develop their conceptions of social authority. There are lifetimes of work to be done on this topic, and a beginning can be made here. The children's attempts to construct coherent, defensible stances have no place in Canter's classroom, where the teacher must be the "boss." No doubt Sue is leading the little band of guerrilla philosophers, but "boss" is hardly the word to describe the way she leads.

* * *

It does not take a discipline problem or acts of violence to occasion dialogue on the psychology and ethics of social authority.

[February 1] The class learns that their principal has received an award. Sue asks why that might have occurred.

"He doesn't be so arrogant," says Joan, whose early snobbish bossiness now rarely shows.

"He talks to children."

"He makes children understand what he says."

"Most principals would say, 'Listen to your teacher, I haven't got time,' but Mr. Parente will listen to you and reason with you," says Peter. "He tells you why."

"He doesn't usually tell us when we will have fire drill. So we are scared, but we get over it and are ready if there's a real fire." Ann appreciates his reasons but, with her deference to powerful authority, finds a case where children must simply trust and obey.

"He's good because he never yells at you and most principals might." Tim still wears his fears on his sleeve.

"He has a loud voice when he's talking to the janitor," counters Ann, consistently seeing the power rather than the reason behind authority.

"Why do you think that is?" Sue knows the janitor is partially deaf, but the discussion races on.

"If they are strict, that's a good principal, 'cause everyone knows he's serious and will make them be good." This is a revealing contribution from Paul, who gives Sue no trouble but can metamorphose and create chaos for student teachers who pass through the class.

"Is that good?"

"Yes," says Ann, who readily resorts to bossiness.

"What is strict?" Sue wants to know.

"It's like when my sister loses library books, she gets in trouble. You do something bad, you get in trouble."

Peter will not accept Ann's reasserted emphasis on adult power. "There are some parents, they think they know everything and kids can't talk back. But there might be a reason [for the kid's action].

They don't even listen." He is passionate as ever for consideration of the reasons for action.

"What is strict?" repeats Sue.

"I think it's when people yell at you," suggests Joan.

"It's when you just do a little problem, and they yell at you," clarifies Vicki.

"When I do something wrong and I cry, she [mother] doesn't yell at me." Ann remains concerned with dealing with power. Speaking truth to power is not one of her ways. Sue gives her the environment to exercise her First Amendment rights, but Ann does not consciously recognize the rights she has been accorded.

"Are there times," asks Sue, "when parents or teachers might have a good reason to yell at you?"

"You might be doing unsafe things."

"If they say *why*, it helps," adds Peter, not to be drawn off his point.

✻   ✻   ✻

[February 16] Sue has been reading the class Keo Felker Lazarus's (1970) three novels about children's encounters with travelers from space. The themes of war and peace are under discussion.

Ann says, "I think about when they were in the Intergalactic Way Station, and they started to want to be like the others in the station, and the others came up and said they could join the Federation if they could show they were trustworthy. [They weren't trustworthy, but] Monaal could zap them and make them be peaceful."

"Let me ask you this," says Sue. "Can anyone make you behave? Can people make you be good?"

"No?" says Ann slowly, uncertainly, sensing that Sue is trying to get her to recognize something she has missed. Though preoccupied with deferring to the power of authorities, she senses that she can respond to Sue's reason rather than her power. She strains to grasp the challenge in Sue's question. Mutual respect does not mean blindly accepting everything another says. It means attempting to comprehend, negotiate, and live with differences. Ann's openness conveys an implicit recognition that she has this respect from Sue. But she is unable to state the principle of their relationship.

George has no such problem. "It's our decision what we do," he calls out, as if this were as obvious as the rain outside the window.

"They can make us eat breakfast," says Tim.

"A grown-up can put pressure on you to do things."

"Can a child?" asks Sue.

Opinion is divided.

"They can kick you." Tim speaks for the affirmative.

"Is that a good way?"

"No!" "No!" cries the chorus.

Adult interventions are explored; then Jack raises the question of physical dominance.

"A kid that used to be my friend and he isn't my friend if he doesn't do what I want and keeps doing it. I can deck him."

The chorus goes into a turmoil of excitement, which Sue seeks to turn into dialogue.

"What's the *best* way to get a behavior you want from a child?"

Peter elaborates his theme. "Sometimes my mom wants me to stop doing something, and she sends me to my room. I get madder and madder." This is easy to believe—the very thought has him quite "mad." "She should sit down and explain why you shouldn't do it."

His message is missed by many.

"Sometimes the best way is to punish them," suggests James.

"Be strict with them," says Joan, who can go either way.

"I like to play with computers," notes Alan. "You could take that privilege away."

"I'd say, 'If you do it you'll get extra dessert!'" Ann's penchant for coercion is consistent.

"Can you think about this?" asks Sue, taking another tack into the prevailing wind. "Monaal would like Cyclo's behavior to change so he can join the Intergalactic Federation. What can Monaal do?"

"Nothing!" Peter is emphatic.

"But didn't he do something?"

"Let him go?"

"Does he talk to him?" Sue leads.

"Yes." "No." They are unsure.

"He talked to him."

"OK, Jack. What did he say? Remember when . . ."

"I think," Dan butts in, "what he says was, ah, you know, ah, 'It's never going to work until . . .'"

"Until what?"

"Ah . . ." Dan is digging deep. "Ahh . . . until you're . . . trust-worthy." The boy most likely, according to initial reports, to be troublesome leads the way in the understanding of troublesome behavior.

Peter, another candidate for prime troublemaker, must have been reflecting on the earlier discussion of bribes. "Like what Ann says—you give a treat. But then they'll want a treat every time."

"Can you reward someone without giving a treat?" Sue is pleased to have Peter's ideas to work with. Ann still inhabits another planet:

"You could let them stay up a whole hour later."

"What kind of reward do *I* give you for good behavior?"

"Not gumballs," calls Jodie. (A student teacher used some.)

"Notes."

"You gave me a pack of gum."

"No. That was Miss Johnson."

"You tell us, 'Good job!'" says Tim.

"I remind you and say I'm impressed."

Peter persists with the problems of exogenous rewards. "If the teacher gives them stickers and notes and then doesn't have time [to keep it up], the kids could get mad."

"Really, Peter!" Sue agrees. "What we find in this room is, I let you know when you do good. And, like Peter says, telling why helps you know what to do."

Peter's insights are obviously not shared by all, but all seem content with Sue's summation.

"So," she proceeds, "was there anything else that Monaal might have done?"

"He could show an example."

"Like you teach a baby?" asks Sue.

"Yes."

＊　　＊　　＊

"When fiction becomes thought," wrote John Gardner (1978), "the writer makes discoveries which, in the act of discovering them in his fiction, he communicates to the reader" (p. 109). "Real art creates myths a society can live instead of die by, and clearly our society is in need of such myths. What I claim is that such myths are not mere hopeful fairy tales but the products of careful and disciplined thought: that a properly built myth is worthy of belief, at least tentatively" (p. 126).

These children assume fiction has a moral purpose. They need no prodding to extract the moral from a story. But to describe, as Gardner does, a writer as communicating her discoveries to readers makes the readers passive recipients of these insights. The second graders are industrious and discriminating in using tales to make their own tentative but serious ethical discoveries.

Children's understanding of social authority becomes more sophisticated with age (Damon, 1977). Peter's emphasis on the scrutiny of the rational basis of an authority's directives marks his conception as more advanced than that of Paul, who identifies power and authority. Evelyn's recognition of the importance of parents' greater experience suggests an intermediate position. Joan's fluctuation between emphasis on reason and power suggests she is in transition. Sue does not need to know the details of the research on conceptions of authority to sense the diversity of understanding that emerges in these discussions. She takes advantage of this diversity to provoke everyone to scrutinize their own positions. The children listen to one another and present their views with vigor. This is hard intellectual work, but it flies along. This session is likely to promote the growth of higher levels of social and moral knowledge.

But this is no abstract exercise in understanding of authority or moral principles or mastery of logical thought. "Reflectiveness, even logical thinking remain important; but the *point* of cognitive development is not to gain an increasingly complete grasp of abstract principles. It is to interpret from as many vantage points as possible lived experience, the ways there are of being in the world" (Greene, 1988, p. 120).[4] It is also to constitute in this classroom a community that will promote further shared, lived experience and its spirited interpretation.

These explorations are hardly likely to produce children who will see the assertive discipline program as reasonable, effective, or just.[5] The more advanced children, like Joan and Peter, are the most likely to reject that system. They might bow to a teacher's assertiveness, but they will not easily identify with it.

These second-grade discipline theorists want to make sense of questions of social authority and obedience. The more they try to make sense, the more they will move in the direction of Peter's more advanced understanding, and the more their classroom will become a community of moral explorers. Though Peter can easily cause a teacher problems, he does not want chaos. He wants things to make sense. Here, things usually do, and he is a robust and vigorous citizen of the class. Are such students so threatening to the academic and social order that their ruminations about authority must run underground?

*　　*　　*

[March 21] Sue has had to leave the room. A moment after her departure, Dan notices her absence. He peers around the room.

"Who's in charge?" he calls. Each week, someone is given the job of being "in charge" if Sue must leave the room. No one responds to Dan's call. Children keep on with their work, some talking quietly about it. All is normal.

"Who's in charge?" repeats Dan. Peter joins him.

"Who's in charge?"

Others start to attend to them. Someone recalls that James is in charge. He looks up from his work, even paler than usual. Paralyzed by his awesome responsibility, despite the prompting of Dan and Peter, he does nothing. It is not clear exactly what needs to be done, as there is no real disorder.

Peter and Dan take charge of the person in charge. They prompt James to go to the light switch and nudge him to turn it off—the local signal for calm in the room.

"Why can't you just all sit and be quiet?" asks James plaintively. Little changes. Joan is now walking around holding a globe above her head, contemplating some geographical problem. She is absorbed and bothering no one, but the attempts to create order have instead created small ripples of noise.

"Dr. Nicholls is here. He's an adult," Evelyn observes. But no one else thinks this is relevant, and she gets the point.

The three boys' powers of judgment in matters of discipline are not great. They might just as well have kept on with their own work, as most of their classmates did. But many a student teacher has had trouble with such decisions. The potential troublemakers, Dan and Peter, are, nevertheless, committed to the established system. If there is going to be a discipline problem, it will not come from them.

*   *   *

[April 12] Ann's mother has sent Sue a note saying that Ann is unhappy about her relations with other children. Suspecting that Ann's bossiness is involved, Sue initiates a class discussion.

About 10 minutes into it, Ann reveals that she is having trouble getting a cheerleading club organized. She also reports, "I used to have a friend who I had fights with lots of times. I don't know why, but maybe it's because she's bossy."

This triggers a discussion of whether clubs need bosses. Peter scorns Dan's suggestion that they do. Clubs, he argues, are "for people to get together and have fun playing together. Clubs are for people to get along with each other, and to learn to decide things." His resistance to imposed authority is consistent.

Sue directs the question back to earnest Ann.

"When I try to have a club, everyone is wild and talking. When I was in cheerleading club, everything was under control. But when I have a club, everything crazy goes on. I guess people don't think I'm strict."

"Then you can't get their respect," suggests Joan.

"What do you need to get respect?" asks Sue.

"You need to get shades and have a whistle and blow it a lot." Peter intends irony.

Vicki takes strictness seriously but is cynical about adult responsiveness to children: "When adults are around you have to listen and be good 'cause you get in trouble if you don't. Nobody listens to children anyhow." For a while, after her initial fear of school faded, she was a barbarian. She later lived on the boundary between engaging expressiveness and annoying intrusiveness. I, as well as Sue and the children, encountered this. Once, as I sat scribbling at a round table on the perimeter, she alighted, like a wiry bird, on my knee. "What are you writing?" "Well, I'm just writing things down so I can remember all the things that happen here." "Oh." She snatched my pen and wrote "Vicki Maldinado" in large shaky script on my clipboard. For a while, she alighted daily to draw a picture or write her name or some small message. For several weeks she insisted on carrying my clipboard when I went with the class to recess, and teased by keeping my pen. She is still quirkily energetic, but no longer the outsider.

Sue asks again about the meaning of respect.

"Parents don't scare me," says Dan. "Other kids tell on me but I just stand there." We have no trouble believing him. He will not submit easily to power.

Now aligned with Dan, Peter picks up the theme: "You don't *have* to respect parents. I'm not going to stop *just* 'cause *they* say. Some parents need to learn things and some don't."

"Parents deserve respect 'cause they've done a lot for you," argues Joan.

"They're *your* parents, you have to respect them," chimes in James.

"I don't like the President [of the United States] because they don't give you freedom. You have to obey your parents." Peter extends his challenge to the top.

"It's freedom within the rules," Sue suggests.

"I don't like the rules!" cries Joan, switching sides.[6]

Evelyn tells a joke of some relevance to the topic, and Paul contributes his experience:

"I've been the leader of a club. Sometimes people are silly. The best thing to do is act like," he puffs up, "'I'm so strong,' so they're scared and I'll have their attention."

"So, you have to be strong and scare people? . . . What do you think about all this, Claire?"

"I think Dan is saying you don't have to respect people who aren't in your family."

"So are there other people you respect?"

Many contribute examples, mostly involving relatives and school authorities. Evelyn adds, "Heavenly Father and Jesus."

Less deferential, Joan proposes a qualified humanism. "Everybody! You have to respect everybody! Not my sister, though."

Jodie's mother's boyfriend qualifies.

"Respect people your age and older."

"And younger," adds Peter.

"Are you scared of younger people? Is respect something that happens only when you are scared?" probes Sue.

This crystallizes something for Vicki. She snaps upright in her seat.

"You respect people and they respect you back."

"Why?"

"They like you and want to be good to you," explains Vicki.

"They treat you the way they'd like to be treated," adds Joan. The relatively sophisticated ethic of mutual respect gradually gains adherents.

"So if you are a leader, how do you get respect?"

"Respect them and treat them how you want them to treat you," says Joan.

A little later, Ann proposes, "I could bring my jump rope, and people could use it if I was there to watch them."

"Ann! You're too bossy." Joan is right. Ann doesn't seem upset, but Sue is conciliatory without denying Joan's lesson.

"Give her a chance. I think she's got quite a lot to think about. I think we all do."

After recess, Ann, Elizabeth, Vicki, and Jodie want to "do a little cheer" that they have practiced. Their performance is well received. As they leave for lunch, I ask if they had wild arguments in their practice. They grin knowingly. "Only a little bit," says Ann, as they bounce off discussing the cheers they will practice.

Progressive education is sometimes taken to mean sentimental concession to childish impulse. That has not happened here. Sue played the chair, but also presented her own position in the form of questions and challenges. The children have challenged one another robustly and passionately, yet they remain the family Sue wanted. Their differences occasion vigorous and exciting negotiation. It has been a good day for what Dewey called conjoint communicated experience.

CHAPTER 6

Workbooks and Intelligent Work

[September 21] Before the bell rings to signal the beginning of the school day, there is much cooperative activity. Groups and pairs of children fold paper planes, do origami, play cards, and read. When the final bell rings, Sue notes all this. "This morning I noticed a lot of you got busy before the bell. There were lots of people cooperating, sharing ideas. You girls were playing cards. What game was it?"

"Uno."

"Does anyone not know how to play that?" Hands go up.

"Well, here's something you can share with others."

"Alan, I saw you making paper boats. Where did you get the idea?"

"By reading *Curious George*" [a book about a monkey].

"Was that a surprise, to find out about paper boats in *Curious George*?"

"Yes."

"Alan learned that, so later, when you have time, you might ask him to help you learn that." Sue continues around the class labeling the constructive activities, encouraging cooperation and initiative in learning. "You have the 15 minutes before the final bell to do what you choose."

When the bell rings, Sue says, "You chose well and helped each other. Very impressive! Now that the bell has rung, we must stop. You have been learning and sharing, but when the bell rings, we have to do formal learning." I twitch and, catching herself making a categorical distinction between schoolwork and the work they have been doing, Sue qualifies. "We have to learn other things now."

Today, this distinction is destined to blur. Evelyn leads off show-and-tell. With her most whiny, attention-getting tone, she displays a tawdry collection of possessions that elicit little reaction. Then she mentions a trip to the Indianapolis zoo. Suddenly the class is alive. Evelyn has fingered the topic for the morning.

Tim, who had been waiting to tell about his "Alf" [a television character] cards, talks instead about a trip to Chicago's Lincoln Park zoo. From then on, the topic is zoos, animals, and museums. Sue ignores her planned assignments and rides this wave.

"You had so many ideas to share, let's do some writing about your ideas. This is a perfect time for some writing about a zoo or a museum—a time to write about those ideas. You don't have to make sentences or a story. This time it's different. This is the challenge—to write down your ideas, the things you want to write. We are going to write ideas only. For instance: the eagle, the alligator, the cave [at the museum], the turkey buzzard. Just a list of your short ideas."

"Can we draw?"

"Not now. Spelling is not a problem 'cause you are just getting down ideas . . . as many ideas as you can."

"Can we write on the back of the paper as well?"

"Can we use markers?"

"Can we write cursive?"

"Is this the only thing we are going to do?"

"What are we going to do next?"

After these questions are settled, there is 25 minutes of concentrated work. As the momentum declines, Sue puts the students in groups of three, admonishing them to share ideas and come up with more they might write about. Discussions are generally animated. Jodie and Claire listen while Martha says, "I like the elephant, I like the birds."

"You gave me an idea."

"I like the lions. I like the seals. I like . . ."

"The alligators."

"How did you know?" Giggles all around, and on they go.

Sue points out that they have brainstormed and shared ideas and, instead of suggesting, asks, "What could we do now?"

"Start writing."

Sue encourages them to write something using their ideas.

"Gee, that's hard. I've got 16 ideas," says Evelyn.

"You don't have to use them all. Choose the ones you like best—the most interesting ones."

"This time do we write in sentences?" Peter used some at the outset but seems to want this to be made legitimate.

There is no need to urge them to work. Enthusiasm and concentration are everywhere—except for Yong Kim, who has trouble with English. Sue calls him over, and he dictates a story of which he is very proud.

Some are content to guess at spelling, but others seek help.

Quiet, serious Claire has need of a comma and wants to know if its tail goes up or down. I tell her, and she inserts one at the start of her story: "Have you been to New York. Well, in New York there is . . ." For Claire, "punctuation was thus wedded to meaning" (Mayhew & Edwards, 1936/1965, p. 257).[1] She makes this convention speak for her. Everyone is busy communicating their experiences and, like Claire, grappling with the conventional forms our language provides for this purpose. The momentum lasts up to recess, the whole exercise taking almost two hours.

This episode nicely illustrates what Dewey and many others, including those of the whole-language movement, hoped for in schooling: that mastery of the conventions whereby we communicate might be accomplished as a part of the process of communication of matters of consequence to students.

In the afternoon of the same day, Sue distributes a small mound of purple crystals to each student. "We are going to be scientists and figure out what is in front of us . . . Most scientists don't taste things they aren't sure about. Can you tell why?"

"It could make you sick."

"OK. Now, no guessing, just tell me what you see." Many interpretations are volunteered, but Sue directs them to describe and lists their words on the board.

"Crystals, sparkly, pointed, purple, sticky, smells like grape . . ." But guessing cannot be restrained.

"They are magnets."

"Why?"

"It sticks."

"What to?"

"Itself—well, it's not magnets, but it sticks to itself."

"Is it alive?" asks someone.

"It jumped up."

"How can you tell if things are alive?" Suggestions, including movement, are offered.

"Electricity makes it move," suggests Alan.

"How does the electricity get to it?"

"The light from somewhere gets to it and gives it electricity. Things make electricity from light power."

"Do you think it's alive?" A chorus of "yesses" follows. Alan qualifies with "Well, not alive and snorting like an animal."

"How many don't think it's alive?" Six hands go up. Some are uncertain. Everyone is involved.

"Now the next thing to do is put a little bit in your mouth." The room erupts in screams and cries. "Shhhh! You know I wouldn't ask you to do anything that would hurt you." She demonstrates and they follow. The Pop Rocks taste of grape and fizz in the mouth. The class fizzes with them.

"It's driving me crazy!"

"I'm gonna kill these things!"

Sue lets the excitement taper off and says, "I wouldn't give you something alive to eat, so maybe you can forget the theory that it's alive. What was happening inside your mouth?"

"It was moving."

"It popped . . ."

"What might have made it do that?"

"It's wet."

"What did the wet do?"

"It dissolved."

Glasses of water are produced. "Some of you said water had something to do with it. Right?" "Yes." "Shall we see what happens with water?" Each group puts crystals in water and observes them bubble, dissolve, and color the water blue. A lively discussion of these results follows. As it tapers off, Sue asks why someone should make things like these and Rice Krispies. This precipitates further lively discussion. "To make people buy them" seems the most favored opinion.

Finally, Sue charges them to write about the things they saw happening and to see if they can explain them.

"Do I have to write down what it is? Because I want to give them a few questions and let them think." Peter recognizes and appreciates the way Sue ran the lesson. He writes only questions: "What happens when you put water on it? . . . Is it alive? . . ."

Carlos, who struggles with spelling, sits by me so he can ask for assistance, which he does only when stumped. When the bell ends the session, he picks up his half-filled page, pointing to the bottom of the second side. "I'm going to take it home and write all down to here."

George wrote, "I liked the science active. it was nete bekus it popt. It was weird. . . ." He surely wrote for them all. Their enthusiasm to write is almost equal to their involvement in the discussion and exploration.

The contrast between these two episodes and workbook and worksheet sessions is striking. The dramatic, dialogical lesson cannot be reproduced by workbooks. The fact that, in their writing, children can find something they want to say and devise a method of saying it can hardly be irrelevant. In workbooks, the question posed is often of marginal interest and imperfectly comprehended, and the form of the answer is constrained.

An energetic and excited class departs for their buses, leaving Sue to wonder aloud whether she led the class across the line between excitement and disorder. Her one-eyed observer hastens to say she did not. Both sessions involved topics that captured the curiosity and interest of the class. The children raised the first topic, and Sue rode the wave with them. She initiated the second one. But in each case they addressed questions that were, for them, complex, offering some sense of adventure, and that involved them in the mastery of the more banal matters of conventional forms of written and spoken communication.

*   *   *

Individual differences in competence are present and obvious in every subject. In reading, grouping students of roughly similar ability is the traditional response to this. When a group sits with Sue to read, the students talk a lot, often about personal experiences that bear on the stories they are reading. They ask their share of questions and offer their own observations. These are lively little communities of text interpretation and dialogue about the world. As many observers have noted, however, the activities typically assigned to those not reading with the teacher are often less engrossing.[2]

[October 10] While Sue works with a reading group, Carlos starts on the assigned coloring, cutting, and pasting sheet. He bends over, concentrating, coloring the first of eight panels in a vivid orange. His interest fades after this panel. He pops, fizzes, and buzzes with his fingers in his mouth, grins to himself, and bounces happily in his chair. Peter joins him and they set out to explore the range of sounds that can be made with a human mouth and hand. They then discuss their recess soccer games. Carlos, a dashing, macho soccer lover with little concern for the bottom line, claims to have scored one goal.

"No, you got at least five one day." Peter is always keeping score. "And I got four one day . . ."

"Excuse me, Peter," Sue interrupts. "Could you move and let Carlos finish?" Carlos moves ahead intermittently, with the quality of his product steadily declining. At the last panel he looks around, dreaming, coming to only when I pass by saying, "Hey, you've nearly done that."

Later the same day, in a session when everyone has been assigned the same worksheets, Alan notices Paul has a different assignment.

"Why are you doing that?" he asks, loud with surprise and outrage. Paul tries to explain that Sue has given him a unique assignment, but Alan keeps asking his question in an accusing tone until Sue calls for quiet and explains.

For Alan, who hates most worksheet and workbook activities, the notion that everyone should be doing the same worksheet appears strongly established. There is nothing Sue and I can think of that has made this an explicit rule, but it is consistent with the notion that worksheets are a kind of test, where everyone must do the same work. Alan dislikes these regimented sessions but, here, collaborates to impose uniformity.

[October 17] "This morning there are three morning papers [worksheets] and some reading [workbook] assignments." Sue points to the list on the board. "*Towers*, you have these pages in the workbook and these in the bonus book."

"Ah! That's a lot," mutters Alan as the assignments for his group are pointed out.

Low moans float up from unidentifiable sources.

"This looks like hard, tough work," says Dan, scanning the worksheets.

"Goodness, Dan, it's so nice to hear your pencil talking and not your mouth." Sue easily quiets him, but the groaning affects her. Teaching requires the consent of students, and discontent will not be chased away by the exercise of power. To make the task appear reasonable, Sue adjusts.

There are three worksheets. At the top of the first are six rhymes to be completed. One reads:

"What a good idea for stew I've got.
Where's that big old iron _____?"

"Pot" and five other words to be chosen from among float in a pot at the bottom of the page.

Sue quickly goes through each question, having someone find each answer.

"Now we know what it's supposed to say. When you get to this place, you put it in."

She walks them through the sheet, pleasantly enough, but with no spark from her or the students. This resembles the fragmentation strategy some high school teachers use (McNeil, 1986)—they reduce complex topics to lists of easy-to-learn, easy-to-test bits of information. This does little to help students understand the complexity of the world, but it helps keep them quiet and in their seats. Students know exactly what is expected and the course content appears rigorous and objective. The evaluation of student work seems fair and unpolluted by teacher bias. When school is seen as a test, rather than an adventure in ideas, students can adopt this limited vision of fairness: Teachers are fair if they specify, in listlike fashion, exactly what must be learned to gain a satisfactory grade.

With this implicit contract in place, it is difficult for teachers to promote exploration of the many sides of ambiguous, controversial topics. Students will stop fidgeting and mumbling and will diligently take notes if the teacher gives up discussion of diverse perspectives on the causes of the Civil War and instead lists those causes that will be on the test. The result is schooling that is fair in the restricted sense that everyone knows how the teacher will evaluate them. It is, however, unexciting, unenlightening, and irrelevant to the students' personal knowledge of the world. They learn the lists and expect that this will help them gain good grades and even paid employment. But they do not expect the lists of arid details to help them interpret life (McNeil, 1986). Such schooling is unfair in the wider sense that it prepares students to pass other peoples' tests without strengthening their capacity to set their own assignments in collaboration with their fellows. The concern with grades can blind them to the triviality of the questions they address and the larger injustice of an unexamined life. Thus can students themselves help prevent their academic activities from gaining scope and coherence.

Workbooks and worksheets offer packaged, fragmented knowledge. Sue does not intentionally introduce them to maintain control, but she faces a common dilemma: When you work with one reading group, what do you do with the other students? In this sense workbooks serve to maintain order. But, for whatever reason they are introduced, they dictate much of what follows. Sue feels compelled to simplify the tasks (if they are too hard) so the students will see them as fair and doable. She cannot make workbooks and worksheets seem an adventure. She is captured by the students' interpretation of them as tests and struggles to make the test less fearsome by walking them through it.

As Sue leads them through, the moaning ceases and they become calm. This is not the same teacher and these are not the students who were scientists examining purple crystals and naturalists discussing and writing about animals. Only the names remain the same.

The second and third assignments are introduced. Sue asks if there are any words that the students can't read and explains those. The second sheet involves choosing synonyms for underlined words—for example, "Do Halloween ghosts *scare* you?" "Frighten," printed on a bat at the bottom of the page, is the expected choice. The final sheet is titled "Ghostly Little Riddles." Sue elicits the meaning of *riddle* from the students, then introduces the task. When solving the riddles, the children do not relate the answers they find back to the riddle. This is answer-finding rather than riddle-solving.

Sue calls the *Moonbeams* reading group up to read with her. Alan, who is in another group, comes up to point out that Sue has made a mistake in his group's workbook assignment. When Sue releases his group from the assignment, he looks as if he had been released from prison. Two days earlier, after he had finished his workbook assignments, I asked how he liked that work.

"I mostly like to be finished with this work," he said with a sigh. Normally he is very active in class discussions. He loves intellectual puzzles. He avidly follows the stories Sue reads and sparkles with interest in reading groups. He cannot be termed lazy. He is close to nuts about anything to do with computers. He does not even say he'd rather not do the workbook assignments, only that he likes having them done. A few weeks later, he assigns himself the task of copying a story he likes from a reader. He works at this in his spare time over two weeks. It is workbook work, not all intellectual work, that Alan wants to be finished with.

Normally industrious, Jack sits at the back with his workbook. As directed by the instructions, he completes the sentence "Stan told us about an _____ story he has read" by crossing out "interesting" in a list of possible answers and copying it into the blank. He daydreams briefly, then completes "Madeline has been _____ stamps for a long time" by crossing out "collecting" and printing it in the space. He stares blankly at the wall for some time. Claire, from the same reading group, plows through seven such items while Jack travels unknown seas. When he does work on the assignment, he spends more and more time elaborately blotting out the words he chooses. His heart is not in the work. He makes several mistakes on the last questions though they seem no harder than the rest.

[October 19] As Sue starts the *Moonbeams* on the story "Nate the Great," Peter, sitting alone with his worksheets, pops up in his seat. "Oh, that's a really great story," he calls out. Shortly, from the back of the room, Wole says, to no one in particular, "Oh, no! I know this one. I know what's happening." He follows for a couple of minutes before returning to his work. Peter keeps listening and commenting quietly as the story progresses.

The *Towers* are next to read with Sue. Dan sits ignoring his worksheet, listening to their discussion of Indians. He turns to me to say, "We are going to study Indians in Cub Scouts two weeks from now," and goes back to listening. The workbooks cannot compete for his attention.

On the same day, in a unit on spiders, a worksheet has a series of boxes:

Add 4			
3	1	4	5

Add 3			
2	7	3	1

Carlos is confused about what to do. On the first one he is supposed to add 4 to all the other numbers: $3 + 4$, $1 + 4$, $4 + 4$, and, finally, $5 + 4$. He eventually takes the "Add 4" as an instruction only and does not think to add the "4" after the "Add" to each other number. He adds the 4 on the line between the 1 and 5 to the 3, then to the 1 and finally to the 5. What to do with the 4 itself is a puzzle. He adds the 5 to it, thus getting the wrong answer under the 4. He maintains his interpretation of the task until he encounters an instance where the number to be added is not included in the four numbers below it. Now he is stumped. He added easily and accurately. Nevertheless, someone who had not watched him would be likely to assume that his "incorrect" answers reflected errors of addition rather than an idiosyncratic but not unreasonable interpretation of the question.

[October 24] A math worksheet entitled "Creepy Concoctions" shows a witch's cauldron full of subtraction problems (or facts) such as $9 - 5 = \_\_$. Above the cauldron are bubbles with answers such as $\_\_ - \_\_ = 4$. The instructions are: "Fill in each bubble with subtraction facts from the witch's pot. Cross off each fact as you use it." The students are accustomed to the crossing-off strategy, but the task confuses at least a third of them. The simplest approach would be to solve each subtraction problem in turn, then look for the bubble with that answer in it. But they are stumped because they start with one of the numbers in a bubble, then look for a subtraction sum that gives that answer. They are slow at subtraction and become frustrated after getting correct answers to a succession of subtraction problems without getting the answers they are looking for. Many ask me or Sue for help. The suggestion that they answer any problem in the cauldron and then look for the bubble that has that answer enables most to do the job easily, but with little sense of why. What is achieved?

"This is too hard," mutters Tim. He puts the "Creepy" sheet aside and starts one of the others assigned for this session. This also proves hard for him. He asks me for help with words he cannot read. He and many others have trouble with the names of people on this sheet (Leilani, Herbie, and Georgie) and with other words (medicine, aloe, foxglove, faint).

On this work, they often seek adult help. They generally assume they should not collaborate. Today at least three children put their hands over their work when another appears to be looking at it. One calls, "No cheating!" But Evelyn tells me that she and Jill are going to share the work—"She's going to do this one, and I'm going to do this one [and so on]." Instead they collaborate on each item.

[September 20] George is doing a worksheet requiring alphabetizing of lists of words. I ask, "Is that a good thing to learn?"

"No, because my hand hurts."

"We've done a lot of work," Alan adds. He lists the assignments and concludes, "I call that too much."

A week later George is, on his own initiative, writing a story in cursive script. Everyone else is printing. They have had no instruction in cursive.

"Cursive writing," I whisper. "Is that hard?"

"No."

"Does it hurt your hand?"

"No." He laboriously copies cursive letters one at a time from a chart on the wall. The work is slow, deliberate, and intense, surely a difficult manual task. Yet the subjective experience of effort is not to be compared with that of worksheets, where he has no say in selecting the task or in how it is executed, let alone in defining the meaning of the activity.

Whole-class instruction is sometimes thought of as "bad traditional" instruction. But it can be dramatic, thought-provoking, and more engaging than most seatwork, especially the way Sue usually does it: with a dramatic sense and with responsiveness to the children's own questions. There is little danger of any individual's failing to complete work or falling far behind. No one is put on the spot. Those not participating will be called on and gently encouraged. If they cannot contribute, they are not embarrassed. If their attention flags, Sue modifies her approach. When this does not work, she leads them to another topic. They are stimulated, prodded to stretch for insight and justify their answers, but not pushed beyond their strength or understanding.

[October 10] "I want to talk about a problem people had a long, long time ago. . . . They had trouble telling who owned bits of land. They had to find some way of measuring. . . . The King made his foot the measure. . . ." She calls Peter up and asks him to measure the length of the room by walking heel to toe from front to back. The class spontaneously counts. By the time he reaches the end, in 45 "feet," all but Jodie and Carlos have joined in the counting.

Jodie is called up and takes 44 steps. "But she left spaces between her feet at the end," an observer notes.

Wole begins to step out the distance. Carlos and Jodie are now following with everyone.

"His feet are the same," calls Dan as Wole reaches 20. He is almost right. Wole records 45 steps.

Everyone counts George's progress. He takes 40 steps.

"He's got bigger feet."

Joan takes a turn. Again everyone is involved. Sue stops her at 45—3 steps short of the wall—and continues the student-initiated discussion of the problems involved in this method of measurement. She raises the unfairness of dividing up land if different feet were used on different occasions and the impossibility of using the King's foot for all measuring.

"I know—you could use a baby," suggests Peter.

"What do you mean? Plonk a baby on the ground and turn it over and over?"

This is greeted with laughter. Peter, who had not intended humor, persists. "You could use a stuffed baby."

"Oh—like a doll that wouldn't get hurt," says Sue.

A discussion of measuring sticks and units of measurement follows. Then, "I'm going to give you a unit that is this long." Sue holds up a paper clip. "You can use this to measure your desk." (The desks are all the same size.) All receive two clips and quickly set about measuring by alternately advancing the clips across their desks. The answers range from 16 to 20, with 18 most common.

"Let's see what mine show," says Sue, and starts laying out one after the other, with everyone (including Jodie and Carlos) counting until she reaches 18 at the edge of the desk.

This has all been by way of introduction to a mathematics book unit on measurement. Shortly after the beginning of this introduction, everyone is actively involved, and they stay that way. The book, however, lacks this power to engross, even though it depicts measuring operations of the sort the class has been actually doing. Apart from the fact that the book makes students more passive, its arbitrary visual conventions produce confusions that were not evident in the public lesson. Sue acknowledges the fading focus. "I've got a feeling we've lost it here. Would you close your books and put this away."

[October 12] Two days later, a discussion of rulers leads to an exercise in the text. The task is to measure and mark specified lengths on pictures of sticks. Small bug-eyed creatures printed on the page announce the length to be measured off on each stick. Each creature emits a speech bubble with a length ("7 cm" and so on). In most cases, the speech bubble is between the creature and the indicated stick, but some creatures look at "their" sticks, others look above them, some below them and some in the opposite direction.

After explaining the task, Sue asks who does not understand. Seven hands go up. She explains again. Hands keep going up. Peter, an unusually analytic interpreter of directions, asks me about the possible interpretations of a particularly confusing pair.

Most can do the measuring, but the obscurity of the instructions forces them to depend on adults. Like many tasks in this text, this one leaves them with no meaningful outcome. They do not know the length of their desks, of the room, or of anything of relevance to their lives. Nor do they gain a sense of the ways one might measure things in the world. The task is problematic without being enlightening. Mastery of the arbitrary conventions of specific computer programs can lead to the capacity to do new and useful things, but the main gain from completion of these idiosyncratic tasks is the release from the need to do more of them.[3]

Responding to the children's confusion with the instructions, Sue comments, "See, they [the authors] are trying to see if you can follow the directions"—a charitable interpretation of the intentions of the writers, but probably the best one could offer to help make this work meaningful. But shouldn't the ability to detect foolishness in tasks also be encouraged? In attempting to use these materials, Sue is more or less trapped into discouraging critical thinking about the value of the tasks her students tackle. The measurements are finished with good humor, but can hardly be as meaningful as the paper clip and foot measurements of the earlier day.

The next day, Sue decides to make her way without the math book. She has devised a variety of measuring tasks, printed out on cards, that children tackle in pairs. They have to choose among foot rulers, yard rulers, decimeter rulers, meter rulers, and measuring tapes. There is lively discussion of the different scales before they start. The difference between width and length has to be clarified.

As they work making and recording measurements, many other problems arise. Is it better to measure the length of the blackboard at the level of the chalk shelf along its bottom or to find a line across somewhere above this? The first impulse is, usually, not to take advantage of the shelf to rest rulers on and keep them straight. The advantages of a long ruler when measuring a plant's height are not immediately obvious to a pair who start by trying to hold foot rulers stationary in the air beside the plant. One pair sets off measuring the distance to the drinking fountain, alternately laying down two rulers on a line that wanders back and forth across the hall. After some confusion, they recognize the problem and achieve a straight line by following the cracks between the square floor tiles. One reminds the other to keep the ends of the rulers together, "like with the feet." Other problems that on the face of it appear simple, such as measuring one's waist, require serious negotiation over the instrument to use and the way to use it accurately.

All come together to compare and discuss their findings. The fact that these do not always converge heightens awareness of the problems of measuring. These are not easy problems for second graders, but they are edifying—a world away from the workbook.

[October 21] In groups of three, children read and discuss drafts of stories they have written for Halloween. Carlos reads last in his group and is embarrassed about having trouble making himself understood—he has a slight lisp and a trace of a Chilean accent. He fools around briefly, rejecting solid, caring Elizabeth's offer to read his story for him. He does, however, seem pleased with his story and determined to practice reading aloud as, after Jodie and Elizabeth turn away from him, he reads it to no apparent audience.

When writing, he sometimes asks how to spell a word, but copying never seems to appear as a possibility. When groups disband to do further work on the stories and associated drawings, most of them are absorbed.

Dan brings his story up to me. "Look," he says. Before I can respond, he reads it aloud. It is full of dialogue and quite expressive. Before I can comment, he rushes back to his seat to write on.

Jill is more alive than usual, copying from a draft of her story and then expanding it.

"I'm going to make a lot of copies. I'm going to make one for each person at home," she announces to me. Instead, she keeps adding to her story. As she tapes a second page onto her first one, she announces, "There! I'm doing a big story." We do not hear such comments about workbook or worksheet assignments.

"I see the ideas are really flowing here," comments Sue as she passes by.

Sitting next to Jill, Martha has more trouble than most spelling the words she wants to use. She asks me for help and becomes passive, hoping I will take over. On other work, she often gives up and seeks to copy or get someone to tell her what to do. Now I will not help, so she barges ahead. Her spelling is flawed, but she becomes active and involved. Unlike tasks from the math and language workbooks, this one offers the promise of a coherent accomplishment. Martha does not have to be able to spell every word to write her story. She does not have the experience of being stopped in her tracks while others get further and further ahead on worksheets.

Dewey sought a theory of experience that would guide education. He strove to avoid experience that increases specific skills, but confines life to a narrow course. He also sought to avoid experience that is exciting or fun but does not strengthen the disposition for increasingly complex and meaningful experience. The educative experience he sought would foster interest and excitement, strengthen skills and widen horizons, and make knowledge more coherent. This experience would involve "an organic connection between education and personal experience" (1938, p. 25).[4] It would start with personal concerns and expand these to encompass the wisdom, knowledge, and skills of the child's culture. These should truly become the child's property, that she might enhance its value. Not inert property, but material from which to fashion new experiences—intellectual adventure for the child and for society.

A week after the Pop Rocks session, Sue and I sit down to discuss her philosophy and to review progress. "When I set up writing activities," says Sue into the tape recorder, "I make sure I draw on common experiences so they're meaningful and so [students] have a wealth of vocabulary to draw on. Then the experiences [of writing] are not traumatic. They're exciting and the children are eager to go on and relate whatever it is that they've experienced. . . . I'll either provide the experience or they'll go ahead and indicate that they have experienced the same thing. . . . They have the common experience and yet they'll be able to show individuality. . . ." When it is clear that the purpose for writing is there, "Usually I give them about three qualifiers. So if it's a thank-you letter we are writing, they'd have to get in the thank-you. They'd need to say what they liked and what they learned." Her rationale and practice, which are in this respect similar for mathematics and science, have much in common with Dewey's theory of experience. There is a constant search for the topic or question that is meaningful, and then for subtle ways of using this to launch new questions and gain new knowledge and skills.

The workbooks and textbooks do not fit easily into this picture. "I don't see that the basal readers and our follow-up activities in the practice skill books or the bonus books have the fire [that the Ramona books can spark]."

"So does this mean that the curriculum materials as such are not so important to you?"

"I think so," says Sue, not wholly meaning it. My question oversimplifies, implying a dichotomy between the child and the curriculum materials. Sue clarifies. "My focus is on the *learner*. ... So whatever curriculum material I'm presenting to the child, I want to make sure that it's relevant. And I want to make sure they can handle it, manipulate it, work with it, understand it, solve whatever the dilemma might be. ... I guess I have a great deal of concern about whether they have totally become involved in the learning process. ... Unfortunately, quite often the follow-up [workbook] activities that the basal company has created are so formal, and they only permit one correct response. ... It's more accountable ... and we do have that factor to come up against."

"I [have the children] do more discussing than I do writing. I don't think there are many teachers who spend as much time discussing as I do. That's because I really want a picture of what's inside that child's mind. ... If I can give them an opportunity to express themselves, then I can tell how much they've actually applied to themselves and gained as new knowledge. ... We've relied too much on paper and pencil for feedback. I get feedback from personal comments, from body language, from glib remarks that come out later in the day. I have to be constantly listening, sorting, sifting, and storing."

"All I am is a stimulus. I'm not necessarily the 'educator.' I might just stimulate a thought that carries that child on his own. ... I don't look upon my role as being totally a provider of information. If I did, I think it would be a really sad environment—if I were the lecturer, the authority, the only one who would provide information. I want them to know that I can learn from them as much as they can learn from me."

All of this is manifest in Sue's teaching, but rarely when textbooks and workbooks are used. Sue does not feel she can discard them entirely, but when she expounds her philosophy of teaching, there is no real place for them. Her preferred approach is more consistent with the whole-language perspective than with the mechanistic thinking underlying workbooks and worksheets.[5] When she uses workbooks and worksheets, she finds herself in the role of a coach trying to improve aptitude test scores. When she does try to justify them, she reaches for Benjamin Bloom's taxonomy of educational objectives, which provides a sort of justification for teaching discrete bits of information. As Lipman (1988) puts it, this taxonomy is a "Gibraltar-like pyramid of cognitive functions, of which the recall of grubby facts formed the ignominious base and of which analytical and evaluative skills formed the exalted apex" (p. 4).

It is a view of knowledge that sits well with the mentality of worksheet constructors, who seem to be providing the grubby base of the pyramid on which the apex of pure reason will later shine. It is incompatible with Sue's respect for the experience children bring to the class and their growing ability to evaluate the nature and significance of their own intellectual activities. They do not need to be persuaded that "basic" skills and information are important, but it does not follow that such skills and knowledge must be mastered through worksheet exercises before significant thought is possible. Sometimes the class becomes engrossed in a worksheet. A task of coloring and matching words is sometimes just what they want. Then crayons and pencils rubbing on paper make the only ripples of sound in the room. But this is rare.

PART III

Disciplines Disciplined by Students

CHAPTER 7

Curriculum Theory: What Knowledge Is of Most Worth?

From the outset, Sue seeks student views on the value of different types of knowledge. Initially her concern in doing this is to make assignments seem as meaningful as possible. On the first Friday, a discussion precedes the first language workbook assignment.

"Why do we need to know words?" asks Sue.

"So we can talk to people."

"What's important about talking to people?"

"We can communicate. We can know what they mean."

"What does 'communicate' mean?"

"It means you get together," says Wole. "Like, 'Hi, Tim. How are you?' and he says, 'Hi.'"

Other methods of communication are discussed, including pictures and symbols. The advantages of words emerge.

Alan volunteers that "If you didn't know English, you couldn't learn your schoolwork."

"How do babies learn?"

This leads to a discussion of different languages and of problems of communication across cultures.

"Why don't they all speak the same language?" Peter wants to know. "Then it would be easy."

"They can't agree on which one to have," says Sue.

"Well, why don't they make up a new one?" asks Peter.

The students see the conventions of language as created by humans and as potentially changeable, but they also see consensus as essential for communication. This understanding is evident in a discussion of the conventions of arithmetic.

[September 7] Sue writes "8" on the board and asks, "Is that a number?"

"Yes."

"Is there another way to write 8?" A volunteer writes "eight" on the board. "Is this the number 8? Is 'eight' '8'? Yes or no?"

"Yes."

"I can't understand how they can both be 8," says Sue, deadpan.

"I can do it another way," volunteers Jodie and goes up to write "VIII."

"What have we done?" asks Sue.

"I know another way." Tim writes a differently shaped "8."

"Well, that's close to this [8]," comments Sue, "so I'll not count it." Jack writes, "2 + 2 + 2 + 2 =   ."

Evelyn writes "K" and announces, without conviction, "It's a German 8." The others let this pass.

Most are preoccupied with getting a turn to put an answer on the board. "0 + 8" and "7 + 1" go up. Claire, who is from Japan, puts up the Japanese symbol for 8, which is received with much interest. They keep trying to suggest more ways of writing 8 after they have run out of ways.

*   *   *

Because students see language and symbols as tools for communication, it is meaningful for Sue to encourage standard forms in writing—for example, by matter-of-factly misreading words they have run together.

"Does this say . . . ?" Or, "If you write . . . the reader will be confused and not know what you are saying."

[October 10] Alan reads aloud, "She stopped near the water . . ." Sue repeats this to him.

"Look at it. Is 'She stopped near the water . . .' the same as 'She stopped. Near the water . . .'?"

"Oh!" Alan gets the point of the period and rereads the passage correctly.

[January 10] Sue points to the sentence Martha has written and brought up for scrutiny. One *b* is poorly formed. "An *l* and an *o* pushed together make a perfect *b*, but the way you've got them separate, I'd read it and think it was '*lo*'." Martha is easily crushed by hints that she is wrong, but her expression says, "Oh, yes!" She returns to her seat and quickly corrects the error.

Sue's treatment of these errors is more than a correction. It highlights what the children recognize as the essential function of words and writing. It prompts the students to discern what they need to do by considering whether their writing communicates.

"That's not right" would be coercive without conveying the reason for the problem. "That's not right" is also more likely to make a child feel that her competence, rather than the task of communication, is the issue.

Children understand the point of intellectual conventions rather well. They do not need to be persuaded that these conventions should be mastered, and they leap to correct mistakes and communicate more clearly. However, like most adults, they see the details of conventional methods of communicating as secondary in importance compared to the substance of one's knowledge. They are eager to master cursive script and do not have to be persuaded that there is a point to learning spelling, but this is not the real meat of intellectual life, even for second graders (Nicholls & Thorkildsen, 1989).

* * *

As the year passes, Sue involves the students in increasingly complex discussions of the nature of knowledge, the value of different types of knowledge, and educational methods. For a democratic society, these are basic questions. An education that strengthens students' ability to negotiate and decide what is worth doing is one that produces citizens. If students are only stimulated to think about efficiency, about how to do things, they are being trained for technocracy. There is much research on students' knowledge of *how* to learn, but students' conceptions of the nature and value of the types of knowledge they might acquire in school has been accorded scant attention. The term "metacognition" could refer to beliefs about what knowledge is of most worth. In practice, however, it refers to a flourishing field of study of children's conceptions of how to learn or remember assigned tasks.[1]

In view of this, our plan had been that, when the school year was well under way, I would interview students about the curriculum and discuss my findings with Sue, after which we would observe the results of any adjustments she might make. I began but did not continue these interviews. A researcher interested in children's views about their schooling can be a pleasant surprise for children who are unaccustomed to being consulted. They are often impressed that an adult is interested in their views. Individual interviews are not necessary, however, to get Sue's students to speak freely. Furthermore, asking them to speak about the class outside of it, I felt like a friend asking a loyal family member to discuss family matters behind the others' backs.

Our question, in any event, was whether dialogue about the nature and point of what children are learning could be a vital part of their education. This, not the "independent" researcher's questions or individual students' answers, is the point. I am relieved as, when the moments are right, Sue starts discussions on topics I had hoped to discuss with students and others. Now the children do not merely have their say, as they might when interviewed by an outsider. Their ideas are challenged, worked over, and reconstructed, and all this helps constitute the ethic of the classroom. We begin with science.

*   *   *

[February 22] "What's the best way to learn about science?" asks Sue.

"Have a scientist instructor."

"Science projects."

"I like to see pictures," declares Dan. "Not just people telling. And it is neat how people can share ideas. Like, some of my friends have weird ideas. Ulp! I don't mean they're stupid. I think they are silly, but then I think about it, and it makes sense." He does not have to be taught the value of dialogue for fostering insight.

"Read books."

"Have a scientist here."

"Have a movie."

"We could have an hour or 30 minutes and *do* things about science. Then we can write about it and tell it," says Peter, developing Dan's ideas.

"I think we should have experiments in the room," says Dan.

"How would you do it?" asks Sue.

"Use measuring things."

"Make time bombs and see what would happen," says James.

"How would you do experiments?" Sue repeats. "Would you want me to do them?"

"I want us to do it. Like on our desks," says Dan. "We could have a center and probably make a book about it."

"We could get paper and everyone can make a picture of what happens."

"We could send notes home asking for help to get materials," says Evelyn, ever looking to adults.

"I'd like to do them safely," urges Tim, thinking of the time-bomb proposal.

Model-making is proposed.

"I'm putting together a *Challenger* [space shuttle] kit. It really helps me understand the engine and how it works," says James.

"We wouldn't have to talk only about space," says Dan. "My friend has a good model of an aircraft carrier."

"What did you learn by looking at the model?"

"Not much . . ."

"What is science?" asks Sue.

"Learning."

"What happened in the past," says Claire, puzzling Sue for the moment.

"It's what happened in the film [we saw]."

"Wires."

"Engines."

"Water."

"Space."

"History."

"Can you explain more how history and science are like each other, Claire?"

"Like about the dinosaurs."

"Oh, yes!"

"Science is what you're thinking about and what you discover," says Peter. He seems to know, as William James (1907) put it, that scientists have not "deciphered authentically the eternal thoughts of the Almighty" (p. 56), that their theories are only "a man-made language" (p. 57), that "no theory is absolutely a transcript of reality" (p. 57). Peter's thought resonates.

"You go on trips and try to see what happens . . . you put a straw in water and . . ." says Alan.

"One thing I like in science is things from the past," says Paul.

"Maybe we can put all the information in the computer," suggests Alan, always seeking to use the magic machine.

"How will you know," asks Sue, "if the information is accurate?"

"Get different books and read them and get models and compare."

"Why would you want to go to more than one thing?"

"Computers don't know everything."

"To see if everyone thinks the same thing, and if they do, it's probably true," suggests Vera.

"So you could read lots of things by many people we'd know? Peter, what do you think?"

He has been waving his hand to say, "Sometimes we like to be surprised. We like it if you do like with the Pop Rocks." Independent though he is, he appreciates what his teacher can do for him. He recalls an occasion when she made learning an adventure, even though she knew, and he knew she knew, where the journey was going.

Dan reveals his enthusiasm for the emerging possibilities. "We don't always have fun at recess. We might stay in and do it. I mean, stay in and do science, not math and stuff."

"I have a book on air-cushion vehicles." Possibilities proliferate.

"Should I teach science like reading?" asks Sue, to provoke clarification. A chorus of "no's" indicates the inappropriateness of the idea, not a dislike of reading.

Peter leaps to rule out workbook-type tasks. "We should really do it in life. We get tired of answering lots of questions. Scientists aren't inside doing worksheets. They are in the world finding things."

"Peter, do scientists write things?"

"They write after their experiments," says Peter, blissfully ignorant of the problems of writing to gain funding for research.

"So you want to write afterward?"

"We could write lists of what we want to do and then do them and then write it or maybe type it and then tell it," suggests Dan, who a couple of weeks earlier had been resisting any form of writing.

"Sometimes writing things down means you don't forget," says Sue hopefully.

"And you could keep those ideas and that would tell you what children think about." Dan, even with his "reading problem" and propensity to be a troublemaker, recognizes this as an issue for educators. This is not an isolated occasion. He often takes the teacher's perspective.

Ann proposes the learning of different sections of a book by different students, who would then teach one another.

"You know what Peter said," bursts out Dan. "We don't want to read [about science] all the time. We want to do real things."

Ann is a little startled at this response to her good intentions.

Before Sue can think of a way out for Ann, Evelyn diverts attention. Often eager to be seen to do the right thing, and assuming that the right thing must be dictated by books, teachers, and preachers, she brightly waves the science book, which all were issued but which has barely been used. "It gives experiments in your science book."

Everyone takes out their science text. Sue suggests they decide what topics they most want to study. They discuss the book and the issues among one another. Sue thinks she has a chance to sit for a moment and catch her wits, but quickly people crowd around to say what they are interested in.

"I like animals. I want to be a vet," says Claire with her book open to pictures of animals.

Into the gentle clamor of preferences, Dan brings his review of the textbook. "What do they think we are?" He points to a picture of a calf that has the caption "What happens if an animal has no food?" "This tells you things I already know. Some of these things my grandfather already told me." He has his own science books that are more complex than the one the book-selection committee has blessed him with.

The bell for recess terminates this flurry of interest and comment. We are both impressed with the class's lively sense of what science is. During recess, we decide Sue will challenge them further.

When they reassemble, Sue asks, "Do you think you will know enough to teach each other?"

"That's not what I mean," says Dan, groping for the conception of experiment and dialogue he articulated earlier. "We could tell each other stuff, what we did learn."

"So, you just want to be reporters," says Sue, pushing harder.

"No, no," says Wole. He has said little so far, but senses that Dan and Peter have a more complex case that deserves consideration. "If we're right, we can tell people."

"Don't you need a grown-up to tell you if you're right?" Sue challenges.

"If you read a book and you're sure it's true, you could tell."

"Mrs. Hazzard, you don't get what I'm saying. We can give them information." Dan appears to imply that others can evaluate the information themselves.

"How can *I* tell you got it right?"

"We can prove to you by doing something—like making a light or something. We could do it by attaching wires and showing you."

"Only grown-ups have good ideas," asserts Sue, strong but deadpan, contradicting her everyday practice of taking their ideas seriously.

"Some kids have good ideas," calls Joan.

Peter is suspicious.

"Oh, you're trying to get our brains to brain-work. You're trying to trick us into thinking."

"I'm really interested . . ." Sue protests. They are both right, but Peter is slightly disgusted.

"You always act like this," he exaggerates.

Ann sees other sides to it. "If you're going to be the teacher, it helps you understand and it helps our friends be able to help each other."

"Know who else it helps?" Dan pauses until everyone looks expectantly at him, then turns to the back of the room. "Dr. Nicholls!" I have to stop scribbling to acknowledge this brief digression from the main show, which then rolls on.

"Other kids can be knowing something a teacher doesn't," claims Joan.

"Since when?" Sue challenges, now with a trace of a grin.

"Do you know anything about judo?" says Dan, advancing threateningly, glaring up from just below Sue's waist.

"What team does Rafael Palmiero play for? Who did he play for before them?" Peter calls.

"What's the name of my piano teacher?" calls Evelyn.

"I know you're not going to be mean to me," says James. His expression says he is joking about Sue's mock-assertive challenge to student judgment, as he claims to know his teacher well enough not to be fooled by her. Sue acknowledges his insight with a fleeting wry smile and a raised eyebrow. He smiles quiet satisfaction with this delicate exchange as Tim, who speaks some Armenian, calls,

"Teachers don't know Armenian."

"So," blusters Sue, in mock confusion. "So, I don't know everything. That became obvious real quick. Since teachers don't know everything, it wouldn't hurt to share ideas that we know well. And, as you've said, if you don't know things, there are ways we can learn. Remind me of those ways, then we'll think of what science to study."

They recapitulate their suggestions for methods, and Peter repeats, "Can't we do it in real life?"

"You have my mind swimming with ideas," says Sue. "You want to be explorers, and what will I do?"

"Help us."

"Sit around and wait."

"What for?"

"For us to finish."

*   *   *

[February 27] "We talked a lot about science and how it should be taught. When it comes to reading, is that different? Do you have any ideas about reading?"

"I like the way it's taught." Vera is eager to register her vote.

Unlike some of the others, Vera did not look scared or distressed at the beginning of the year, but she was very self-contained. Within a few weeks she looked perfectly relaxed, with an air of physical and emotional robustness and grace. At that point, she appeared a possible barometer of the ethos of the class. She spoke little, but her body and eyes said much. By December, Vera was often more than merely relaxed and secure. She wore a quiet, twinkling smile as if she carried some secret, surprising gem—perhaps the conviction that school is safe, interesting, humane? I then wondered if the class might have reached its ideal, final working state. With other duties pressing, I contemplated ending observations shortly after the half year. But there was no significant plateau for Vera or the class. Now graceful and strong, Vera sparkles with enthusiasm for school and interest in her classmates. She is an articulate, determined, considerate contributor to discussions.

"What about reading groups?" asks Sue.

"You don't go too fast, so we can get used to it. And you tell us lots about the story," says Evelyn.

"And if we can't get it, you tell us," adds Vicki.

"I like it when we have our silent reading," says Alan.

There are complaints that they haven't had reading groups very frequently. "That's because we've had the student teachers," Sue explains.

There is wide approval of the way reading is conducted. But workbooks haven't been mentioned. Sue asks, "How could I teach the stuff in the workbooks?"

"You know the stuff that's in there, and you just review it and tell the teacher," says Peter. "The reading book is showing you words to learn, and the workbook is showing and telling what you did when you read." Workbooks, he is saying (or close to saying), test rather than teach. He does not miss much. Vicki waves her hand vigorously and backs him up. Is it an accident that she too showed early signs of rebelliousness?

In a chapter justifying and suggesting improvements in workbooks, Jean Osborn (1984) starts her list of "properties that are unique" to workbooks with "Workbooks provide the teacher with what is often the only clear and uncompromised feedback about what each student can do" (p. 181). To Vicki and Peter, this is no strength.

Sue makes a couple of appeals for the workbook. Dan echoes Peter's theme. He will hear nothing good about workbooks.

"How did people learn the vowel sounds?" asks Sue. "James, did you learn that from the workbook?"

"I learned it in the family and other places. I have a good memory."

Tim returns to Dan and Peter's theme. "I like writing on paper or reading books. Most of that stuff [in workbooks] we know. It's kind of boring to go through it again."

"In the first grade, Mrs. Roberts let us do the workbook by ourselves," volunteers Vera, referring to the practice of giving workbook assignments and expecting children to proceed on their own.

"Did you like that?"

"No."

"Why?"

"I don't think she should do that 'cause some children couldn't understand."

The discussion now focuses on the difficulty of the workbooks. The students have trouble identifying what makes the workbooks easy or hard. Nevertheless, as among teachers, a common "complaint about workbook tasks is that they are either too easy or too hard" (Osborn, 1984, p. 164). The point of the workbook activities gets lost in this technical discussion—an ironically appropriate development, given the arid nature of the workbooks.

Alan pinpoints a common difficulty. "Sometimes the instructions are difficult. Like there's lines and there's blanks and you don't know what they are for."

"It's scary when it's on a page and you have to answer it," says Vera, "but it's good when it's reading."

A mistake in reading group is never a source of embarrassment. Children never leave a visible trail of mistakes, as they can in workbooks. The reading mistakes are public, but they don't hurt. Might the fact that the discussion of workbooks keeps returning to the question of whether they are too hard or too easy—which doesn't happen with other topics, such as science—reflect the fact that workbooks focus attention on competence? The children recognize that the reading workbooks test their knowledge. Thus their preoccupation with difficulty and competence.

This also helps explain the preoccupation with copying—the work-covering, which arises most often in workbook and worksheet assignments. These are tests more than they are learning situations. Small wonder if, after a diet of this, high school students see school learning as a series of testlike multiple-choice exercises. Although they see such work as irrelevant to their lives, they pressure their teachers to make school like this—to water down teaching to clearly specified, easily learnable, unambiguously right or wrong bits of information that will make school-that-is-a-test both fair and unthreatening. Small wonder that they resist collaborative inquiry about big and fuzzy questions like what is science, what is it for, and how should it be learned? Some of these second graders are going to have to give up deep commitments before they will fit into high school class-rooms like this.[2]

Dan comes back to Alan's point. "Mrs. Hazzard, I think the directions make no sense."

When Sue asks, "Is there anything about the workbook that is good?" Elizabeth has an answer.

"I'd like to say they are good 'cause they help you be a better reader."

"How do they help?"

"'Cause you read directions." Elizabeth, a true trooper, echoes one of Sue's suggestions. She turns the problematic directions into the task itself and declares it useful.

Peter will not let this pass.

"It's better if you read a story. You don't see people out there," he waves at the windows, "reading directions. We should read some-thing like in real life."

"Is there any time you need to read directions?"

"Yes, sometimes," he concedes. "But you already know how to read directions. You don't get directions that say to put words in A-B-C order. It would be okay if we read things like stop signs but not A-B-C orders." This task demands a use of the alphabet that is irrelevant to many everyday tasks such as using dictionaries and phone books.

"Do you have to read directions to put models together?"

"You can guess," calls Dan, losing grip on reason in his bluster to avoid losing ground in the attack on workbooks.

"You don't want to guess." Alan wants nothing to do with work-books but cannot accept this invitation to chaos. "You could ruin a computer if you put it together that way."

"Aren't there times you do need to know how to read directions?"

"Not those kind." Peter has stretched himself heroically to clarify his ideas and, for now, can say no more. He does not mean he wants to learn to read stop signs. Everyone in the class knows he can do this. His is an appeal for learning that makes sense and for learning instead of testing. He can do the workbooks easily, but how many years of them can he take and still respect those who keep piling them in front of him?

Sue accepts his point, for the moment at least. "If I don't use the workbooks, what can I do?"

"Just use the reading book."

"Papers."

"Dittos?" (which are usually like the workbook).

"I think the computer would be better," says Alan.

Peter makes it clear that his objection is specific. "If you give us papers, don't give us ones some company made up. You could make ones up for us." This leader of the loyal opposition respects his teachers' pedagogical knowledge.

"So you want papers that are meaningful to you?" says Sue to nods and yesses from the community.

She explains that the schools are choosing new reading programs and might choose new books. When she describes the selection process, Dan is disgusted.

"Why can't teachers teach how they want to and not all the same?" Sue lets this pass. But, again, Dan shows he does not seek to avoid intellectual work or to advance a narrow, self-interested view. He sees how these discussions can help teachers, and he accords them the responsibility for their work that he seeks for his own.

Ann, showing new signs of autonomy, backs him up. "Like in this [personal journal] book, if you see something on Nickelodeon, you could say you saw that TV show. Like an animal show. People could act out parts so we know what it is like, and we could go to the library and find, like, a book [on the same thing], and see how different it was."

*   *   *

"There is, I think," wrote John Dewey (1938), "no point in the philosophy of progressive education which is sounder than its emphasis upon the importance of the participation of the learner in the formation of the purposes which direct his [or her] activities in the learning process" (p. 67). Dewey knew that this sort of statement was easily, but inadvisably, interpreted as supporting unimpeded self-expression. He wrote *Experience and Education* to distinguish his vision from those that emphasized individualistic conceptions of freedom as untrammeled choice rather than envisioning school as part of a culture that draws strength from and contributes to social diversity. For Dewey, the only freedom of enduring value was freedom of intelligence,

> the power to frame purposes and to execute purposes so framed. Such freedom is in turn identified with self-control; for the formation of purposes and the organization of means to execute them are the work of

intelligence. Plato once defined a slave as the person who executes the purposes of another, and . . . a person is also a slave who is enslaved to [her or] his own blind desires. (p. 67)

Hence the importance of educating those desires by securing "the active co-operation of the pupil in the formation of the purposes involved in [her or] his studying" (p. 67).[3]

Potential rebels, Dan and Peter lead the charge to define the purposes that might govern their learning. They scorn their workbooks. They want to do experiments, to see what happens, to record the results, and, in the clash of ideas among friends, to recognize what makes sense. They embody the scientific spirit that resists arbitrary external authority and egocentric personal impulse alike, a spirit of open-mindedness disciplined by systematic observation, rational reflection, and open debate, and renewed by novel hypotheses. No matter of individual self-expression, this is a social discipline. None is more demanding, more exciting, or more liberating.

Though many have been inspired by the same hope as Dewey, there are few instances of schools where vigorous debate about what to learn and how to learn it are found. Dewey's laboratory school in Chicago, for example, is described (somewhat romantically) as seeking to regain a time

> when there was no rift between experience and [school] knowledge, when information about things and ways of doing grew out of social situations and represented answers to social needs, when the education of the immature member of society proceeded almost wholly through participation in the social or community life of which he was a member, and each individual, no matter how young, did certain things in the way of work and play *along* with others, and learned, thereby, to adjust himself to his surroundings, to adapt himself to social relationships, and to get control of his own special power. (Mayhew & Edwards, 1936/1965, p. 21)

The concern for connected learning is apparent in this description. There is, however, little hint of why Dewey might be called "the prophet of intelligence as an adventure" (Kallen, 1940, pp. 15–16). Nor is it argued that students should negotiate what knowledge is most valuable.

Some such negotiation might have taken place in Dewey's school, but Mayhew and Edwards do not reveal this in their account of the school or its associated theory. Part of that theory, the expanding horizons notion, was that younger children find topics that are closer to their home life more interesting and more comprehensible than remote topics. Thus, as in many contemporary schools, social studies started with home and neighborhood and gradually widened the horizon.

An 8-year-old in Dewey's school asked his teacher, "Which do you think . . . is the best way to study geography—to begin with your own place and go out, out, out, until you reach the stars, or to begin with the stars and come in and in until you reach your own place again?" He was told that people differ on this matter, but that this year the class would study his locality. He agreed, but murmured, "But I shall get a book about the stars, anyway" (Mayhew & Edwards, 1936/1965, p. 289). An opportunity for students to participate in the formation of the purposes governing their learning was lost. The places where students live may not be the most intellectually challenging. The worlds of the stars, dinosaurs, witches, and ghosts may, partly because of their obvious remoteness, be more alluring and challenging. Young children may be poised for more intellectual adventure than the teachers in Dewey's school allowed, and those teachers appear not to have been truly ready to involve students in the formation of the purposes that governed school activities.

A gap between Dewey's declaration that students should participate in the formation of the purposes that govern their learning and the actual negotiation of those purposes by students is evident also in the schools Dewey and his daughter Evelyn described under the title *Schools of Tomorrow* (Dewey & Dewey, 1915). At Fairhope, for example, "each pupil may do as he pleases as long as he does not interfere with any one else. The children are not freed, however, from all discipline. They must keep at work while they are in school, and learn not to bother their neighbors, as well as to help them when necessary" (p. 25). Variants of this theme are found in today's alternative schools. Choosing is not the same as actively negotiating the means and ends of one's education. Mere choosing embodies an individualistic, smorgasbord conception of freedom.

Though they are rare at present, there have been a variety of schools where students chose what and how to study. Schools where students routinely discuss the nature and point of what they are learning seem rarer still. Matters of personal conduct and social rules are negotiated by the community in some alternative schools, but questions about the nature of knowledge, about what knowledge is useful, and whether a topic should be studied in a manner consistent with the principles that governed its choice are rarely matters for students' dialogue. Yet these questions are central to any community committed to democratic life.[4]

The interesting Sudbury Valley School also seems not to provoke inquiry about what knowledge is worthwhile. "Do not intrude yourself upon your neighbor. . . . This is the rule that underlies the educational policies of the school" (Greenberg, 1973, p. 136; Gray & Chanoff, 1986). Though students participate in constructing the formal rules and practices that govern much of their life in the school, these dialogues appear not to extend to the intellectual work that occurs there. Yet, to gain a diploma from the school, a student must convince the school members that she or he is ready to function competently and responsibly in the outside world. The challenge this presents is not comparable to the usual requirement to pass a set of courses prescribed by remote authorities. Mere diligence will hardly suffice. Students must take responsibility for the nature of their work and become not mere choosers but curriculum theorists. This might promote reflection and discourse on the significance of the work done in school. Without this, the participation of learners in the formation of the purposes that govern their learning is incomplete.

CHAPTER 8

Life and Literacy

On the third day of school, Sue says, "I want to share a story [*Beezus and Ramona* by Beverly Cleary, 1955] that is one of my favorites. It's about a 4-year-old. Does anyone have a 4-year-old brother or sister?"

Right away a dialogue about siblings begins. This sets the tone for the reading of Ramona's story. Story sessions sometimes involve more discussion of children's lives and their knowledge than listening to the story. But these are not digressions. It is as if Ramona and her family have joined the classroom conversations on topics as diverse as feelings on starting kindergarten and the meaning of the word "exasperate."

When, in a subsequent story, *Ramona the Pest*, Ramona—the tough, inquisitive, adventurous, spunky little heroine—has new boots and wants to go out in the rain and splash in puddles, Sue's students wave their hands, eager to describe the times they have done this.

When they have had their say, Ramona plods along in her new boots.

"What is plodding?" asks Sue, stopping her reading again. Alan gets up to demonstrate a heavy plod. Entranced, George and Wole join him in a plodding dance. The little sideshow stops as Sue continues reading.

Ramona encounters worms out on the sidewalk.

"Why," asks Sue, "should worms come out when it rains?"

"They love mud."

"They want to float in the water."

"They don't like the rain, and they are trying to get out."

"Oh! Oh! I know! I know!" Jack is bursting with his insight. "They're flooded."

His insight seems to solve the problem for everyone and, back in the story, Ramona wraps a worm around her finger and declares it an engagement ring.

"What does engagement mean?"

"Love."

"Ugh!"—from two boys.

"Married."

Sue clarifies and reads on until an arithmetic problem comes up: Twenty-nine kindergarten children have boots. How many boots does the teacher have to worry about buckling? When they solve this for one class, someone asks how many there would be for two classes. There are lots of suggestions. Peter finally announces that $50 + 50 + 8 + 8 = 116$.

Back in the story, a character is prancing.

"What animal prances?"

"Elephant."

"Not really."

"A horse."

"Right, when a horse prances it puts its knees up."

Suddenly five children are prancing. When Sue points out that the class downstairs might be disturbed, they come to a stop. Sue begins reading, but Dan cannot stop from prancing. A chorus of "Shh!" from the others, who want the story more than prancing, halts him. Making no comment, Sue proceeds like the Pied Piper, with all following.

The story of the Three Billy Goats Gruff enters this story. Claire tells the Billy Goats' story with some help from others.

Ramona decides to be the Little Billy Goat Gruff and "trip-traps" around her house. A demonstration of vigorous trip-trapping is interrupted by a shrill alarm calling for a surprise fire drill. When the class returns, dark clouds are gathering in the sky of the story.

"What often happens when dark clouds build up?"

"Tornadoes."

"Rain."

Ramona finds some mud.

"What do you think Ramona will do?"

"Stomp"—and she does.

"Do you have any idea of what will happen next?"

"Yes!" they cry, and, sure enough, Ramona in her new boots gets stuck.

"What can she do?"

"Wait until it dries, then break it."

"When a car gets stuck, what do you do?"

"Get a tow truck."

"Get a bigfoot with a pulley."

"What kind of mud is that?" Jack wants to know.

"Just the muddiest mud you could think of."

Ramona is eventually saved, but her boots remain stuck.

When Ramona's teacher asks what she has to say for her savior, Ramona complains that her boots are left in the mud.

"What was she hoping Ramona would say?" asks Sue.

"Thank you."

Sue has read Ramona books to her classes for 18 of her 20 years of teaching. She enjoys giving each character a unique, dramatic voice. Early on, Vicki (whom the class recognizes as being "like Ramona") asks, "I like listening to stories. Do you like reading them?" Contemplating the mystery of what has bewitched her, she reflects on the joys of reading and pays Sue an uncalculated compliment.

Shortly after Sue began reading the first Ramona story, students took books from the series out of the library. They are difficult for most, but Wole has soon read far ahead of Sue. When she prepares to read, he moves his chair to the side of his desk, so that instead of facing the side of the room as he usually does, he looks directly at her. He does this only for these sessions. While she reads, he grins, "oohs," "aahs," covers his head with his arms, and waves them as events he has read about unfold again.

At the beginning of one session, Jack announces that every night he tells his mother what has been happening with Ramona.

My high-speed, scribbled field notes, which only I can decipher, are compared to Ramona's attempts to write. When someone in the class uses a mild disruption to gain attention, a voice from the back of the room notes, "Like Ramona," and the wrongdoer is gently curbed. When Ramona begins kindergarten, the children reflect on and reconsider their hopes and fears at the start of this school year and how these feelings have changed. Ramona faces the dilemmas involving adults, siblings, and peers that Sue's children face. Literature gives meaning to shared lives and, in turn, gains meaning from life.

[January 17] A day after Sue finishes reading *The Gismonauts*, she initiates a discussion of how, in that novel of space adventure, people knew a spaceship was coming, what it looked like, communication devices, and how languages were translated. Throughout, the lively discussion covers imaginary possibilities and related real-world matters.

"You all have so many interesting ideas," comments Sue. She suggests they could write a story about a spaceship. "Here's the scene. You're at home with earphones on, listening to the radio. You hear

news that a spaceship has landed on the school playground." They buzz excitedly. "Once you get to the school yard . . ." Sue waits for the hubbub to subside. "Once you get there, you describe it. Think about the shape, color, size, and anything else. Then do you get to go inside? What does it look like? Think about the good ideas you had for equipment in the spaceship. Then, where did it come from? I want you to think carefully. What do you see? How will you start the story? . . . Remember, we don't have to worry about spelling. And if you make mistakes you can cross out . . . just get the ideas on paper."

Calm prevails as they begin writing. When someone wants to ask a question, Sue whispers to them and they whisper back. Though released from the need for correct spelling, a number quietly seek guidance. Alan has started writing about, not one, but two spaceships. He comes to whisper proudly and point out this innovation to me. Some sit in pairs and quietly exchange ideas. As their stories take shape, a number bring them to Sue, who encourages with questions and comments on unique features of their work.

"Oh! I can just see what he looks like."

"The way you wrote this is great. You can't stop now. I want to see what happens."

"When they talked, did they have a different language?"

Peter wants to read his story to the class. Some keep writing. Most listen, then return to writing.

"In a minute we'll share our stories," says Sue.

"Oh, Mrs. Hazzard!" pleads Elizabeth. "I still have a lot to go." Sue acquiesces. After 35 minutes, they form their own groups for reading and discussing the stories.

"I hate to do this to you," Sue announces a little later, "but it's recess." She fields a chorus of groans. "We can come back to this right after recess."

When they return, Jill and Vera crawl into the legspace under a spare teacher's desk, pull a chair against the opening, and read and discuss their stories. Wole, Tim, and Carlos find enclosure on the carpet in a corner under a table. They digress briefly on ages and birthdays, then read, listen, discuss, and write more. Some still seek help with spelling. Others illustrate their stories. When the lunch bell rings, half an hour after recess, all are still involved.

"Oh, no! It's not fair. I'm not finished," calls Alan, the boy who despises workbooks.

*   *   *

[January 23] Dan has been having problems. It begins to look as if there were substance to the concerns his father expressed to the principal as the year began. He has been involved in fights at recess and has caused problems in class, especially in writing sessions.

Today, topics for a letter to a potential pen pal are being discussed.

"What things do you like that would be good to tell?" asks Sue.

"I don't like anything," says Dan.

He regularly leaves the room for what is known as special help in reading and writing. His difficulty is most apparent in writing, where he has problems with spelling and reversals (writing the mirror image) and transpositions of letters. Why is he upset now, when he started the year so well? The trouble is not always there, but keeps reappearing.

* * *

[January 24] The class is writing about animals in their journals. The topic is very popular.

"How do you spell 'my'?" Carlos asks his neighbor Wole.

"You don't know?" Wole is surprised but tells him.

Carlos starts his story, printing carefully, eyes fixed on his paper. "My dog at Argentina . . ." As he steadily lengthens his story, Wole, far superior at spelling and an avid reader, sits uncomfortably, unable to begin. Everyone around him is writing. For all his ability and love of reading, he is awkward and incompetent when creation with words is called for. If the task is not reading or a cut-and-dried worksheet-like assignment, he is lost—trapped, it seems, by his theory that school is a test where answers are right or wrong. We are now five days beyond the class discussion where Wole was the only one arguing categorically against "copying" and resisting the distinction between receiving help and copying.

Quiet, unassuming, often sad, Jill blossoms in her journal.

My dog is funny but she is big now. She is black and white. win I come back from school I will go over to the fields and play with her. But now she is gone I miss her so much and I hope I get her back I hope I can get another funny dog just like her.

When she has finished she comes to tell me how she loves and misses her dog and how she sometimes calls it "he" though she knows it is "she."

Claire writes,

Animal story. Once my goldfish named Golden Rocks fell in the sink and my brother was shouting and shouting, so I went into the bathroom and I saw my fish in the sink! then my dad took it out and then my brother was shouting again then I went back and I saw the fish in the toilet then I fell into crying then my dad took it out and no more accidents happened and I gave it food. The End.

When Claire reads her story to the appreciative class, several children approve of her phrase "I fell into crying." Next day Claire has changed it to "I cried." Perhaps she realized her original construction was unconventional. When Joan discovers the change, she argues for poetic license.

"It sounded more like you were sad the first way."

Claire seems unconvinced but changes the wording back.

The children have much to learn about language, but they can shape and communicate significant emotions. They are sensitive critics of one another's work. Writing can be living, not mere preparation for making a living.

*   *   *

[January 27] Joan discovers that the paper plates that had been used at a class party can be stuck together to make flying saucers like, she says, the spaceships from *The Gismonauts*, which Sue has been reading. Enthusiastic invention follows. Elizabeth's craft has a door that opens to show a face inside. Paul's has a trapdoor and a folding paper staircase that drops down from the trapdoor. Joan hands hers to Sue, saying, "Mrs. Hazzard to Earth." Sue's smile acknowledges Joan's construction and her recall of Sue's technique for gaining student attention.

The next day Dan has produced a space city of paper plates, cups, and straws. The others are impressed.

"Dan doesn't belong in the second grade," Ann announces. "He should be in the future designing space cities."

By the following morning, most of the table-tops are engulfed by space cities with flying-saucer landing platforms, staircases, and many other ingenious features.

When class starts, Sue notes how much sharing of ideas there was. Dan, consistent in giving credit and avoiding bragging, agrees. "It was Alan that gave me the idea, and look what he started."

Dan's group has first turn to discuss their city. Dan has emerged as leader, but his generosity continues.

"Jill made a lot of mine. I got the idea for the steps from Alan." Paul introduced this invention, but this fact is overlooked, and Paul apparently has no sense that he started it. Alan, not listening to the acknowledgement of his contribution, is at the back of the room quietly trying to point out to me the oxygen pumps and other parts of his new construction. Dan continues, "Claire made this, and I don't know what we are going to use it for."

"It will be a jail," she says.

"Oh, yes," agrees Dan.

James's city has an elevator and a safety chute. Others want to know how people will escape in the event of a fire, and eagerly volunteer suggestions.

Jodie is the last to describe her construction.

"Which is mine?" she quips in mock confusion as she tries to separate hers from the cluster of cities on a table. "I'm not a very good explainer but I'll do my best." Despite the disclaimer, she is alert and relaxed as she faces her active, questioning audience.

Space cities are an obvious topic for writing.

"Your ideas need to be written down before you forget them," says Sue.

"But," calls Joan, who does not have to be reminded that eternal vigilance is the price of liberty, "we have these so we can just look at them and remember." Her quarrel is not with writing, but with Sue's rationale.

"OK. Get into your journals and start writing."

Joan and Elizabeth run to crawl into the enclosure under the spare teacher's desk and collaborate. Alan tells me an involved story about his construction plans, then declares, "Now I'm going to write it all." He bounces off to get his journal and, after a moment's pause, produces a steady flow of words. "I feel like making a real satellite city right now," he says to no one in particular.

Beside this overt enthusiasm, Paul appears restrained. His expression is almost solemn. He has cut and shaped paper plates to make a gracefully menacing, scorpionlike spaceship with curled-up tail and pincers. His absorption during construction was deep, interrupted only by many spontaneous compliments from the others on his vigorous, animalistic creation. Now, holding his pencil firmly, he is a poet in his own world, recording the impact of his peers' assessments of his construction.

When I mad this Spis ship I thot it was a little bit dem [dumb]
bet I fad out thet the spis ship was rile good so he spsiship cod
do anei thing.

This aesthetic epic seems to have made his script and spelling
shakier than usual. But if writing is the communication of experience, his is a dramatic success. As Sylvia Ashton-Warner (1958) writes,
"legibility and expert setting run nowhere in the race with meaning"
(p. 193).

Could a teacher have done anything to match the impact of his
classmates' spontaneous comments on his ship? It would be misleading to say they have boosted his self-esteem. The current egotistical
preoccupation with self-esteem is not of this quality. One can boost
one's self-esteem by finishing worksheets faster than others. When
his self-esteem was threatened by Yong Kim's faster progress, he and
Carlos tried to bring Yong Kim down to their level and, when that
failed, abandoned the worksheet. Now, it is not himself that he writes
about, but his "spis ship." He is learning, not that he can do a worksheet faster than others (he cannot), but that he can do work of
artistic integrity—work that communicates. His achievement does not
diminish the others. Their pleasure is part of his reward. This reward would be debased and oversimplified if we described it simply as a boost for Paul's *self*-esteem.

For most, constructing space ships is easier and more engrossing than writing about them. Speaking with pencils is still hard work.
But this time even Dan is an eager author, explaining his space city
in his journal. Only Jodie has trouble starting. She repeats, in her
slightly theatrical, ironic fashion, to no apparent audience, "I don't
know what to write." Suddenly overcoming inertia, she writes,

I made a space ship, and a space station. The space station has
a . . .

until the bell for recess rings.

All this has sprung from a conjunction of Sue's reading of the
Monaal story, the story she had them write about a spaceship in the
schoolyard, and the rash of construction of space technology precipitated by Joan. Literacy can be part of the social life of school, and
life can be an adventure when the journey is jointly directed by the
participants. Administrative mandates and teachers' lesson plans can
hardly anticipate such adventures.

*   *   *

[February 2] As Groundhog Day nears, Sue reads to the class stories written by children from previous classes who pretended to have interviewed the proverbial groundhog. Now, slowly, carefully, Carlos is writing a groundhog story. He looks at what he has done, shakes his head, and erases his last two words, saying, "I'm not going to write messy." He redoes them with total concentration. He writes little, but there is no doubt about the seriousness of his purpose.

Carlos's concern is consistent. Six days later, in a discussion of choice of writing topics and methods of developing themes, his contribution is, "If you write fast, the letters get messy." The former cheat is totally reformed, determined to learn to spell and write. A week earlier, before class began, he came in and saw George and James busy on spelling worksheets. He sat beside them and began his sheet. "I found these words," he announced shortly. When George began to show him more, he protested, "I want to do this by myself." He persisted, searching for words despite announcements over the intercom and a class discussion about these. As Sue called for order, Carlos announced, "I found 'sick,'" and turned around, repeating it to me.

Nearby, Alan and James leave trails of invented spelling and shaky script in their concern to get the first drafts of their groundhog stories recorded. Sue will encourage them to produce this story in a polished final version, to be added to the collected works of previous classes.

Parents sometimes misunderstand why teachers do not immediately stamp out invented spelling. The mother of a Chicago first grader objected to the school's failure to do this. She complained that her son hadn't learned "to spell anything yet. . . . When you learn math, they tell you two and two is four. They never let you say two and two is five." Said another, "My daughter is being taught what is wrong is right" (Zorn, 1987, p. 7). Young students know that misspelling a word is akin to writing "two and two is four" in an unconventional fashion. They do not see it as akin to claiming that two and two is five. They also believe that getting the content of a message right is more important than the precise form of its delivery (Nicholls & Thorkildsen, 1988; 1989).

The next day, Vicki is bent on reading her groundhog story to me. She is a small cyclone not to be resisted. In the middle of the story she stops abruptly.

"I wonder where words come from," she says to me.

"I often wonder that too."

On she reads. When she finishes, she turns energetically to expanding her story. She consults her dictionary and forgets her story, swept away by words. She reads "stepmother," a word of potential relevance, as her parents are separating. She mutters away about the definition. She plays with "stepladder" and "stepmother" and goes on to other words before leaping back to her story to add four more lines. Full of the vigor of creation and mastery of words, she insists on reading me her story over from the beginning.

They are all writing stories about groundhogs, but have made of this assignment many assignments. For Carlos, spelling and script are important. Vicki, with her multitrack mind, often goes on excursions in the dictionary, looking for spelling, finding more words, and sometimes forgetting her story. There are many ways to find meaningful work. These assignments cultivate the judgment of students, allowing them to define tasks and, when they stand back and reread or discuss with peers, to scrutinize the implications of their judgments. How remote this is from the planet of workbooks and worksheets!

*   *   *

[February 7] As he has done several times recently, Dan groans as the class begins writing. "Why are you so negative?" asks Sue. "You are dragging us down. Why don't you like school now?"

"I didn't used to like school," he insists, apparently determined that life was always somber.

"What part is tough?"

"Everything. Spelling."

"Is it school that's doing it to you or is it home?"

"It's home." He looks tormented, though with what seems to be a trace of self-consciousness of his tormented appearance. Perhaps he senses that he is creating an opportunity to have his problems considered sympathetically.

"Is it over spelling or writing?" He doesn't respond. The others follow this drama with mild to serious concern.

"Would it get you in trouble if I told your mother you were having trouble?"

"Yes. If I get a word wrong, I have to do it 20 times. If I get one word wrong, I have to do them all over."

"We have to select words that are not so hard—then you'll do better."

"I always choose easy words."

"Let's sit down together and choose. And did you talk to your mom about how making mistakes is a way to learn?"

"You can say that 'cause you're an adult, but I'll get into trouble." He is slowly brightening.

"What if I write a letter to all parents telling them that mistakes help us learn? Would that help?" Dan nods, looking relaxed enough for Sue to carry on with the session.

[February 8] "Some people came up to me," says Sue, "and asked me, 'Do we have to write the story?' How many people had trouble starting?" Enough hands go up to justify discussion of the issue.

"I didn't start," says Dan. "I don't like to write."

"I had a friend in the fourth grade who said 'I like to write, but I don't like writing.' What do you think he meant?" Sue avoids making Dan the explicit focus of her question. His is not a simple response to feelings of incompetence. He seems to be choosing not to be a writer—an ethical decision borne of adversity, perhaps, but his moral choice nonetheless. He might become more determined if challenged. Sue avoids this. She treats him as if he has a right to his decision, unfortunate though it might be, and gropes to provoke a reconsideration that will not leave his life closed off from writing.[1]

"He likes to think of stories," suggests Elizabeth, "but doesn't like to put it on paper."

"OK! What could someone do if they had trouble writing?"

"Get someone to help," suggests Dan, resistant to writing but still part of the class.

"Help them, like put paper in the computer for them." Paul's suggestion leads to discussion of typewriters, Dictaphones, and secretaries. Peter is puzzled about the technology that makes the difference between his crabbed script and the immaculate text he finds in books. After a while, Sue brings them back. "Now Dan is not alone. Some people tape-record their ideas. Does anyone else have trouble?" Vicki has her hand up. "Why?" asks Sue.

"Because of the thinking. 'Cause I didn't want to write, and I didn't have that much ideas."

Wole volunteers. "I had trouble *choosing* what to write."

"What can we do if I put up three ideas and you can't choose?"

"Start on all of them," suggests Evelyn, eager to please.

"Oh! You could use all the ideas?" Sue is a trace quizzical. She goes on to note the diversity of their approaches to writing. "Joan thinks while she talks or writes. Paul thinks before he says anything. Jodie is like that, too. She sits and sits and thinks and thinks and then she writes. Every writer has trouble getting started sometimes."

"Even me?" asks Joan, puzzled by the idea that she might ever have trouble gaining momentum. After more discussion, Joan—ever the champion of freedom—asks, "Why can't we write our own stories?"

"Yeah!" chime several.

"Like Dan could have written about his grandmother on Tuesday," says Sue. "He had lots of things to tell about her, but I said to write about the groundhog. Alan came in last Friday, all excited about his birthday, but I didn't give him a chance. What if I give you a choice . . . ? How does that sound?"

"Fair!"

Murmurs of approval greet this assessment. What is fair depends on the context (Thorkildsen, 1989b). On a test, diversity and choice can look unfair, and helping is out of order. The observation that choice is fair is an observation that this is not a test, but an occasion for the construction of one's own meaning. Commonly, in schools, writing is used to find out what students have learned—it is part of the testing process. Britton (1982), among others, has argued that "Writing can be learning in the sense of discovery" (p. 110). When the children greet choice as fair, they probably agree that writing should be discovery. Dan, however, hovers at the point of choosing not to use writing at all.

"You could suggest girls' ideas and boys' ideas," calls Peter, ever conscious of the difference and in no hurry to discover anything not masculine.

"What I'd like to do with my book of writing," says Paul, "is to write about 10 stories or 20 stories or something. I'd like to write stories 'cause I like to write."

He is clearly less competent than most at the so-called basic literacy skills, but he is committed. When student teachers visit the class, Sue has the children introduce themselves and announce their interests. These remain much what they were on the first day, but Paul introduced a new item after Christmas. "I like soccer and I like learning," he said in a serious, faintly winsome tone. He repeats this each time the class introduces itself to a visitor.

Two weeks later, in another discussion of topics for writing, Joan announces, "I'm interested in two things."

"I'm interested in everything," says Paul.

Today's discussion leads Sue to ask, "Why do you write your journals?"

"To put our thoughts down."

"To learn to write."

"But I don't want to be a writer," insists Dan, not about to be swayed by all this.

"OK. So why do we write?"

"Just for the fun of it," says Tim, who finds the physical act of writing hard. On another occasion he says, "Writing makes my hand sweaty."

"If you never know how to write, you can't write for your mother or grandmother," Paul says, deeply earnest.

"What would you write them?"

"Letters."

"So we can," Martha volunteers, answering the "Why do we write?" question.

"I was going to say that [we write] so we can read," says Wole.

"To practice handwriting," says George, the self-motivated learner of cursive script.

"To write stories or books," says Dan, drawn in despite himself.

"So we know how to write when we get older."

"When we go to the grocery, we write lists."

"If you use different screws and stuff—like making things."

"OK! So you can write to explain things."

"To communicate," says solemn Jack, often a source of big words.

"That's all communication," says Alan, with a touch of scorn, hinting that Jack has said nothing.

Looking at Alan, Sue acknowledges his point: "That's right!" Then Jack's: "He gave me one big word for all of it."

Although Dan precipitated this discussion, Sue has not addressed him directly. Now she does.

"Let's stop for a minute. I'm very concerned about your attitude today. I hope the discussion has helped." There is no thought of concealing her hope to influence him. Now she speaks to the whole class. "We talked about reasons for writing . . . How to get started . . . You've all given it a lot of thought. More, I think, than a lot of high school students."

This stimulates Vicki to observe, "If you don't learn to write, you'll be out of work [when you grow up] and sometimes you can't get people to write for you."

"If you're slow, that's okay as long as you know how to write," says Elizabeth.

"This morning for your journal . . ." begins Sue.

"I'd like to do a groundhog story," interrupts Dan. As they return to writing, Dan is restored. He is relaxed and active, working with Claire. With Dan at her elbow following, suggesting, and negotiating on theme and details, she writes their story.

[February 14] On returning from his remedial reading session, Dan is far from himself. He is tense and uncomfortable, with a faint air of trying to decide whether he is really disturbed. He folds his arms and hangs his head forward. He chews the strap of his overalls, slumps down in his chair, closes his eyes, and flops his head back. He looks as if he were trying to use his body to compose his mind. When the lunch bell rings, his forehead furrows as he shuffles up to Sue.

"I don't want to go for lunch."

"I'm sorry, I can't stay back with you. There really isn't any choice." Then, after a little negotiation, "Dan is feeling a bit lonely today. Is anyone going to be with him for lunch?" There are many volunteers, and Dan leaves looking close to normal.

*   *   *

[February 22] There is general interest when Sue introduces some new library books. Part of the discussion focuses on colored versus black-and-white illustrations. Sue holds up *The Round Trip* by Ann Jonas (1983), which has black-and-white drawings.

"This is one of my favorites . . ."

"Looks like it will be boring," says Peter, peering up from the front row.

"Why?"

"It all looks boring. It's looking like it'll just be a camping trip." Sue does not argue. Peter is not trying to create difficulty. He has strong views and announces them. Sue reads the book to the class. It depicts a train journey. At the end of the book, she turns the book over, revealing that each picture is a different picture when viewed the other way. She continues the trip back to the front of the book and asks, "Was that a boring book?" It is already evident that even Peter no longer thinks so.

"Could they have done that with color illustrations?"

"No. No."

Summing up, Sue says, "I'm glad you thought it was interesting. Now, how can you tell if a book is interesting, Peter?"

"You have to read it," he acknowledges. He will not be pushed about, but he is ready to listen and weigh what he hears.

"OK," nods Sue. This is no victory for the teacher because there was no battle. This is just one step in the exploration of books and of the children's relationships to them. Sue proceeds.

"But what if you don't have time? If you're at the library choosing a book, you can't read them all."

"If you read one of an author's books and it wasn't good, probably that means the others won't be good," says Dan.

"The name of the book might give you a clue."

"Yes," says Sue. "Some of the Hardy Boys books have really exciting titles."

"You could ask friends who [had] read it," says Peter.

"You can look through it."

"Ask a librarian."

"My sister looks for teddy-bear books."

"I go and look at the [table of] contents."

"Why?" asks Tim.

"He'll look there to see if there are things that are interesting."

"I take a section of the library like "Space" 'cause I know it's exciting."

"I don't like Nancy Drew books," says Ann. "But I have Hardy Boys books, and I know I like them."

"Have you ever been in a store and looked on the back or inside the dust jacket?" asks Sue and illustrates by reading from the jacket of the *Just So Stories*, some of which she has read to the class.

"If you're in the boring part of a book, you can skip and go to the end and go back, and you might like it then," suggests George.

"I wouldn't do that!" says Wole.

"If there aren't pictures, it makes me want to read it," says Dan.

"The pictures give the story away," adds Tim.

"I used to think books without pictures were boring, but I don't . . ." says Paul.

They move on to free-choice reading. Sue allows those who wish to go down the hall to the drinking fountain, but Dan dives into his book.

Tim reads the *Just So Stories*. They are hard for him, but he persists. If he can make progress, he is not afraid of challenge. It is not so hard now being a second grader.

A month earlier he chose relatively big words for his personal spelling list. I commented on this.

"I like it," he said. "I like challenges. Especially video games. I don't know why, but I like it." He finished his list without looking up and turned to reading a book of his choice. This proved difficult. He plugged away, sounding out words and occasionally asking for help. But in the effort of reading words, the story was lost. He found something closer to his level and was absorbed until the bell rang. He does not need a teacher to test him to find out what tasks are challenging for him. Children who want to learn also want to select their own challenges and can do this.[2] What sort of challenge, in any event, is it to meet someone else's goals?

*   *   *

[February 27] For show-and-tell, Dan presents a helicopter he has made from a kit. Sue comments, "You really used your imagination, didn't you!"

"No," he replies. "It shows you how to do it [on the box]." His stance shows pride in his work, but he wants no false claims.

Later the same day, the discussion turns to mothers.

"Mine thinks I'm stupid," says Dan.

"She's not trying to do it on purpose, I think," Joan consoles. "She probably wants you to learn but just wants you to learn too fast."

Shortly, when someone suggests workbooks should be more challenging, Ann says, "I'd get some wrong. Then I'll get in really deep trouble at home."

Later, Sue initiates a discussion of reading—what things are helpful and interesting and what are not. Amid the discussion of things the students like, Dan strikes a discordant note.

"I don't like it. I never get a book I like . . ."

"I like chapter books," says Vicki.

"What about those, Dan?" asks Sue.

"They are long and take a lot of work. I'm no good at reading." He is tense and awkward.

"Why do you think you're not a good reader?"

"I'm not fast. My mother calls me names. She says, 'You need special education. You need special help,' just because I don't always know the answers."

"Do you think you are different from everyone else?"

"No. Most kids don't know it all."

"Could you say, 'Fine, I'll take special help, and then I'll learn faster'?" Dan's problem remains, so Sue makes a suggestion. "I can say that in the class here you've learned a lot. I could tell your mother."

"You know my [younger] brother. He says he's the best, and now, to try and get attention, he says I'm dumb. He goes on and on."

"It's good you can see through the games he is playing," says Sue.

Dan seems able to name the sources of his affliction, but his equilibrium comes and goes.

[March 16] Students are writing in their personal notebooks. Dan sits doing nothing.

"Can I read your stories?" I ask. Dan has written few over recent weeks and, except for the groundhog story, on which he had help, they are short by his standards.

"I'm wondering why you aren't writing."

"I'm stupid."

"Yes," I say, looking at his account of his space station. "I remember this space station. I can tell that only a really dumb person could make a station like that."

Alan, who is not inhibited by the conventions of spelling, has been writing about computers. He interrupts to chatter about his story.

"I wonder if Dan isn't writing 'cause he is worried about spelling words right," I suggest. "Alan doesn't worry about that. He gets some words wrong, but people can tell what he means."

"I'm just not born to write. I'm not going to write when I grow up."

"Well, I guess the cavemen didn't write. Oh, maybe they did on the walls of their caves?"

"I'm going to be a scientist when I grow up."

"Yes, I've seen how you make all sorts of things and how you read books about animals and how things work."

"No, I'm going to be an astronaut. That's what I'll be."

"Well, they do a bit of science too."

"I know what I'm going to write about. I'll write about my crazy [baby] sister." He writes with unselfconscious involvement for the few minutes until recess.

*   *   *

[March 17] After a silent reading session and discussion of the books they read, Sue asks, "Where do you think authors get their ideas?"

"From doing experiments and seeing what happens."

"By reading other books."

"Isn't that illegal?" The complex question of cheating arises again.

"From their life."

"How do you mean?"

"If you get in trouble, you can write about that."

"Or," suggests Dan, "if you were blind and couldn't hear [like Helen Keller, about whom he has been reading], you could write about that."

"You could write about your favorite thing."

"I'm going to make a baseball card dictionary," says Peter, who dominates the baseball card exchange.

"Where did you get that idea?" Sue asks.

"There is this book about baseball, but it doesn't tell the names and positions of the players, so it gave me the idea."

"Sometimes, they [authors] go to their past and find experiences—like if they smoked—and write about that."

"You can ask other people about where they've been, like over the Bermuda Triangle."

"They wouldn't be around if they went over there."

"You can use imagination."

"Where do you think the author of *Where the Wild Things Are* got that idea?"

"From a dream," says Tim.

[March 9] Sue has just finished reading *The Secret Garden*. The class discusses the story, recapitulating it in rich detail. Sue raises the possibility that they might view a videotaped version of the story. Most assert that the video version is unlikely to be as good as the book, but they want to see it. They watch and are captured again. They discuss the differences in detail of plot and explain why they appreciated various features of each version.

Alan notes that the music on the video made a difference. "I like them both," he goes on. "Some things you can't make up, like what the walls [of the garden] look like or how much ivy there is. I didn't think there was that much ivy."

A moment later Ann picks up on his implication that the video might have shown how it really was. "I didn't think it was like that. When you see the video, you know if you're right or not."

Later, Dan declares, of the differences between the versions, "They all could happen."

"They're both right," adds George.

"What do you mean, they're both right, George?" asks Sue.

"Like, they both make sense." He seems to sense that stories are created, that they are not mirrors of nature.

"Was the same picture in your head and Peter's head?" Sue asks.

"Yes."

"No!" calls Peter. "It can't be."

"My picture looked different than the movie," says Joan.

"So did mine," adds Claire.

"I think it's neat that everyone has different pictures," says Dan.

"Did everyone get the same pictures when we read the book?"

"No," they say, happy with their intellectual and aesthetic pluralism.

When Sue asks what makes a book good, Tim says, "If it's realistic," which could imply a match to one true, objective reality.

A moment later, Joan proposes a possibly more subjective criterion. "Some stories don't make sense."

"What do you mean, a thing doesn't make sense to you?" Sue asks.

"Like if there's a key and no door."

They are not all as clear as George, Jason, Joan, and Dan on the interpretive role they play or the multiplicity of possible truths there might be in a world where, nevertheless, not everything goes. But they are all busy analyzing their responses to these stories.

When they move on to silent reading of books they have chosen, Vicki reads a condensed version of *The Secret Garden* she had started before the videotape and discussion. She learns something new. When Sue later asks, "Is it as good as the other ones?" Vicki answers, "Yes." Then, waking up, "Now this is better. When I first read it, I didn't even know what it was about." Her earlier ignorance is no embarrassment. She is electrified by her discovery of new meaning.

The children are expanding their inquiry, increasingly defining literature as personal, social, and cultural stuff. For scholars of literature, the nature of stories and the roles of authors and readers are contentious topics. They also present interesting and challenging questions for these second-grade theorists.[3] Learning to read and write means exploring the place that books, reading, and writing play in the ongoing complex conversation that is our culture. When reading is dominated by workbooks and achievement tests that measure children's comprehension of words and sentences, this world is sometimes easy and predictable. At other times it is difficult, but it is rarely an exploration. Literature can be a challenging object of interest, and making sense of literature means asking the questions that renew social life while examining its connections to the places we have been and the people we have known.

*   *   *

[March 20] A discussion of tornadoes stemming from the experience of a tornado warning ends with Sue's adding this topic to the list of possible writing topics on the board. A few quiet "oh's" go up, indicating that some are reluctant about writing. It is hard to tell why. Perhaps the formula for writing has simply been used too often. Dan's reluctance cannot have helped. A discussion begins about whether preliminary discussions help provide ideas for writing.

Joan extends the scope of the question by asking, "Why can't you give us options, like math or writing?"

"How will I know when you are ready to write or do math?"

"We'll tell you."

The discussion again turns to topics for writing. "Can't I write about baseball cards, not feelings? I don't want to write about feelings," says Peter, who earlier had wanted to write about "boys' ideas," not "girls' ideas."

Peter's wonderful ingenuity and drive does not show in imaginative writing. He is never the one to go spontaneously to his journal to reflect on his emotional life or to create a fantasy world. His writing has none of the richness of Jill's book. Less competent in terms of test scores and much slower to complete worksheets, Jill finds writing part of a life full of feeling. For Peter, writing is usually a slightly boring part of school, and his writing does not match his oral skill or vigor. Jill seeks time to make personal entries in her journal.

On March 16, Jill makes four entries. One tells of a visit to her grandmother. Another is about a sister's birthday. Two are about competence:

> When I give my self a pat on the back I Fil good and I love math and I like reading I don't like braging thow. The time I did well was on the fist day of school. I am good at lost of things now and I am Good at some planets.

On the first day of school, she did not look as if she felt she was doing well, but she lives the day again in her journal.

Next day, before school, she writes,

> My friend is 10 yers old and her name is Amy Johnson and she hits mean the bus some time win I don't play with her a lot now her still hits me.

Jill keeps returning to her journal, where she grapples with the ethics of friendship, love, loss, and competence. Peter writes less and says less. He chooses to write about baseball, but produces short, barren pieces. Writing may be more fulfilling when it serves the moral purpose John Gardner saw for it—the creation of stories to live by—than when it serves more technical purposes. When Dewey argued that education should be living itself, not a separate preparation for living, he was arguing for the involvement of as many aspects of experience as possible in a complementary way. He was arguing for the involvement of the student's diverse abilities and interests in a way that expanded them into a cooperative whole.[4] In writing, Peter lists facts he already knows. For Jill, to write is to weave the fabric of life. Not so for Peter. His ingenuity and social dexterity have no place in his writing. He solves no emotional or ethical dilemmas in writing and writes only when asked to. Jill sits alone addressing the moral, emotional, and intellectual challenges of social life. Writing for her is living.

Though perhaps everyone should learn to write, should everyone be a writer in the sense of using writing to explore and construct a fuller life? In this session, breakaway movements suggest some students do not think so. Some of the resistance to writing might be resistance to writerly writing rather than an anti-intellectual impulse. The question of the place of this sort of writing in school need not be reserved for academic researchers. With the provocative help of classmates and teacher, students can examine and negotiate these positions.[5]

A long list of possible topics, most not about feelings, is brainstormed.

When novel-loving Elizabeth suggests make-believe stories, Wole sparks, "That'd be great." He is becoming a producer as well as a consumer of creative writing, shedding his theory that school is a test.

Joan interrupts. "I think we've got enough [ideas]. We've got more than [there are] children in the class." After a few more suggestions from others, she tries again. "How about options? Can we do math or writing?"

Sue agrees. Six immediately start writing. Elizabeth writes a title, *Jenny in Colombia*, and sets off on a romantic adventure.

On the same table at the back of the room, Dan and Claire prepare to do science experiments from a book they have been reading. They get food coloring and put drops in a glass of water, chattering about the way the color spreads as Elizabeth sits beside them writing. After trying several colors, they depart to a refrigerator downstairs to get ice cubes. They wrap some in paper towels and leave them beside unwrapped cubes on a shelf to see if wrapping affects the rate of melting. They get paper cups and make drinks from food coloring and sugar. They dissolve more sugar and other crystals and leave the container on a heat outlet to see what will happen when the water evaporates.

Dan is the principal investigator, Claire the assistant, working as if their lives depended on completing the experiments before the bell rings. Together they scan the description of each experiment and speed to execute it. Slowly, others are attracted, read the book over their shoulders, and begin imitating their work.

Peter and James have a protracted, animated discussion about the planets. Most of the time they refer to details of a display of the solar system Sue has put on a wall. Jack and Alan depart for the library eager to find some "good books" about planets.

Joan, the initiator of all this, takes her math book and persuades Jill to leave her beloved journal—in which she was beginning an entry—and come to an isolated table to do math. They sit facing the wall and work busily until Sue calls for everyone's attention.

As the period winds down, James is the only person who spent more than a moment not active at something that might be called schoolwork.

"Tell me what you did," asks Sue, who saw most of it. A number changed tasks; about equal numbers indicate they worked at writing, math, and science. "How did you feel? Did you learn?"

"Yes," they chorus.

"Was it wasted time?"

"No!" "No!"

"Were you just playing?"

"No!"

"We played but we learned stuff."

"Is it good for me to let you do that?"

"We still learned a lot."

"How do I know? I'm not really sure you learned."

"Maybe we could write down what we learned," says Dan, the boy "not born to write."

"You could ask us things."

When they begin repeating their themes, Sue asks, "What's the difference between playing and learning?"

"When you play you're not learning much."

"No! You can learn playing checkers. You can learn new things that way."

"So is it safe to say you learned something?"

"Correct!" "Yes." "Yes."

"How many think they learned more than one thing?" Almost all raise a hand. "How many think they only learned one thing?" Only

Jack raises a hand. He tells of frustration at being unable to find the book he wanted on space.

Perhaps they are not all writers, but they all seem to be learners.

Sue's style in this session contrasts with the supportive, encouraging tone she used in the early days of the year. She has let them choose, but this is no *laissez-faire* liberalism. She challenges them vigorously. Choice was allowed only after repeated appeals. After work on their chosen tasks, Sue provokes them to evaluate the meaning and quality of their work. Robust and determined philosophers and practitioners of education as living, they thrive on these challenges to justify their purposes and actions.

*   *   *

[**March 24**] George is moving to another city. Sue leads the class in brainstorming for things to include about him in a farewell note. The suggestions include "He never gets in trouble," "He's very good at math," "He's good at baseball," "He's a good friend to be with," "He's funny," "My mom would say he's a hunk," "He's quiet," "He cares for people," and "He smiles a lot." They are competent observers of one another. They are obviously not describing Peter or Tim. In character, George quietly smiles his appreciation.

As they begin to write cards, Dan says, "George, this is the only thing I want to write about." His message is a compliment for George and a comment on his own recovering attitude to writing.

> Dear George:
> I think that it will seem that you're sick every day. I will miss you George.
> Sincerely,
>   Ann

> Nobody is perfect but you !!
> 1. George is nice.
> 2. George is smart.
> 3. There is so much more I cannot say. George is gone !!
>   Jodie

James draws two stick figures with arms around each other and writes,

> George was the best Friend I could have. He was nice. He was my best friend. For years we have eyshuther. He's good at bas-

ketball, soccer, kickball, plus he liked lost uv people liket him all. Love, James Marsden.

[**April 19**] In show-and-tell, Ann announces, "I wrote a poem. It goes like this:"

April reminds me of robins in trees.
And children playing.
And people swimming.
And my sister's birthday.
And birds chirping.
And eyes watching.
And children at school.
It's busy in April.

"When did you make it?" asks Sue.

"I made it today." She is pleased with her work and can tell she has communicated with her peers.

Later I ask if I can write her story down. She agrees happily, adding, "I might have a poem club and write poems when I grow up."

Wole is next for show-and-tell. He grins and shuffles, anticipating the humor of the poems he plans to read. "I have a poem book. This one is called *Poem Stew*." He reads several poems to his attentive audience and, responding to a question, says, "It has the authors' names and an author index. Some say 'Anonymous.'"

When, for show-and-tell, the children introduce what could just as well have been assigned as schoolwork by the teacher, the boundary between school and personal life is gone.

[**April 26**] In a discussion of learning science, Dan says that you should stick with a topic if you like it but drop it if it's boring. When Sue asks why, he explains.

"Well, there are some things you do have to learn, like spelling. You've got to learn it 'cause when you're older, like working, you have to write things down. There's not a job where you can't write."

He is not as devoted to writing as Jill, but his resistance has died. Three weeks ago he started using a small ring-bound pad—not standard issue—which he holds in the palm of his hand as he writes. He has redefined the world as a place where writing is valuable and himself as someone who writes. A visitor to the class would not now guess that he was "not born to write."

CHAPTER 9

The Philosophy and Conduct of Science

[April 10] In show-and-tell, Dan announces, "These are my dinosaur books, and this is my favorite one. This first page is best." He displays a time chart of different species and the periods when they were presumed to be present in significant numbers. "See, look at all the details. There are some little animals."

"Why is that little one all by himself?" Peter points to one in the period after most dinosaurs had become extinct. Sue steps in to hold the book up higher for all to see and to help field the barrage of questions and comments that is swamping Dan. "Why do you think they are nearly all gone later on?"

"Maybe there was war."

"But were there people back then?"

"No."

"Maybe the book doesn't show all of them."

"Maybe God didn't like them."

"They weren't so intelligent."

"They need a mate."

"It takes a long time to hatch their eggs."

People are standing up at their desks. Some drift to the front to see more.

"Maybe they got smarter and smarter and got to be able to make different kinds."

"God created man after the dinosaurs."

"What if you don't believe in God?" asks Joan. She has asked this before. She is rarely impressed by attempts to justify anything by appeals to God or any superior power.

"In the scriptures it says God created the earth in six days." Evelyn is all earnestness. "On the first day . . ." She receives an attentive audience as she recounts the six days of the creation. Twice, when her memory fails, others prompt her. The juxtaposition of evolution and scripture is accepted as if both were part of nature's plan.

"He made man out of woman," Vicki pipes up.

"The other way around," says Vera.

"What about Joan's question? What if you don't believe in God?" asks Sue. "And even if you do, this is a question that's been around for a long time." She begins an account of evolution but stops as children press urgently with questions.

"It says here that *Tyrannosaurus rex* was in Indiana." Joan has moved to the front and found this in Dan's book.

"Wow!" "Gee!" "Hey!" The troops break ranks and converge on the book.

Surrounded, the leader goes with the crowd: "From all this I think we'll work up a whole center on dinosaurs." The children studied dinosaurs in the first grade, but no one is about to protest, "We already did this."

"You can write about dinosaurs in your journals," proposes Sue. "Write what you know and what you don't know . . ."

There has been much talk outside classrooms to the effect that students should discover or construct scientific knowledge. Inside classrooms, it is more common to find a different ethic. The typical science class requires every student to "complete the same readings, worksheets, experiments and tests—and to come to essentially the same conclusions" (Goodlad, 1983, p. 215). Students almost never pose questions or devise ways to answer them. They are sometimes admonished to discover things, but the meaning of such "discovery" is revealed when student "experimenters" ask their teachers, "'Is this what was supposed to happen?' or 'Have I got the right answer?'" (Driver, 1983, p. 126). Too often, classroom talk is governed by three understandings: "1. It is the teacher who asks the questions. 2. The teacher knows the answers. 3. Repeated questions imply wrong answers" (Edwards & Mercer, 1987, p. 45). This is not the case in Sue's class.

"Can we write our own solutions?" asks Dan.

"Can we use Dan's books?" Tim has a hand on one as he asks.

When Dan and Sue agree, a human wave engulfs the books. Without Sue's bidding, at least half of them sit in pairs reading, talking, and writing about dinosaurs. Sue unearths more books from a back cupboard, and these are snapped up as they emerge.

After 15 minutes, Sue asks what they've come up with. Instead of information, there are questions. "I want to know how long the longest dinosaur is." "How would we survive if dinosaurs were still alive?" "What if they talked?"

"How did they die?" comes up several times.

"Nobody really knows the answer," calls Dan. "But it would be a good one to study."

"I want to say something about Dan," says Paul as the session winds down. "I'm glad he brought the books in 'cause I like things that were a long time ago." A chorus of assent shows he speaks for the majority. "I want to know how they hatch from eggs," he adds.

*   *   *

If students study things that were a long time ago and about which no one knows the answer, the patterns that distinguish classroom talk from the mutuality and multiplicity of everyday conversation can hardly develop. The emphasis in science education on questions for which there are agreed-upon solutions may stem in part from an enthusiastic misapplication of Piagetian developmental psychology to the classroom. Piaget was interested in children's failure to see as axiomatic or logically necessary various things that adults see as axiomatic or necessary. He sought to understand, for example, how children come to see as natural or necessary that the total number of counters in a set does not change, whether the counters are spread apart or are bunched together. Applied to the classroom, this approach is easily assimilated into the ethic that students must discover the correct answers that are known to their teachers. This is not a necessary consequence of Piaget's perspective.[1] Nevertheless, a preoccupation with questions for which scientists are presumed to have right answers is unduly narrow and can make it hard for students to experience anything like scientific exploration.

Science lessons rarely focus on the unknown, but not because young children can't cope with uncertainty. They know the difference between matters about which we are (for the moment at least) certain and those that are controversial and unsettled—on which no one, teachers included, can lay down the law (Nicholls & Nelson, 1992). Most of Sue's students are ready to explore what they know to be unknown.

*   *   *

[April 25] For part of each day, during a little over a week, dinosaurs have been a topic of reading, writing, and discussion.

"Are there any questions we didn't answer?" asks Sue.

"About the longer dinosaurs—how much they ate in one day and, totaling it up, how much they ate in a year."

"How did they die?" asks Evelyn.

"That's what I want to know."

"So do I."

"That's what everyone wants to know," intones Wole.

"Yes!" cries the chorus.

"If the dinosaurs died," argues Alan, "you're talking about cells and how they change the body. You're talking about how a person would come to life then."

After some discussion, Sue discerns and explains to the others that Alan is asking how human evolution differed from dinosaur evolution, so that humans are still here whereas dinosaurs are not.

"Some people believe God made dinosaurs and some don't." This is a variant of one of Joan's themes—"If you didn't believe in God . . ." But she has another puzzle now. "I thought they came from little to big so they can't come from big to little. People would have to be first."

Size increase among dinosaurs is discussed extensively.

Peter focuses on intra-group diversity. "You know how dinosaurs changed kinds. So did men. I'm just saying dinosaurs changed and so do we. One man couldn't be all the kinds there are, so we must have changed."

Alan suggests that the sun makes different people's colors. Ann takes the topic back to species transformation.

"I think if man is brought by animals, then birds must be from pterodactyls."

"No! Not pterodactyl." Vicki, the pterodactyl lover, intervenes. "It has rubbery skin and wings."

Joan brings to the front Dan's chart indicating time periods when different dinosaurs predominated. As children take turns to get a drink in the hall, she discusses it with Sue and the crowd that grows around them. Soon the only ones not in this group or getting a drink are Vicki, who is sorting cards with pictures of dinosaurs, and Jill, who is playing with a model dinosaur.

When all are back, Sue draws the less loquacious students into a discussion of the chart. She points out that Joan has detected similarities among dinosaurs from different time periods.

"What is similar about these ones, Paul?" She points to Triceratops and similar creatures that appear in several time periods.

"They have shields and horns."

"Carlos?" asks Sue.

"The shape of their heads."

"Their tails look about the same length."

"On *Triceratops*, all the heads look similar."

"Oh, I know!" Jack is excited. "They're all armored." Sue continues around the class, drawing in everyone. Then, out of the blue Paul declares, "That [chart] says *Stegosaurus* and *Tyrannosaurus rex* were in different times, but the film [from the day before] showed they fought each other."

"Which is right?" asks Sue.

"People who write books, they don't write things about things that aren't right. There is more in a book that we know is real," says Dan, owner of the book.

"Books say exactly and a movie says, 'maybe,'" offers Joan.

"So if it's written in a book, it must always be true?"

"No!" they cry.

"They'll tell you if a book is make-believe," says Joan.

"Books don't always tell the truth," says Vera.

"How can you tell if they do?"

"You see if it makes sense," answers Vera. Perhaps she is groping for a thought expressed by William James (1907): *"That ideas (which themselves are but parts of our experience) become true just in so far as they help us get into satisfactory relation with other parts of our experience. . . ."* (p. 58).

James's pragmatist approach to truth does not satisfy everyone, but it is hard to improve on. Sue, however, puts the tough question: "How do we know if something doesn't make sense?"

"You can tell," claims Joan, "Like if you write 'Joan' with an *i* you can see it doesn't make sense."

Murmurs of doubt are heard, and Joan nods agreement when Dan says, "There's lots of Johnsons, and I've come to realize that they're not all spelled the same." Students recognize the arbitrary nature of the conventions of spelling. They see that these are not established in the same way as the substantive claims of science (Nicholls & Thorkildsen, 1989).

"Sometimes," says Vera, clarifying her position, "you can tell 'cause if it tells you something you know isn't true, you know to not believe."

"You can look in different books, like the dictionary," adds Jack.

"So, if it's in the dictionary, is it true?"

"Books usually have labels that tell you whether it's make-believe or nonfiction. Fiction is what's make-believe, so nonfiction is real." Peter's logic seems to satisfy him fully.

"So this book is nonfiction. So is it or the video right?"

"I went to the bookshop, to the history books, to the 'for sure' books," says Dan. "If they get the books scrambled up, it's their fault."

Ann raises the question of the author's motives. "Maybe the person who wrote it wanted to be right when they were little, and when they grew up they learned the way it really was. Then they would know."

"I think the book is true," proposes Claire, "because the video might be old and the book is newer."

"Sometimes a movie says when it was made," observes Vera.

Though eager to battle over slight variations of their suggestions, they are unable to progress much further.

"So," asks Sue, "why are people interested in dinosaurs?"

"Because it's an unknown thing, like an adventure," says Dan.

"So, if it's unknown, it's more interesting?"

"Just like space," he says.

"It's like we're guessing," chimes Joan buoyantly.

"Like scientists!" calls multitrack Vicki, flourishing her arm, as if she were one of the Three Musketeers. She has been flipping through a dinosaur book, appearing not to be following the discussion. But when she detects a problem (about the evolution of birds, for example) or a point that needs enhancement, she is wholly focused, deftly inserting her contribution into the mosaic of discussion and inwardly smiling at the art of it all before turning back to the book.

"First we're reading the books, and then we're guessing, and then we see if we're right," says Joan.

"It'd be more of an adventure if we could find out on our own." Dan repeats his theme.

Peter has a different problem. He points to the time chart. "*Stegosaurus* and this [later] one might be related, so why are there only two of them and so many of the other types?"

"Well, that's a tough question," says Sue.

"Like Dan was saying," Peter again supports Dan, "I think we should go out and dig and see what we find."

Others do not object to his intent but doubt the advisability of ruining "our yard" and ask, "Where are the tools?"

"I don't think it was a real *Tyrannosaurus rex*," says Paul, returning to the videotape, "so I don't believe the movie."

"Why?"

"'Cause dinosaurs can't be around."

"Turtles are dinosaurs and they're around," says Alan.

"So why did big ones die and not the little ones?"

"They could have fought, and the little ones kept safe and the big ones killed each other," Ann suggests.

"There is big turtles still alive," says Alan. His eyes are popping with determination to communicate the enormity of the one he saw at a zoo. "It could eat one whole banana ... at ... probably," his eyes roll, "two bites."

"The big ones died because when you get old you die," suggests Claire, apparently confusing the age and size of individuals with the evolution and size of species.

"Little ones can dig holes and hide."

Vera, like Claire, attempts to connect her knowledge of human life to the remote but pertinent lives of dinosaurs. "The big ones might have died because they were fat and the little ones didn't."

"Maybe the big ones' brains were not so smart," proposes Vicki. "And the little ones were smarter."

"I read a book that said the little ones didn't have big brains," says Dan.

The possibility of climatic change is raised. They refer to different books they have read that implicate both higher and lower temperatures.

"What if it got hot?" asks Sue.

"Maybe they get sweaty and plants would grow more. And they could get burned. Maybe their skin was light like mine," wonders Vicki.

"Maybe they die when they get sweaty," says Jack.

"Maybe they aren't extinct. Turtles and jellyfish are alive. Maybe it's the land ones that died," says Peter.

"So only the land ones disappeared?"

"But there were water dinosaurs that died," Peter recalls, changing his mind.

"Maybe a comet hits the earth and spins it around and the animals spin off and fall back broken so only little ones are left." Jodie gestures to evoke this disaster. "Maybe that's how those rocks in space [asteroids, which they studied earlier] came."

"They could have frozen in space," says Wole.

"Cold and snow killed them." Jack holds up a book showing dying dinosaurs in snow.

"So how could it get cold?" asks Sue.

"The rings of Saturn are made of ice," says Peter. "If comets can flash by the earth, perhaps Saturn or its rings can?"

Hot and cold and their effects are discussed until Ann suggests, "Plants could die, plant eaters die, and meat eaters have no food so ..."

"They'd have to eat each other," interrupts Wole.

The possibility that the earth's water could have evaporated, how evaporation happens, and its likely effects are explored.

Tim refers to earlier themes. "I think that some comets have an ice middle, and if something rushes past you fast, it makes a cold wind." He is certainly working to bring this part of his experience into satisfactory relation with other parts.

They discuss the effects climatic changes would have and what colors the dinosaurs were, and then go back to evolution.

"If there was no changing cells we'd all be the same," reiterates Alan.

"The Bible doesn't say that." Jack is authoritative. His back is straight, his expression firm.

"So the Bible tells us the whole answer?" asks Sue.

"Yes!" Jack is determined. "Because God made the whole earth."

"If people came from animals," says Ann, pursuing Alan's theme, "and we are from Indiana, where *Tyrannosaurus rex* was, we'd have some of *Tyrannosaurus rex*'s blood."

"Claire, what do you think?"

"Man came from God."

"Where did the animals come from?"

"From Jesus. I believe in Jesus."

"I'm confused. God and Jesus made different things? I thought they both made all the same things?" Joan presents this as a question, but her manner gently implies that Claire's idea makes no sense.

"It says in the Bible . . ." Peter begins, but Joan cuts him off firmly.

"It never said he made dinosaurs."

"But he made *all* the animals, and dinosaurs are animals, so," Peter strikes back, "*unfortunately*, you are wrong." This is the only moment in this hour and a half of discussion when a touch of personal venom appears.

Jack is adamant about God's role and accepts no challenges. He says he has seen dinosaurs in a book about how God made the earth. But he bears no animosity toward the Darwinians and Lamarckians of the class. He assumes that natural explanations can also be valid. He follows and contributes robustly to discussions on these matters—now championing the ice age theory, now arguing another position.

"How did the first dinosaur get on earth?" James is earnest. God's act seems an incomplete explanation for him.

"God made the animals and the people. They were made separate, at different times."

"Who believes God made the dinosaurs and everything else?" Every hand, Joan's included, goes up.

"So how would a person who doesn't believe in God explain all the dinosaurs and animals?"

"I know what you're doing." Peter stands up, pointing at Sue. "You're trying to get us to think. This is not doing us any good except to get us ready to think hard." What indeed is he thinking? We are both puzzled by his earnest and emotional challenge.

"Is it good to get you to think hard and maybe change your mind?" asks Sue, but the class is too interested in thinking hard to answer her question.

"They say there's no dinosaurs left. How do they know?" Paul questions urgently. "How do they really know?"

"Yes," chimes Peter, suddenly not the person who just questioned the value of thinking hard. "How *do* we know?"

"Some things *look* like they were a long time ago," Vera suggests.

"You saw on the film how some scientists put together a dinosaur's bones, and years later someone found they had the wrong head on it. How could they know that?"

"By the imprints in different parts of the bones," says Peter, who seems unable to stop thinking hard.

"They could have another, and it looked better on it," proposes Evelyn.

"They saw that the head of the new one could go on it," adds Paul.

The bell for the end of school rings. There is no sign of flagging interest. Sue proposes that tonight they should think about how one knows one is right about something and how scientists know when they are right.

[April 26] The suggestion that one can tell whether a claim is correct by asking experts makes sense to several speakers, but Peter will not hear of it.

"Their source is not your source. You need to *do* things. You need to go to your sources, not their sources." He is passionate in his demand that one's knowledge of science should not rest on faith in experts. Some others are not persuaded. Sue refocuses the discussion:

"Who is an expert?"

"Scientists."

"My grandpa is an expert at woodwork."

"How do you become an expert?" asks Sue.

"God is an expert," contributes Evelyn.

"He was already an expert," adds Vera.

A long list of experts at different things follows. Jack claims expertise at baseball and explains, "I practice a lot. Practice makes perfect."

Yesterday Dan implied that if you got the right type of book, what it said would be true. Today he was ready to rely on experts. Now he has second thoughts. He recounts a visit to a doctor who "never gave us any medicine, so we had to go to a better doctor. Scientists seem like they're rich and know everything, but they don't." Like the Wizard of Oz, the scientist is just a person like us.

"You can't know everything," contributes Peter. "There are some things people can't know. It's been proven that we can't know everything."

Others reassert the limits of knowledge until Sue asks, "Should scientists give up?"

"No, they just keep trying."

"Some things you think are impossible you can do if you just keep on trying."

"Like bringing dinosaurs back to life? You can't do that," qualifies Dan.

"Does science ever stop?"

"No, it can't. Like 100 years ago, maybe they didn't know about dinosaurs," says Dan.

"Why?"

"Maybe they didn't have the stuff for digging them."

"Like the guy who invented the telephone."

"What do you mean, Vicki?"

"People said you couldn't talk like that, and he made a thing like a record and an earphone and he talked through it. I don't know how." She does, however, know that the incomprehensible might eventually be comprehended and the impossible be made possible.

The conversation soon returns to how one knows if one is right.

"You study on it," Alan offers.

"How?"

"Use tools," he suggests.

"You use your brain. You think and figure it out for yourself," says Vicki.

"It's like a big mystery to scientists," declares Alan. "It's like a big maze you have to find your way through."

"It's like you're this small and trying to drive a bumper car and can't reach the pedal," suggests little Tim.

They get back to diversity of scientific opinion.

"What you get most of is the best one," proposes Dan.

"It's like voting," chimes Vera.

"Can you make the wrong decision voting?" asks Sue, but the specific intervenes again as Peter goes to the globe and suggests that one could check the theory of continental drift by cutting up a map and seeing if the pieces fitted. A number decide to look at home for maps they could do this with.

Timid Martha must have been reflecting on Alan's maze metaphor, because she now tries to relate the mirror maze on the television program "Double Dare" to the discussion.

"No," says Wole, "Alan is thinking of the maze that's in 'Fun House.'"

"I meant," says Alan, after Sue questions him, "That you can't find all the answers. There are bits you can't find."

Peter elaborates the metaphor. "It's like there's lots of doors, and as soon as you get the information, it fits together and you've got a key and it opens a door and you go through and there's another door. When you get to the last door, you know it all."

"Are we there?" Sue asks.

An enthusiastic chorus of "No!" leaves no doubt how much they relish the idea of science as a never-ending quest.

*   *   *

"When the first mathematical, logical, and natural uniformities, the first *laws*, were discovered, men were so carried away by the clearness, beauty, and simplification that resulted, that they believed themselves to have deciphered authentically the eternal thoughts of the Almighty" (James, 1907, p. 56). William James wrote as if this notion were passing. He hoped it was. But the idea that science is most truly science and most to be revered when it reveals eternal truths, unstained by human biases, is still with us. Many see the physical sciences as superior to others, not because they provide endless and exciting quests but because of the abstractness and impersonality of their formulations and the precision of their predictions and findings.

Such contemporary expressions of what Dewey (1988) called the quest for certainty are a far cry from our second graders' quest for excitement. These children seem close to James's (1907) "notion that no theory is absolutely a transcript of reality . . . only a man-made language, a conceptual shorthand . . . in which we write our reports of nature; and languages, as is well known, tolerate much choice of expression and many dialects" (p. 57).

"In the Europe of the 16th century, as in classical Athens, some scholars condemned as irrational *con*fusion what others welcomed as intellectual *pro*fusion" (Toulmin, 1990, p. 27). Our second graders welcome profusion. They are ready, with Montaigne and the Renaissance humanists, "to suspend judgment about matters of general theory, and to concentrate on accumulating a rich perspective, both on the natural world and on human affairs, as we encounter them" (Toulmin, 1990, p. 27).

*　　*　　*

[May 1] At the end of a session in which they have been observing the effects of putting raisins in soda, Alan notices that his thumb appears enlarged when he puts it into his glass of soda. He points this out to Sue, who calls attention to his discovery.

"What makes it so big?"

"Gee!"

Everyone is fascinated. They insert their thumbs and fingers and get the same effect. Vicki insists on shoving my fingers into her glass. In the midst of this experimentation, the bell ending the school day rings, and they reluctantly clean up and leave for their buses.

Next morning, before the bell begins the formal school day, Tim brings water in a glass to his desk. Carlos, Ann, Vicki, Claire, and Dan quickly unite with him to experiment. Many small objects go into the water—crayons, pencils, erasers, paper clips, bits of toys. The outcome of each trial is saluted.

"Oh, neat!"

"Wow! Look how big that is."

"Try the [eraser shaped like a] watermelon."

"Wooo. Look! It's huge."

The regularity of the effect captures them.

When the bell rings, Tim has a wet desk to deal with. Discussion soon turns to this experiment.

"Was everything larger?" asks Sue.

"Yes."

"One of the things didn't work," claims Dan.

"What?"

"I can't remember." No one suggests what might not have appeared larger, but neither does anyone disagree.

"What can we say about this? What kind of theory, as scientists, can we make up?"

"It's very fun to do," offers Tim, for whom the aesthetic experience of the world is inextricably bound up with the understanding of it. He savors his acts of science as if they were treasured poems he had written.

"Oh, I meant, what happens when things go in the glass?"

"It might get bigger. I'm not sure."

Tim and his collaborators are happy to leave the matter there. They were startled by their discovery and feel no need to press to an absolute conclusion. The unpredictability of the world is as fascinating as its regularities. In a few years they will not have to reflect to be sure that the phenomenon is predictable; the suggestion that it might not be will soon seem preposterous.

Right now, Sue could seek ways to convince them of this. She could explain. She could suggest more observations and systematic recording. But she does not. She treats this question as controversial, as a topic on which it would be inappropriate to seek a hasty consensus. The children have done real intellectual work. Sue provoked them to summarize their conclusions. By pressing further, she might convince them of what will eventually appear obvious. But would this turn science into a quest for certainty, without a leavening passion for the uncertainties that will provoke new explorations? Would they forget that science can be "very fun to do"?

*   *   *

[May 4] Sue started reading *The Last of the Really Great Whangdoodles* (Edwards, 1974) the previous day. The definition of "whangdoodle" in their dictionaries is confusing: "*noun, slang*: a fanciful creature of undefined nature." They turn to a larger dictionary from the library, which presents new problems.

"What's 'mythical'?" asks Wole.

They discuss *mythical, fanciful,* and *undefined.*

This stimulates a story from Jodie about a ghostly house.

"Was Redeye in there?" Jack wants to know.

"There's no such thing as Redeye."

"Who knows? Who knows?" Jack advances across the room loftily and firmly, his finger pointing at doubting Joan. "He's a ghost!"

"Are there ghosts?" asks Sue.

A conglomeration of yesses and no's erupts.

"And there *are* witches!" Jack is firm. "On the radio I heard a witch talking to the man."

"How did you know it was a witch?"

"I heard on the radio and they said on the radio that their pure washing color is red."

"When they wash . . . ?" Sue prompts.

"They put blood in it."

"I don't believe it a bit," explodes Joan.

"I've got evidence on ghosts," claims Tim. "I saw it on the news, and I was in the audience. The guy was talking to the man, and some kind of blob came behind him. It looked gooey and red. I'm not sure if it was red, but I think it was."

"Where were you?"

"In the audience."

"Where?"

"In the theater."

"Is it Christian?" asks Jack.

"No. They were broadcasting."

"He's making it up."

"You never know, 'cause maybe it's a regular person."

"How can you tell it's a witch? 'Cause it's on the radio and you can't see."

"This was a Christian radio station, and Christians can't lie, 'cause they'll break a law." Jack is resolute.

"Do they ever lie?" asks Sue.

"Sometimes, but not at this radio station, 'cause they were face to face with a real witch."

Peter distinguishes truth from the experience of certainty: "Yourself, you can be sure, but you can't be positive."

"Yeah! It might be that. He can say that but he can't prove it. How do you know they are really there? Do you have a crystal ball?"

Jack nearly bursts with moral indignation. "A crystal ball is *evil magic!* I don't have a crystal ball. I wouldn't!"

"Does anyone believe, as Jack does, that there are witches and ghosts?" A third of the class raise their hands.

"It was moving across the stage," says Tim.

"There was wheels under it," suggests Joan.

"It was floating. I could see the bottom." Their enthusiasm to offer interpretations overwhelms the normal turn-taking. When calm is restored, Sue calls on Elizabeth.

"It might be someone dressed up like in the movies. People pull them through the air with strings."

"A movie projection."

"They are pretending."

"They sounded like a real witch." Jack is determined and speaks loudly, but not vindictively. "OK," he challenges, striding to the front of the room. "Everyone try to talk like a witch and I'll tell you if it's real."

"People can tell lies as easily as the truth," proposes Evelyn.

"So, do you think Tim and Jack are lying?" asks Sue.

The class is divided.

"How do you [Tim and Jack] know they weren't just tricking you?" asks Evelyn.

"So they could be telling the truth but the people tricked them?" checks Sue. Evelyn nods to this, but wants stronger evidence from Jack:

"If a witch turned him into a frog and he came hopping in here, then I might believe it."

Wole has found *witch* in the dictionary. "It's someone who practices magic," he offers.

"There's no such thing as magic."

"There is!"

"No!"

"It's just tricks."

"You think you're seeing it and you're not. It's not doing what they think."

"It could be a hologram."

"Holograms are just pictures from a special projector," says Tim.

"Yes, but three-dimensional," adds Dan.

Jack too has found *witch* in the dictionary. "It says a witch is an ugly old woman, especially," he points at the unbelievers, "of an *evil* nature." Other dictionary definitions are offered without resolution of the questions.

Martha believes there could be ghosts because she just heard a ghostly singing in the corridor. (Later she will confide to Sue that she discovered it was the fourth graders downstairs practicing for a concert.)

Sue moves to conclude. "I think we found people who have strong ideas, and none has given enough proof to change other people's ideas. This happens often in life. What should we do in situations like this—when someone believes the opposite of you and they won't change?"

"Nothing."

"Ask someone else."

"Let them believe what they want to."

"Yes. There's no way you can change their belief."

"Jack, you presented a strong argument," recalls Sue. "Are you trying to prove it for them or to convince yourself?"

"I already know. I've got proof!"

"Is anyone not sure about this?" About a third of them raise their hands.

"You don't have to believe," suggests Joan, prophet of freedom. "It's like the President. Some people don't like the President we have. But they choose."

Sue concludes with the suggestion Dan made when discussions of science started: If we listen to others, something they say might make a little bit of sense. Though always animated and occasionally intense, the discussion has created no enemies. Jack was very assertive and at times under siege. Though he, more than anyone, claimed certainty, he never stooped to personal attack. He shows no sign of having dismissed his peers or of having himself been diminished. Indeed, he is energized.[2]

The children act as if they knew what the sixteenth-century humanists, William James, John Dewey, and Stephen Toulmin might have hoped they would learn.

> There may be no rational way to convert to our point of view people who honestly hold other positions, but we cannot short circuit such disagreements. Instead we should live with them, as further evidence of the diversity of human life. Later on these differences may be resolved by further shared experience. . . . Tolerating the resulting plurality, ambiguity, or the lack of certainty is no error, let alone a sin. Honest reflection shows that it is part of the price we inevitably pay for being human beings, and not gods. (Toulmin, 1990, p. 30)

All this has been an interlude in the "reading" of *The Last of the Really Great Whangdoodles*. Everyone settles back, warm with anticipation, when Sue says, "I'm going to read a bit more."

The episode is not, however, over. The next day, Joan confides to Sue that, after speaking with her mother, she has decided she may have been wrong. Perhaps there *are* witches.

At the beginning of the year, Joan, who had been unhappy in first grade, would press to tell her own stories to the class without regard for the inclinations of her classmates. Her own voice was the one she preferred to hear, and she directed it at her teacher, ignoring her peers. During these brittle displays, which began to fade after three weeks, I found myself alternately grinding my teeth at Joan's arrogance and marveling at Sue's patience as she tried to get the measure of the girl. Now, Joan has lost none of her determination, but it is a determination to make sense rather than to dominate. When others spoke, she used not to listen, waiting (when she did wait) only for a chance to speak. She is still quick with words, but now she often peers intently into the faces of speakers, listening with an intense, unselfconscious grimace that is close to a smile, as if entering their thoughts.

Two weeks after the Whangdoodle session, Joan's mother relates to Sue a conversation about a class discussion. Joan's mother takes every chance to remind Sue how she appreciates what has happened to her daughter since the school year began. She has said what a relief it is to "have my daughter back"—the daughter who used to lie in bed thinking of ways to annoy her mother. On the evening in question, she asked Joan what had happened in school. When Joan began an account of a class discussion, her mother asked whether the class did any work. She was amused and delighted to report how Joan pounced on her implication that a class discussion was not work: "Mother! You might not realize it, but quite often we get into discussions about things that are very important, and we learn a lot from this." This small piece of human dynamite does not merely think deeply. She thinks deeply about the sources of her own thinking, her assertiveness now enriched by her recognition of the power of conversation.

*   *   *

[May 20] When Sue asks, "Do scientists have the right to guess?" there is diversity of opinion.

"They know the stuff and they shouldn't guess," thinks Martha, who is still, more than most, tight, constrained, and lacking confidence. Her very being seems founded on the notions that some external authority must judge the value of her ideas and of her person and that the logic of these awful judgments is inscrutable.

"We all have a guessing permit," counters Alan, who often presumes that things can be discovered and will make sense. After an inconclusive exchange on this question, Sue asks, "Are you scientists?"

"Sometimes we are."

"You make us be scientists."

"How?"

"You make us figure things out," says Wole. "Like if Whangdoodles exist."

"Anything else I do?"

"By teaching us things."

"Questions! You ask us questions." Vera stands up, arching her back, waving her hand to call her answer. There are murmurs of assent.

"One of the ways you teach us is, you don't tell us the answers. We figure it out," adds Dan.

"How about we ask you the questions and you figure it out?" Evelyn's deference to authority occasionally cracks to reveal an independent, even rebellious streak, but it has taken a long time for her to gain the confidence to offer such a joking challenge. Her proposal is greeted with cheers from the children and mock horror from Sue.

"So what will you ask me?"

"199 times 9," calls Jack.

When Sue works this on the board, there are cries of "Cheat!" "You have to do it in your head."

"Is that cheating?" asks Sue.

"Adults should know," says Ann.

"Yes," say the others.

"Did you teach me anything?"

"We taught you how not to cheat," says Jack.

"What would you ask if you wanted me to be a scientist?" asks Sue.

"What was the first dinosaur?" says Vera.

"We could give you 10 dinosaur books to take home and you should do half an hour of research every day and do some papers, and I'll tell you what's wrong, and you go home with the books and find out your mistakes." Evelyn can challenge the teacher but, for her, scientific knowledge is found in books, and freedom means that she is boss.

"So you'll make me find out the information?"

Evelyn nods emphatically. Ann and Claire suggest similar plans.

Peter is still for exploration: "First, I'll tell you a little bit of information, and then . . ."

"Then what?"

"You'll be on your own."

"We'll take you to the museum and you'll see stuff and we'll tell you what to write." For Ann, like Evelyn, someone must be boss.

"Why can't you choose by yourself what you're going to do?" asks Peter.

"Do scientists decide themselves what they will study?" Sue asks.

"They decide." Peter is adamant.

"Yes!" cries the chorus.

"How?"

"By having clues. They see if a thing fits," says Jodie, perhaps answering a different question. But on they go, generating questions for Sue:

"When do you think the dinosaurs died and how?" "Which dinosaur came first?" "What was the very last thing found [latest discovery] on earth?" "What's the first spider?" "Is God really true?" "What was the first composer?" "What was the first song made?"

Jill comes up to ask Sue her question. She does not want to call it out. "Why, that's an interesting question," says Sue and announces, "What is the very last number?"

Jodie ends the list with evident satisfaction with the aptness of her suggestion: "Try an experiment on anything you want to and write a report about it."

The day clearly belongs to the notion that science involves choosing and negotiating what questions to ask and with finding answers that make sense, rather than merely finding the teacher's answers to the teacher's questions.

*   *   *

Generally, students in our schools come to assume that scientific knowledge is to be memorized rather than constructed in personal and social inquiry. This fact has been of some national concern. So too has been the failure of a majority of students to comprehend the science lessons they have apparently been studying (National Assessment of Educational Progress, 1979).

It may be that science educators have inadvertently gotten what some of them wanted. "Problem solving in a domain such as physics has," according to Eylon and Linn, "the advantage of having 'real-world' features and of being associated with a *well-structured* knowledge domain (principles of physics) and *well-defined* problem-solving procedures. These *attractive features* have led to a cumulative, systematic research effort in physics and mathematics problem-solving" (1988, p. 237; italics added).[3] If science education is primarily a matter of acquiring well-structured knowledge, it is unlikely to be an adventure.

Science can sweep aside intellectual fogs, yet it also seeks and creates puzzles, paradoxes, and ambiguities. In basic biomedical research, writes Lewis Thomas (1974), "What you need at the outset is a high degree of uncertainty: otherwise it isn't likely to be an important problem. . . . There are fascinating ideas all over the place, irresistible experiments beyond numbering, all sorts of new ways into the maze of problems. But every next move is unpredictable, every outcome uncertain. It is a puzzling time, but a very good time" (pp. 118–119).

Jodie and her classmates are not old enough to understand fully that to determine whether a given variable produces a given effect, one must control for the effects of other variables. In this sense, they do not understand what an experiment is.[4] If we emphasize this, they will all look like inferior scientists. Yet Jodie and most of her peers are wholeheartedly with Thomas (1982) when he argues that we should "recognize science as the high adventure it really is, the wildest of all explorations ever undertaken by human beings" (p. 93). If this is the heart of science, they are scientists at heart.

The uncertainty-reducing function of science gets most of the playing time in schools and in research on science education. Perhaps this is why, as Thomas (1982) puts it, "the worst thing that has happened to science education is that the fun has gone out of it" (p. 93). "We might begin looking more closely at the common ground that science shares with . . . the humanities and with social and behavioral science. For there is such a common ground. It is called bewilderment" (p. 91). "Leave," he suggests, "the so-called basics aside for a while, and concentrate the attention of all students on the things that are not known" (p. 92).[5]

Even first graders recognize that there are many phenomena about which we are fairly certain. A spacecraft, for example, will not float up from earth unassisted into orbit. They also recognize areas where disagreement is endemic and legitimate. Is there, for example, life elsewhere in space? (Nicholls & Nelson, 1992). When science means well-structured, noncontroversial information, children can be wrong and stupid every day of the year. But controversial topics strike no fear into these would-be scientists with licenses to guess and to travel in exciting mazes without end.

CHAPTER 10

The Life of Drama

[**May 2**] Sue has been trying out more absorbing and challenging activities for children to do while she works with reading groups. Workbooks and worksheets are put aside. Today, while she works with one group, other small groups read.

Jodie, Vera, and Dan share a single book. At first, Dan hovers too far away to follow as Jodie, then Vera, reads. He moves closer and wants to take over reading. Reluctantly, but without complaining, Vera releases the book. When he stumbles, the girls help him, gently and unobtrusively. When her turn comes round, Vera reads, "... went out crying ..." and asks, "Does that say 'crying'?" "'Carrying,'" says Evelyn. This makes sense to Vera, who proceeds. Here, as with other groups, there is no thought of seeking adult help, as so commonly happens with workbooks. Vera reads until Dan asks for a turn, then submits, sadly but silently, to the imperative to share.

Enclosed in a square formed behind the open door and a bookcase, Alan reads to Jill and Evelyn. Evelyn writes a story in her notebook while listening. Alan seeks to shorten his task. "Let's skip the next page." "No!" cries his audience, suddenly alive, wanting the whole story. Surprised, Alan returns to the task.

When another group leaves Sue, they begin a very animated reading of a play from their reader.

[**May 11**] More groups read plays. Jill, Vicki, Evelyn, and Vera struggle to choose parts for *Small Deer's Magic Leaf*. Jill becomes upset and goes to Sue, who suggests that they draw lots for parts. Pleased, they rush to continue.

Soon they begin making costumes. Jill is still fragile. She smolders, muttering that Vicki made her be Deer instead of Elephant. She will not share her scissors. She denigrates the deer ears she makes, then snaps, "Don't look!" when Vicki glances her way. Vicki looks puzzled but soon forgets, eager to complete her own costume.

"There's nothing wrong with those," says Evelyn, trying to calm Jill. "They're good ears."

When the bell signals recess, Jill goes to Sue saying Vicki broke a promise. Sue suggests Vicki must have thought Jill was very good because she gave her the main role. Jill suddenly sobs, "I don't want to say, 'Ah-choo!' I don't know how." As Vicki sees Jill's dismay, her eyes pop with surprise and concern.

"I can say that bit. Someone else can do it if you don't want to."

Martha comes across the room to rub Jill's back and stroke her hair. Elizabeth hugs her. Martha leads her to get a tissue for her wet eyes. Leaving for recess, the group, including Vicki and Jill, hold hands. Plays raise challenges not found in workbooks.

[May 15] Sue asks for reactions to the different approaches they tried the previous week. Peter quickly objects that his group had the "same old regular thing."

There is some discussion of workbooks. Dan splutters and moans at the back of the room whenever a vaguely encouraging word is said about them. Twice Sue reminds him that "Everyone has a right to give an opinion here."

"Why do we have to do things we already know, like vowels?" Tim supports Dan.

"So," asks Sue, "is there a point where you can stop practicing? Does practice help?"

"No!" blurts Dan.

"All it does is help get it in your mind so you memorize it. You remember it more," says Joan.

"You get speed. You get to go faster," adds Peter.

"In my [South American] country you have to do times [tables] real quick." Perhaps Vera here reveals why she took so long in the year to relax.

A group preparing a play is especially pleased.

"I liked it," says Jodie. "You can decide things you are going to do. They give you ideas and you choose. We didn't have to sit and do all the paperwork. We can plan activities."

"The story was exciting," says Alan.

"I want to do something more active, like a play," announces Dan.

Sue canvasses opinions, which are diverse.

"I like to only read, read the whole day," says Alan, exaggerating his considerable capacity to sit still when absorbed.

"I don't like reading too much," says James. "You sit down too much."

"What could you do?"

"You could have stories and plays."

Others clamor to be heard. Sue asks, "What if I said you could select a story and read it and you could present it to the class any way you want?"

"I'd do a play."

Many proposals about how to organize plays bubble up. "How will we pick?" Sue asks. "Where can you get ideas for plays?"

"In our minds."

"From a book."

"And if there are different ideas?"

"You vote!"

This gets wide support. Suggestions for plays flow. They pull books from their desks and off bookshelves, form provisional collaborations, and negotiate topics, while Sue writes their suggestions on the board. Stepping back to look at the list, which fills much of the board, Sue asks again, "How are we going to decide?"

"Vote!" "Vote!" "Vote!" they cry, wanting to get on with it.

"You are inciting a riot," cracks Sue as the clamor fades.

"What's inciting a riot? What does that mean?" Peter calls, but the momentum for choosing wipes out his question.

Students busily negotiate among themselves, listening with one ear as Sue goes down the list asking what they will choose. Dan, Tim, and Claire opt for a dinosaur story based on a book and audiotape and discuss sound effects.

"I want to do *Andrew*. . . . 'cause there's a robber," argues Peter to his collaborators.

"No!" calls Wole. "There's *three* robbers in *The Bremen Town Musicians*." This settles it. After brief advice from Sue, who is attending to many coalescing groups, this troupe recruits extra players.

Elizabeth has collected Ann, Jodie, and Joan for a play based on a *Sweet Valley Twins* book. "I'll tell them the whole story," Elizabeth proposes to Sue, "'cause I've read the whole book." They go to an empty office next door to prepare. They are back in about 10 minutes to ask Sue to settle a disagreement that seems to reflect Ann's penchant for organizing things her own way. "You've got to listen to each other," urges Sue. They bounce away. In 15 minutes, when I check, they are in the middle of a scene but want to go back to the beginning for me.

"We're not properly organized yet," explains Jodie, but they launch into two short family scenes and one at school. Their dash puts television soap operas to shame. Changes in timing and content are negotiated as the drama flows on. Jodie especially has a sensitive, ironic touch, lively and funny.

Back in the classroom, Wole has charge of the Bremen Town Musicians. "What do you want to be? OK, you'll be Robber One. I'm Dog. Where's Carlos? We want Carlos." When Carlos returns from a session with a speech teacher, they welcome him warmly. Though he is the slowest reader in the class, he is ready. He is folded into the middle of the group, who are crammed together on the floor with their backs into a corner. Getting help when he needs it, he tackles his part with determination. Sharing one book, this group is a miracle of coordination. They quickly have the story moving, helping one another with words and expression.

"No! No! Paul, make your voice rough and mean." Paul, who is Lion, growls out his lines as strongly as his reading skills permit.

Vera and Jill snuggle together on the carpet with *The Scared Little Rabbit*. "I'd like to read it with you," says Vera, whose steady inclusiveness calms the touchy Jill. They take several parts each and, because there is an odd number, share one. Vera is enthusiastic, changing voice for different characters. Jill's depressed delivery slowly gains some of Vera's verve.

"Write, 'We are doing a play,'" says Vera, looking up at me scribbling at a nearby table. "Write, 'We are doing a play,'" she repeats with friendly determination, coming over to check, prompting me to print so she can see that it is done.

The scared little rabbit fears that the sky is falling in. The other characters entering the story doubt this, declaiming a refrain which Vera and Jill chant in unison: "The sky is falling in?" And, with melodramatic disbelief, "I see no signs of the sky falling in."

Dan, Claire, and Tim are in another corner, engrossed in listening to the tape of a dinosaur story, following it in a book, and making plans.

Only Vicki, Evelyn, and Martha are slow to gain momentum. The play is a little difficult for them. They decide to write out a list of characters along with their own names. They have trouble agreeing on how to do this. Martha insists on this ritual. She writes slowly, losing her place and starting over while the others squirm and mutter their discontent. Martha, looking exhausted, finally defends herself, ponderously mumbling, "I'm getting very tired 'cause I went to bed at 10 'til . . ." In mid-sentence she loses all sense of certainty and says, with the tone of a guess, "Ah . . . 9 o'clock." When they eventually complete their list, Martha closes the folder and they consult it no more.

When the bell rings for recess, theirs is the only group that does not want to stay inside and continue. They must all go outside, so the other groups continue planning and practicing there. After recess, with no encouragement from Sue, they continue for the half hour until lunch.

[May 17] After recess, Sue asks if anyone is ready to present a play. Elizabeth and Jodie volunteer the Sweet Valley Twins. They have had one session where Elizabeth told Ann, Jodie, and Joan the story, and they practiced with much animation. Earlier this morning they had a dress rehearsal. There will be two clothing changes—from day clothes to sleepwear to swimwear.

As the class goes next door to see the play, Ann starts sobbing. This is no act.

"We didn't practice all of it," she blubbers. Her outburst looks as if it could have been occasioned by murder. The other three quickly calm her, holding her, patting her back, and leading her along, saying, "Just do your best. It'll be good."

The audience sits packed closely on the floor of the small room, eagerly waiting, occasionally jostling for a view. They are treated to volatile family squabbles, a school scene, and a beach scene with more interpersonal strife. In the end the characters embrace, saying, "Let's be friends."

Audience members pop up on their knees like groundhogs trying to gain more height to see the world. Unconsciously they inch toward the action. The school scene takes place around a table, and several watchers have crept up to put their hands and chins on one end of the table. This is the kind of audience pickpockets pray for. They are captured.

A series of improvised hits occur in conjunction with this show. When this group was planning, Sue asked what they expected the audience to do while they were changing costumes.

"We'll have a commercial break."

"Who will do the commercial?"

"Jack will. He's not in the play."

In the end Evelyn and Vicki take over when Jodie announces after the first act, "We'll be right back after these messages." Evelyn stumbles through a commercial for a rock video, with Vicki giggling with delight as her assistant and advisor. They then create and promote dish-washing detergent:

"And now this new Lemon Drop something."

The idea of commercials needs no further endorsement. Dan advertises car batteries. Tim gives the caterpillar he happened to have in his hand a crawl-on part in his pitch for pest extermination. Wole shows his gains in readiness to produce his own ideas with a wide-eyed pitch for a rocket booster "to get you to school if you miss the bus." Alan invites, "If you're having trouble completing your coin collection, come to Alan's." Peter promotes his yearlong hobby, offering to sell baseball cards.

[May 18] The next day Sue asks whether any other plays are ready. The Bremen Town Musicians, or most of them, volunteer. "But," says Jack, "we were making masks."

"If you're still making masks, we're not having the play now," says Sue firmly.

"We're not making masks," snaps Peter as Sue finishes her sentence, and they are off to make theater in an empty classroom.

This time, costumes are absent and the actors read, most with some flourish. Wole's love of reading flowers in and with his play-reading. He has long had trouble with creative writing, but yesterday he contributed an imaginative and expressive commercial spot. Today he is a chicken whose mistress is ready to dispose of him.

"She is about to make soup out of me," he declaims with a lively, humorous expression of fear. Vera claps and turns around to beam her delight and appreciation to Sue. Wole's cock-a-doodle-doo's also gain wide approval. At the other extreme in reading ability, Paul labors to read his parts, slightly out of his depth but prompted discreetly by Wole and the others and criticized by no one.

When Sue asks for critical comment, Tim volunteers, "They acted like animals, but they weren't really animals."

The approval is general. This stimulates the egomaniac in Peter, who starts to claim that his group was better than the girls'. When the others disagree, he concedes, "Theirs was better. It was more realistic. They remembered their lines. We need a better play."

"I liked yours, Peter," insists Vicki, not getting into whose play was best.

"Can we have time to make masks and learn our lines?" asks Peter, who chose to perform without making masks.

Peter and the others seem not to realize that the Sweet Valley troupe did not memorize their lines, but made them up in practice and approximated and elaborated them in the performance. The strain of reading and keeping the drama going is difficult for most of them. The boys inadvertently simplified their task by overlooking costume and scenery. The three groups that follow try to do everything.

After a little negotiation, those who have performed opt to do a new play, then change their minds to join established groups that need more players.

Martha, Evelyn, and Vicki are joined in rehearsal by new players. Martha, who is the storyteller, will not begin until everyone is
standing quietly in what she regards as the right place. She finally
starts, reads ponderously, and frustrates the others by repeatedly
returning to the beginning after every trivial disruption from the lively
cast. The scene quickly becomes chaotic. Another group practicing
nearby makes it hard to hear. Some threaten to abandon the enterprise. Martha is close to tears. They appeal to me. I suggest they forget the action and costumes first time through and sit close together
so they can hear one another. They gain some momentum. After
another run-through and some nudging from Sue, they put on a performance that the audience finds perfectly satisfactory. After having
haltingly read her opening piece many times, Martha now speaks it
competently from memory. She says "original donkeys" rather than
"ordinary donkeys" and varies a few other things. But she carries
through, senses success, and stands taller.

The next day, after quick and vigorous practice, three more plays
go on. Reading *The Scared Little Rabbit* in practice, Jill had alternated
between confident, expressive reading and crying during moments
of confusion. At one point she threatened to "tell Mrs. Hazzard" and
set off to find Sue. Vicki stopped her, insisting in no-nonsense fashion, "You are always doing that. Come back and let's do the play."
In performance these problems are overcome. The troupe almost sing
their parts, chanting the refrains together and bounding around to
escape from the sky that threatens to fall in. Despite her pouting and
tears before the show, Jill delivers a robust performance. She also
makes three lively contributions to the discussion of the two plays
that precede hers today. This is unusual for her even though Sue
constantly gives her chances to contribute in class. It is hard to avoid
concluding that drama has dramatic effects.

Next Dan, Claire, and Tim perform their play, based on a story
about a visit to a dinosaur zoo. Dinosaurs encased in brown paper
appear from behind a large, sketchily painted background with "Welcome to Dinosaur Land" written across it. The rudimentary but imaginative costumes are identified with delight by the audience, which
spontaneously inserts its own commercials when the actors need time
to regroup. The climax is a clash between *Tyrannosaurus rex* and
Triceratops, whose costumes give special delight.

An observer entering now would not know how much negotiation and how many changes of plan preceded this performance. The
common goal of putting on a show has united the children. As in
the stereotypical band of thespians, there is more drama off the stage

than on, but the plays go on. The most contrived realities are the scenes of the most real experiences for the players.

After the dinosaurs are gone, discussion turns back to the much-admired play based on a Sweet Valley Twins story. Because most seem still not to have realized this, Sue asks, "Girls, did you make up a script?"

"No," says Elizabeth.

"How did you do it?"

"The first part we did like a book [I'd read]. Then we made it up."

"She told us a story and we said, 'We want to change this part to make it more real,'" Jodie explains.

"How many thought they memorized it?" asks Sue. Most put their hands up.

"It wasn't the same each time," says Elizabeth.

"They had to read the book?"

"I read it," says Elizabeth.

"Our play was no good," says Dan.

Others disagree, but he insists on elaborating the faults of his show. Severe though it is, his self-criticism is directed at producing a better show. "Ours was horrible 'cause they had to talk and couldn't remember all the stupid dinosaur names. It would be better if I read it."

"We needed more time to practice."

"Peter and Dan didn't tell us what order to go in."

Paul and Joan describe scenes they liked, but Dan insists, "No! It was horrible."

"Can we do another one?" Vicki wants to know. A discussion of methods spontaneously erupts. Sue poses questions arising from the past sessions. "Will you make up your own story or adapt one?"

"It's too hard to get people's attention [if there is a lot of people]." Several agree with this.

"Maybe that's how the Sweet Valley Twins was good."

Attention turns to sources of topics. Soon, in an enthusiastic turmoil, they are choosing new topics and groups.

All manner of challenges arise. Working with Paul, Jack, Peter, and Tim, Wole becomes upset. Paul and Peter pat and stroke his head. They are planning an action play based on a Nintendo video game. "We'll need to make lots of swords," declares Paul. Spaceship materials are required, and, as the action will take place in space, "How are we going to breathe up there?"

"We'll put air in the spaceship."

"When it gets used up it makes poisonous gas."

"Are any of your uncles a spaceman? An astronaut?" Tim hopes to acquire spacesuits.

"We're going to fly in the air," decides Peter, avoiding these obstacles.

When the evolving plot needs a princess, Tim proposes, "We could have a boy for the princess and then we wouldn't have to kiss a girl." Giggling approval, they move to the next challenge.

[May 25] Joan, Jill, Martha, and Vicki are starting their practice of a play based on the *Ramona* series. As well as constructing a plot about family life, they have props including a box for a television set and straws for toothbrushes. As on the previous day, they have a little trouble getting their concerns coordinated. Soon they are moving along. Vicki steps briefly out of the action to grab my clipboard and print, like an aside in a Shakespearean play, "First it was bad," implying that things have greatly improved. Martha and Jill are much more animated than in earlier sessions. When things don't go her way, Martha pouts, but she recovers when encouraged: "Don't be moody."

The rehearsal is sweeping along. Jill jumps up and down smiling, following the action as she anticipates her cues. Sue comes by to check their progress and Martha chirps, "It's working out fine. I got to be the mom." When Sue asks if they'll be ready to produce a show tomorrow, they all agree and Jill nods her head enthusiastically. She has not been livelier all year. Sue looks questioningly at me. I say, "Their play looks good."

"And I like it," chimes Jill.

[May 26] The Ramona play and one based on the *Gismonaut* are put on. There is high good humor as they prepare. The Gismonaut actors' uniforms include space helmets, each made of four stapled-together paper plates—fashions that seem inspired by Flash Gordon and the Tin Man from Oz.

"I think Wole is turning into Darth Vader," quips Alan.

"This is good," says Dan. They truly look like space warriors.

Trying to move along preparations for the Ramona play, Sue asks, "Do I have to wait 'til 10 o'clock, Vicki?"

"I'm not Vicki!" snaps Vicki.

"Ramona Quimby!" says Sue, on cue.

"Ramona! Stop acting like a baby!" says Martha in the role of mother.

"She is one," declares Joan.

The method actresses have become their roles.

The audience is richly satisfied by both shows.

"I liked how Ramona played her part," says Evelyn.

"How do you mean?" asks Sue.

"She talked like Ramona."

"She walked like Ramona."

"In real life she is like Ramona."

They are generous in complimenting one another but also frank in noting weaknesses.

Martha, having found a line that got a good laugh, repeated it too often. Others comment on this several times. They do not notice Martha shrinking down in her seat.

Vicki does: "Everyone was picking on Martha, but she did good."

They explain that they were trying to be constructive, but Vicki persists in presenting Martha's perspective.

"It *felt* like everyone was saying they didn't like what she did."

"Oh, no!" they protest. They didn't mean that. Vicki persists, distinguishing the others' intentions from their effect on Martha. She lets up only when the others say enough, not to convince Martha she is a star, but to make her look reasonably relaxed.

Wilting Martha often frustrated Vicki during preparations. But Vicki persisted, drawing her back in. Vicki started the year scared, then became almost wild. Along the way her parents separated in chaotic fashion; they remain antagonistically estranged. Their daughter now combines flash, verve, and intellectual passion with a resilient, persistent concern for those without her force of character. These talents will never show on the standardized tests, nor do they grow in the narrow world of workbooks. In the imaginary world of second-grade theater, however, her life is rich, full, and constructive. A day later, a group of boys' Nintendo play goes on. It is largely "mindless violence" that keeps the audience watching but a trifle bemused.

Alan watches, puzzled and a touch disgusted.

"This is a play?" he asks, popping up on his haunches. "I don't know what they are doing."

When the play is discussed, the critic who "didn't think it was too good" speaks for most of them.

Claire recalls a line that got an appreciative laugh. "I liked it when Tim said 'mad dog'" as he attacked a toy dog with his paper sword.

Wole joins the critics. "It wasn't like I planned." Peter, who didn't want to write about feelings, and his band of boys helped produce a Nintendo play that aroused few feelings.

As the class walks back inside, Alan marvels, "I never thought I'd be in a play, but I was in . . ."—his eyes roll as he reflects (he had major roles in two and backup roles in others)—"four plays!"

The same day Jodie, Joan, Claire, and Vicki put on another show in the tradition of the Sweet Valley Twins show. This receives favorable reviews.

"I liked the fight," declares Paul.

"I liked Jodie," says Dan, imitating the pout she acted.

"I liked where Claire was saying, 'Oh, rats!'" says Vicki, imitating her with dash.

These girls give the class a human, moral drama that grips the audience: a wide array of emotions and conflicts leading, once again, to reconciliations all around.

*   *   *

Children's drama receives little attention from researchers. Reading and math loom large in educational psychology texts, but drama rarely gains an index entry. In the clamor about education, few speak for drama. Yet if one wants the wholehearted engagement of students in collaborative activity that engages the emotions, the intellect, language, and the body to develop and communicate complex and subtle ideas, drama has that power. If one wants students to learn to plan, practice, and carry out complex collaborative adventures, drama is ideal. Emotions are engaged without heads being broken.

Jodie lives much of her life as an ironic soap opera. Sitting beside me, struggling with a workbook, she gasps, then sighs. "I thought today was going to be a good day, but things are going wrong. My head hurts. Why do things always go wrong?" She is uncomfortable, but she is also laughing at her own discomfort. This is not obvious in her words but in her soap opera intonation and the small toss of her head.

After Sue shows a videotape of *The Secret Garden*, in the middle of a writing session Jodie says, "Oh, Colin!" Colin is one of the characters of the story, and Jodie's "Oh, Colin!" is a melodramatic overstatement of the tone of the novel. Jodie keeps on writing. Vera, sitting nearby, looks up, beaming appreciative recognition. Uncertain whether I've read this spontaneous subtlety right, I catch Vera's eye and ask, "Secret Garden?" Vera, ever careful not to diminish others, is embarrassed. She nods very slightly, looking awkward on my behalf, because I had to ask. I feel big and clumsy.

Jodie's subtlety and irony are obvious to her appreciative peers. Vicki in the role of Ramona gets their applause, as does Wole when he plays the chicken about to become soup. They become more wholly engaged in drama than in anything else. And, in drama, they are sensitive, constructive critics of one another. When their comments hurt Martha, the effect is unintentional, and Vicki persists until they see the hurt they have done. At the same time, most impose sensitive but stringent standards on themselves. Dan certainly got his wish for something more active than the workbooks, at which he has no desire to measure up. Here he reproaches himself harshly and can barely contain his determination to produce yet more dramatic shows.

*   *   *

Peter recognizes that the Sweet Valley Twins troupe and some of the others have a power that he has not matched. But the boy who didn't want to write about feelings cannot find a theme or voice to excite or capture the audience the way Jodie and, less compellingly, Tim do. He is full of wonderful ingenuity about the technical questions involved in staging a play about space travel, but he cannot make it theater. He recognizes, after his attempt to brag elicits a prod from the others, that he does not measure up well on the stage. Yet even he vigorously returns to the task of creating new shows.

Peter's skills are the ones that parents generally ask teachers about: the skills that "the" tests test. His are the skills that politicians think need to be improved so the country will, they imagine, become more economically competitive. The wider band of competencies required for these theatrical shows are not assessed on the tests that the nation is so preoccupied with. It is probably a good thing that they are not, because these subtle displays would wither if reduced to the format of tests and used as criteria for admission to college or promotion to the next grade. But now they wither from simple lack of attention.

There are a variety of ways of introducing students to drama. In some, teachers play leading roles.[1] But here, the immediate impulse and much of the organization came from the children. Jodie explained how plays enabled them to plan. Peter didn't want the same old workbook thing, and Dan wanted to do something more active. They helped spark the full-blown preoccupation with plays. Yet the seeds were evident early, in the children's absorption in Sue's dramatic readings of Ramona stories. Early in the year, even the slower readers quickly saw the point of bringing characters of the plays in their readers alive and were ready to leap into fuller-bodied productions and to impose ever more stringent standards. These second graders make their plays no mere preparation for life, but life itself.[2] Here is yet more reason for the fuller participation of students in the formation of the purposes that govern their activities in school.

PART IV

Possible Futures,
Present Lives

CHAPTER 11

The Ethics of Achievement: Ending Threatened by Beginning

At the beginning of the year, concerns about competence were strong, and Sue's concern was to allay them and foster unselfconscious involvement in tasks. As the year progresses, the preoccupation with competence itself becomes grist for the mill of classroom discussion.

[March 20] "Why can't we have A's and B's instead of P's and P+'s?" Joan wants to know. "It would be more of a challenge to have more than a P+ to work for. P and P+ don't tell much."

"Is there anything else I can do to show how you are doing?" Sue seeks to deflect the preoccupation with grades.

"I don't think I'm going to get a good grade," announces Dan.

"I want to have A's and B's 'cause my mom will give me $10 if I get an A," explains Joan.

"My mother will give me $15," says Evelyn.

"I'm worried about not getting all A's," says Ann.

"Nobody can get all A's," declares Peter, whose chances are as good as anyone's.

"My mother makes a big deal about it when I don't get everything right." Joan is rethinking her initial request.

"No one can get everything right," observes Tim earnestly.

"Why do mothers make such a fuss if you don't get everything perfect?" Joan now conveys a hint of accusation.

Sue explains that parents are human, love their children a lot, and want the best for them, but sometimes forget and have trouble remembering how it feels to be in the second grade. "It's hard being a mom, too," she concludes.

"Mothers," declares Dan with conviction and a trace of conscious hyperbole, "are a different form of humans."

"And they're always sick," adds Jack solemnly.

"Why are they always doing that?" asks Joan, altering her stance. "—Making a big deal about getting everything right."

"They are trying to make you perfect, but no one's perfect," says little Tim, not quick at his schoolwork, but reflective, serious, and sensitive.

Tim has become steadily more secure. On National Teachers' Day he brought Sue a small present with a note on which he had printed, "Thank you for the key to learning." This delicate charm is typical of him. He takes an artist's pleasure in the intellectual and emotional adventures that occur in school and is a busy creator of his own endeavors. On the more mundane assignments, he doggedly does his best. Even when the effort of writing means his "hand sweats," he does his duty to his family. Do they know how he can feel the pressure from them? They show every sign of being devoted parents. They are delighted with what Sue has done for their son and often make this plain. But they seem not to realize that much of it depends on Sue's strategies for calming him down and convincing him that his parents' evaluation of his work need not be feared. If she had not managed this, he might have been allergic to more than the star-spangled banner.

Now Tim has himself well in hand. His insight about parents' reasons for pressing for perfection helps him as well as the others to cope with the pressure for high scores that can turn their heads and squelch the aesthetic delights of the arts and sciences.

*   *   *

[April 7] The previous day, Sue was away. She suggested to the substitute teacher that the class have a math "mad minute"—a speeded test on arithmetic facts. Now Sue wants to know how it went. She asks Jill, who is often unsettled by evaluation, "Did you feel okay?" Though looking a little glum, Jill nods.

"If someone else gets more than you, you feel no good," volunteers Joan.

"So," Sue asks, "if we do it today and you can do a bit better than yesterday, will it matter what someone else gets?"

"If someone else gets done, you don't know if they got it all right." Vicki wants to distinguish time needed for completion from number correct.

Joan persists with the problem of social comparison.

"But if someone missed two and you missed four, you don't feel very good."

"Well, Claire, how did you feel?" asks Sue.

"Kind of good, but other people tried to cheat."

Tim volunteers that Alan kept working when the substitute said to stop. Alan defends himself:

"I was right in the middle of a number."

"Did you do more than that one?"

"No."

"How did you feel about that?" Sue asks Claire.

"I felt cheated."

"I felt cheated when I saw Jodie do it and I didn't. If we can't do it, why can they?"

"How did you feel, Vera?" Sue asks.

"Not good."

"Bad."

"This is not a challenge," argues Joan. "It doesn't feel fair. I see people going ahead . . ."

"If I watched more closely to see everyone behaves the same, would you be willing to try again? How many people like speed things?"

About half of the class put their hands up.

"How many don't like them?" A smaller number vote with Joan, who adds, "I like doing it at my own speed."

"You said you want a challenge," argues Peter. "You could challenge yourself to get more than someone else."

"But maybe a person is trying all they can and can't get up higher," Joan answers.

"Everyone learns things," counters Peter.

"But," Joan insists, "they might have done best as they can and can't get up more." More than the others, except perhaps Peter, she seems to realize that one's present ability limits how well one can perform relative to others. She is concerned that people will feel hurt if they do worse than others, and, more than most others, she seems to recognize that some will inevitably score worse when tests have time limits.[1]

"You can just keep on trying," says Peter. "If they just say they can't do it and quit, in a few years they'll say, 'I don't have any money,' and they'll sit around saying, 'What'll I do?'"

"They can just do their best," suggests Alan.

"Their best is all they can do," adds Dan.

Alan wants to claim more. "If you believe you can do a thing, you can."

"Sometimes I don't believe I can do a thing, but I can." Again Joan sees more complexity.

"You do the best you can and you get better as you get older. If you're not good at it, you know that, but you get better." Dan recognizes that inequality is endemic. He has had to come to terms with a forceful assertion of his own relative incompetence. He emphasizes, however, that one can always learn. He recognizes his relative incompetence as a writer but the fact that he can get better is more powerful.

"But everyone wants to be like Peter. They want to be in the highest groups." Joan persists, confronting her dilemma: Everyone can't be number one.

"You don't have to worry about yourself all the time." Peter is partly defending himself.

"It's hard," Dan notes, "when other people get done and say, 'I'm done.'"

"There are other people that are much better than me. There's lots of people in other classes that can do all sorts of things I can't," Peter replies.

Dan sees another side. "People might be miserable if they got in a high group and they weren't ready for it."

"I feel unhappy 'cause Peter is always bragging," says Ann.

"How is he bragging?" Sue asks.

"He is saying like he's got his math book done."

"But he's better than he was at the beginning of the year," says Dan.

Peter is spluttering.

"So you don't feel like you're bragging?" asks Sue.

"No!"

"But you do do it!" declares Joan.

"I'm the same as him [in attainment], but do I brag?" Though less egotistical than he was at the outset, Jack conveys no irony.

"It's hard to ignore when other people say they've finished, isn't it?" says Sue.

"You can't stop a person from saying, 'I'm in the highest reading group,'" says Joan, not seeking simple solutions, keeping many dimensions of the problem in view.

"All through life," says Sue, "someone might tell you they're better than you. This happens to me. What can you do to help yourself get through this?"

"You can walk away," suggests Carlos, who has much experience being bested in schoolwork.

"But, like Joan says, you might still hear it."

"Walk further away," Carlos persists.

"You can say, 'Good for you,' and walk away. Like my brother comes bragging to me and I just say, 'That's real good.'" Dan, who appears not to have been speaking of anyone in particular, notices Peter listening with a pained expression. He quickly adds, "I don't mean *you* do it all the time, Peter."

"Like Joan says, it might still be in your mind," notes Sue.

"You still have the feelings," says Dan. "I know some people who aren't so good at work, and they got put in a separate class. But they know when they go outside [at recess] that they aren't so smart. You can't forget all the time when people show they are better than you, so leave it alone."

"So you can't forget all the time, but life can go on?" Sue queries.

"I bang my head on the wall to make myself forget," declares Tim.

"I don't brag. In that way I'm better," says Ann.

"Well, my brother is smart and brags," says Dan. "But I don't brag. [When he brags] I say to him, 'That's good.'"

"If they brag, they might be good at that thing, but you might be good at something else," James observes.

"Like Dan. He's better than Peter at judo," says Joan.

"Is that all you think about?" Dan is annoyed. Although proud of his skill at judo, he is consistent. He does not wish to be exalted above others.

But Dan is only one example of Joan's theme. She adds, "Like girls are better than boys at gymnastics."

Peter still seems to be taking the discussion as a personal attack, so Sue asks everyone, "What if you were the one who got everything right fast?"

"I'd hate it, 'cause if I'm the best in my family, when I ask my mother or dad things, they don't know and I can't find out," says Tim, who wants to learn and values social solidarity.

"Alan, would you like it?" Sue asks.

"No. Sometimes it's right to be wrong, 'cause you think, 'I'm best . . .'"—the sin of pride.

"You hurry too much and get it wrong," suggests Tim.

"It's like you're trying to get everything for yourself. It's kind of wrong to other people. They'd give up," Alan clarifies, developing a case against egotism.

"It's good to be wrong so you can learn what you got wrong," confirms Joan.

"Yeah!" chimes Alan.

"Jodie, would you like to be the one who got everything right?" asks Sue.

"If you knew it all, you couldn't learn," says Jodie.

"You don't have to worry 'cause no one knows everything. You could skip a grade. You could go outside and learn or go to a library." Peter sounds a note of sophistication about the limits of knowledge. He has just switched from thinking of school as a contest in which the challenge is to show oneself superior in ability to challenging oneself to expand knowledge—a task that never ends.

"If you learned everything [in an assignment] you should still listen because you might have missed something." Evelyn is in character, publicly announcing reasons for being the good girl and working hard, even though, when there is any option, she has less ardor for finishing assignments than do most.

"It's good to make mistakes 'cause if you knew everything, you wouldn't need a mother or dad or brothers or sisters." Tim repeats his theme of solidarity and learning.

Sue asks them to think of times they have made useful mistakes.

"I make so many . . ." Dan's self-deprecation is offered lightly.

Evelyn relates how she and her sister failed to clean the kitchen properly and had to do it again.

"So you learned something? Will it benefit you in later life?" But Evelyn's world intrudes into the line of the discussion. "I cleaned it on Monday and Wednesday and Thursday and my sister makes me do the dishes. When will she have her turn? She's 10."

"Nothing turns out good when I do things bad," says Ann.

"If you were perfect, life would be miserable," says Peter, who often wants to be surprised by the teacher and to have adventures. "You'd know what would happen all the time."

"Sometimes you want to do everything and sometimes you don't," says Alan.

"I think some people worry about themselves too much," says Dan, who has recently recovered from just such worry. "I don't want to be the best at things. I just want to be a normal kid." There is none of the smug moral superiority of the reformed smoker, but conviction nevertheless.

"Would you like to do *your* best?"

"But not if it was different from everyone else. I wouldn't want to show it."

Reductionists might attribute Dan's identification with the common man to earlier assaults on his sense of competence. But should we dismiss a person's work for the homeless because it began with his earlier homelessness? We may hope that Dan will eventually find a moral basis for doing his best even if it means he is not "the best," but his solidarity with the "oppressed" of the schools seems the product of an examined life and no mere exercise in self-protection.[2]

In the afternoon of the same day, the topic of Siamese twins comes up. This produces much interest and puzzlement.

Martha is perplexed. "If they are Siamese twins, how can they sit?"

"They would have to come to their house to go to the bathroom. They'd have toilet problems," says Joan.

"You could have bigger toilets," Tim suggests brightly.

"I think moms would hurt if they had Siamese twins," says Joan.

Paul wants to know, "What if there were three?"

"I don't think they should have to go to a regular school," argues Peter, "'cause people would laugh at them."

Dan is aware of a dilemma that cannot be avoided: "They'd feel different if they *didn't* go to school. But if they did, like Peter says, they'd feel different anyway." Now, having recovered himself, he is consistent in acknowledging others' ideas as well as considering their feelings. Today Peter also acknowledges the plight of those we shunt to the margins of life.

[March 3] "Jill, you have a good sentence. Would you read what you wrote?" asks Sue.

"No," breathes Jill.

"May I read it?" Jill says nothing but nods her acquiescence. This is common for her. We initially presumed this diffidence reflected mere shyness or self-doubt, but there may be more to it.

[March 16] Jill makes four entries in her journal. One is "When I give my self a pat on the back I feel good and I love math and I love reading. I don't like braging thou."

Earlier in the year, during a discussion of reading books chosen by the students themselves, Jill contributes, "Just because you read slow doesn't mean you can't enjoy it." Is her ambivalence about having her work shown in front of the class partly a function of her ethical objection to bragging—akin to Alan's objection to egotism?

She has not always objected to displaying her writing. On a large sheet of art paper, she wrote a description of her lost dog, drew a picture of it, and wrote "Read this" in bold letters. Then, with an expression of singleminded assertiveness, she posted it in the hall outside her classroom. This was not "braging thou." It was an appeal for the return of her dog. She can and will go public with her writing.

Though she plays a small role in discussions of the ethics of achievement, she follows and has her own thoughts on the topic. We cannot say whether her objection to bragging is partially a defensive justification of her timidity. Even if it is, she has a point. She and Dan are wrestling with similar demons.

✱   ✱   ✱

Related to the ethics of tests and comparison of abilities is the question of whether school should emphasize the types of knowledge most easily measured.

[May 5] Beginning a reading workbook assignment, Alan makes a discovery.

"I've only got 27 pages left in this book," he announces proudly to me, waving the book around to show the completed pages. "I've done more than 100."

"Did you learn a lot doing all that?"

"Not really."

"How do you mean?"

"'Cause I knew it already."

"So what is a good way to learn?"

"Studying things by yourself."

"Anything else?"

"Having conversations helps."

He makes very little progress with this assignment. Part of it requires him to write the names of objects displayed on one part of the page under pictures of the type of shop they are most likely to be purchased from. He writes three names, then alternates between dreaming and observing classmates. He then starts playing with answers he knows to be wrong, saying to himself, "Grass seed in the kitchen store. Plants in the kitchen department. Cheese in the garden department," and so on. He chuckles to himself, making no progress on the assigned task.

After recess, Sue asks who has finished. Alan is one of those who have not. Sue gives them 10 minutes to finish and suggests, ironically, that there will be "awful consequences for those who do not finish." Alan makes no further progress and has to put the assignment in his box to do as homework.

While Alan is drifting in workbook purgatory, Dan, James, and Paul are engrossed in making codes in a different workbook. Called a bonus book, it has more than a collection of testlike demands for discrete bits of information.

"She [Mrs. Hazzard] doesn't have to grade these pages. She just has to look at it," says Dan. "We could take this home [to keep using codes] as soon as she looks at it."

When I ask how interesting this task is, Dan declares this book is better than the other one "because there are more things you do—like this." For Dan, the usual workbook does not have "things you do." But the boys are too busy to elaborate. James is staying over at Dan's place, and codes are part of the fun they are planning. Workbooks are not dismal failures when they have "things you do."

Dan and Alan are vocal critics of workbooks and advocates of conversation, controversial topics, and active learning. They remain committed to their stance, but others, thinking of their future in grade 3, are uneasy.

[May 30] "If you were talking to some first graders who were coming to the second grade, what would you tell them?" asks Sue.

"Don't be scared," says Tim, who was.

"I'd tell them how to do math problems," says Martha, who long felt unable to understand them.

"Don't worry," says Claire. "It's easy once you get used to it."

"Don't be scared of it. Believe in yourself," adds James.

"Teachers are nice," says Vera.

"If you get Mrs. Hazzard, don't worry, she's cool," says Tim.

"Neat."

"Awesome."

"She jokes a lot," adds Ann.

"Pay attention to the teacher," says James.

"Mrs. Hazzard is the best teacher in the second grade, so don't worry," calls Jodie.

Sue moves quickly on to the prospect of the third grade: How do they feel about that?

"I don't think I'm ready, 'cause we haven't done all the books," says Vera, again revealing, it seems, why she took so long to relax. "Maybe we talked too much."

"In Japan," says Claire, "they're memorizing the whole times table."

Others are more upbeat. After they have their say, Sue asks, "What are some of the good things you'll want to remember about the second grade?" James volunteers, "The dinosaur video." "The movie about space," adds Dan. "The plays," calls Vicki. "The books you read—*The Gismo*," says Alan. "I want to remember my play," says Vera. "Ramona," calls Vicki.

Peter precipitates another flow of approval for Sue by saying, "The friends and the teacher." Perhaps most telling are Joan's observation, "You were like a counselor to us," and Evelyn's follow-up, "You were always there for me." Tim says, "When you [student] were having a bad day, you got better when you [Mrs. Hazzard] read the story."

"Yeah. You get more relaxed," adds Dan.

They return to how they feel about going on to the third grade. Peter echoes Vera's concern about too much talk—one of his intermittent themes: "There's so much work and you're always doing conversations and I'm not learning anything. In kindergarten I got information like a computer would. I can't do that now. I knew all I had to know for first and second grade in kindergarten. It's conversation, conversation, and we hardly get anything accomplished."

Others point out that earlier in the discussion he had said work was sometimes hard. They list things he learned in the second grade, but his ardor is undimmed. On one earlier occasion when he made this point, he was immediately drawn back into the tide of the conversation he had just disparaged. But in this conversation about the third grade, he is unusually concerned.

What prompts his concern about learning like a computer and his derogation of the conversations that he, as much as anyone, initiates and sustains? This is Peter, who, like a postmodern philosopher of science, declares that scientists choose what they will study, that "science is what you're thinking about and what you discover," and that "you should go to your sources, not their sources." It is also the boy who declares that this conversation is "doing us no good at all. All you are doing is to get us to think hard. We are not learning anything." The student most articulate in his challenges to arbitrary adult authority now wants an adult to pump him full of information he cannot question—information that could offer no challenge to his restless ingenuity.

In a study of college students, William Perry (1970) reports that many undergraduates have conceptions of knowledge akin to that which Peter seems to endorse when he wishes he could absorb facts like a computer. One, for example, said, "A certain amount of theory is good but it should not be dominant in a course. I mean theory might be convenient for them [the professors], but it's nonetheless—

the facts are what's there. And I think that *should* be, that should be the main thing" (p. 67).

Perry argues that, over the college years, most students gradually discard the notion of knowledge as a collection of facts that are out there in the world waiting to be noticed by humans. This conception is gradually replaced by a recognition that knowledge is a human construction and always reflects the diverse concerns of the humans who do the constructing. There is some support for Perry's thesis (Kurfiss, 1977). Down here in the second grade, however, Peter seems to display both conceptions. Though usually less articulate than Peter, others also see knowledge as a thoroughly human construction rather than a mere human discovery, like finding a shell on the beach. It seems impossible that this adult conception of knowledge should occur in second graders who also display, within the same discussion, what Perry terms a less mature conception of knowledge.

The key to this puzzle may be that the category of concepts children use varies with their concerns. When children are thinking about controversial questions, like why dinosaurs died out, whether there is life in space, or what is a proper education, they recognize that various answers are potentially legitimate. Even the experts will disagree on such matters. Children recognize that, when dealing with such controversial topics, one cannot simply memorize the answer but must make a choice—try to see what fits one's priorities and live with the fact that others will have other ideas. Children know that scientists choose and disagree about their questions as well as their answers.

But when children worry about the third grade and whether they will measure up, their conceptions of complex, controversial topics are irrelevant. Relevant are their conceptions of intelligence, of how one gets to be superior or inferior to others at intellectual tasks. In our society, the question of how competent one is cannot easily be answered by posing questions about matters such as why dinosaurs died out. It is too hard to tell whose answers are right and whose are wrong. Intelligence tests never employ such questions. They are full of questions with unambiguously right or wrong answers. Furthermore, these questions are not chosen by the children. Someone else has always decided what questions one needs to answer to show how intelligent one is.

When children worry about how they will measure up in third grade, they worry about being unable to get enough right answers to questions that have already been posed by someone else. When children of about Peter's age think of intelligence, they see it as a matter of accumulating bits of information. They have a quiz-show conception of intelligence (Nicholls, 1989).

High school is often like a test that students see as fair when the teacher makes explicit what must be done to get a good grade (McNeil, 1986). It is not surprising that students accustomed to a diet of workbook-like, testlike tasks arrive at college looking for more of the same, wanting to know exactly what they must do to get an A. In Perry's open-ended interviews about college, this preoccupation makes students appear as if they conceived of all knowledge as being of this black–white, right–wrong type. Their apprehension when professors ask them to deal with controversial topics or to frame their own questions need not indicate their failure to recognize that much knowledge is contested and reflects personal and cultural priorities. Well before the college years, students understand that much important knowledge about the world is controversial and that everyone must take some responsibility for their own beliefs on such matters. Perry's picture of a gradual change to a conception of knowledge as constructed and as reflecting personal or cultural perspectives may be misleading. The apparent change may instead reflect a gradual acceptance of a shift in emphasis from noncontroversial to controversial knowledge in the classroom—a shift from the view that school is fair if it emphasizes unambiguous, factual matters to the idea that school is unfair if it emphasizes such topics.

Teachers and students can collaborate, sometimes unwittingly, sometimes reluctantly, in banishing ambiguity and pluralism from school. It is presumably no accident that it is Peter who interrupts his own absorption in conversations about matters on which uncontested answers are not forthcoming to announce that he is not learning or getting smarter. He, more than many, has moments of egotism, when he is preoccupied with getting ahead. He is prone to see school as a test or a contest. A few days before this incident, after school, Sue overheard his father congratulating him on hearing his account of what amounted to a swindle of a less knowledgeable peer out of a valuable baseball card. A week earlier, when Dan showed his card collection at show and tell, Peter interrupted to tell how he had gained a good trade from Dan without Dan's awareness. Now, in the valley of the shadow of third grade, concern with getting ahead is heightened. What lies beyond the third grade—the college of his choice? his parents' choice? His concern about becoming more intelligent has him advocating learning of the very noncontroversial, worksheet-like information he deplores when, as often happens, his independence and vigorous curiosity about the world are stronger than his desire to absorb more information than others and to measure up as superior.

Wole lacks Peter's egotism, but he had defined school as a test in which collaboration was wrong. He became lost when there was no text to follow or list of right answers to find. The idea that he might help construct the questions that guide his learning had no place in his cosmology. He expanded his vision, but now, as the third grade threatens, it narrows again.

When school is construed as a test or a contest, even students like Peter and Wole, who can safely expect to be near the top of the pack, can resist the prospect that education might be a collaborative adventure. Such resistance must long have puzzled and frustrated teachers with the romantic notion that children are "naturally" disposed to explore. Children can also—when faced with achievement tests, mad minutes, and the next grade—be disposed to measure their worth against their peers' competence. Then the idea of adventure or exploration can have the appeal of a ride over Niagara Falls in a fragile barrel.[3] The security of workbooks, which the teacher can be induced to lead them through, becomes alluring. These cut-and-dried assignments avert immediate worries about abilities and seem to offer a way to accumulate the answers children think they will need to pass the tests that guard the narrow way to status and self-esteem.

*   *   *

[May 31] Before school begins, Wole, Vera, Jack, and Claire are busy, working at top speed, determined to finish the last pages of their reading workbooks before the all-but-finished year expires. Some of this group use other opportunities during the day to finish. Peter does not join the effort.

Alan still has no respect for workbooks and, with some others, makes no special attempt to finish them. They have no place on Tim's agenda for the day. He has brought to school a cardboard box that once held 12 wine bottles. The producer's advertising is all over it. In show-and-tell, Tim announces his intention to make a castle from this improbable artifact. He wants to know if anyone will help him. During breaks, he is absorbed in transforming it with intermittent help from others.

Before everyone returns from lunch, Joan and Evelyn, with help at the end from Dan, write across the board in large letters, "You are the best teacher!" and draw a large heart. They sit down so their identities will not be known.

When all are assembled, Tim has made enough progress for Sue to ask if he wants to explain his castle to the class. There are doors of different sizes, internal floors, and walls. The castle is full of traps. Across the open top rubber bands are stretched.

"Right here," points Tim, "are power lines and, like, I'll show you, if someone tried to climb up—Fizz! Or what if they came parachuting down! And there is an alligator pit."

Interest is high, especially among the boys. Peter, who played a minor role in construction, tries to take over with his louder voice. He steps back reluctantly when Sue suggests, firmly, "Let's let him explain."

"Why don't you put rubber bands right around?" Dan asks.

"We're going to have a force field."

"Why don't we have a big plastic dish over it?" Peter, hovering, can barely keep his hands off the construction.

"The bad guys can crawl in there," says Paul.

"That's where the alligator pit is." Tim is slightly testy under this barrage. "You're not thinking."

"If you have a force field, why have the rubber bands too?" Dan challenges.

"What if they turn it off?"

"It's the castle of what?" asks Jack.

"G. I. Joe's. It's the G. I. Joe fortress."

*   *   *

Tim is always working his imagination on something. Though far slower than Peter at the aspects of schoolwork that are captured on standardized tests, he constantly brings things into the class to work with. Tim is the scientist poet. The aesthetics of things are important to him. Peter would not have seen a fortress in a cardboard box. Once the fortress begins to emerge, he wants his name on it. He appears genuinely intrigued, but his interest is heightened when the castle gets public acclaim. As with Yong Kim's origami, the bottom line, the chance for cash or credit, attracts him. He will spend his spare time trading baseball cards, as fascinated by the information on them as he is careful to make a good trade. But he will not be the one to bring to school a fossil found in the gravel near his home. He will not tie a piece of cotton around a stone and observe how nearly invisible the cotton is, or the stone's erratic bounce as he pulls it across the playground blacktop. He will not make paper boats or speculate on and experiment with their buoyancy. He will not begin an experiment on the effects of immersing objects in water. Peter will join and take over, but Tim initiates all these aesthetic adventures in science.

Tim reminds us that students do not have to be academically superior or see themselves as above others to be committed to asking their own questions and making experience expand, glow, and cohere. Tim thinks about the world, how it looks, feels, works—what he can do in it and what it does to him—more than he thinks about his standing in the class. He derives satisfaction from communicating art and meaning more than from acclaim or feeling superior.

It is common to hear the claim that motivation is important because it increases achievement. If that is why motivation is important, then curiosity, aesthetic appreciation, and pleasure in challenge are but means to the end of high test scores. If achievement as the tests define it is, in the end, the important thing, Tim is a failure and Peter the ideal student. If schools and parents communicate this to Tim, how will his vigorous and sensitive commitment to constructing a humane, artful, and interesting world survive? It is a triumph of second-grade spirit—a too rarely celebrated secular miracle—that students like Tim, much less able than Peter on the tests, remain imaginative creators, wily inquirers, and thirsty savorers of nature.[4]

"What avail is it," asked John Dewey (1938), "to win prescribed amounts of information about geography and history, to win ability to read and write, if in the process the individual loses his [or her] own soul: loses his [or her] appreciation of things worth while, of the values to which these things are relative; if he [or she] loses desire to apply what he [or she] has learned and, above all, loses the ability to extract meaning from . . . future experiences as they occur?" (p. 49). With the third grade looming, the question of whether they will measure up crowds out the question of whether the second grade will help them appreciate what is worthwhile and extract meaning from future experiences.

CHAPTER 12

Authority in Education

How might the idea of education as a collaborative adventure, in which students and teachers negotiate the destination and details of the journey, play in other places? This school's standardized test scores put it clearly above the nation's average. Sue's students had their share of economic, family, and personal difficulties, but most were sheltered from the truly harsh living conditions that might crush one's individuality. Economically disadvantaged students generally experience less education and more training, less inquiry about controversial questions and more emphasis on noncontroversial "basic" information and skills (Knapp & Turnbull, 1990). Would students from the meaner streets of some of Chicago's low-income African-American ghettos agree that everyone has a guessing permit and that science is a maze the ends of which will never be found? Would they, like Vicki, Dan, and the others, want to be like scientists and dramatists, who do something more active than worksheets permit? Would they want to help chart their own courses?

I and some colleagues (Nicholls, Nelson, & Gleaves, 1992) put similar questions to such students. We explained that our job was helping to teach people to become schoolteachers and that by the time people are old enough to learn to be teachers, they have often forgotten what it was like to be elementary school students. Our idea, we said, was that people would become better teachers if they knew more about what students thought about the things they learn in school. "Could anyone find out what students think about the different things you could do in school without coming and asking you?" we would ask. "No!" they would tell us. Then, after discussing any questions they raised, often about how one becomes a teacher, we would launch into our interviews with individual student volunteers.

In one interview, we spoke with students about the difference between studying to try to decide controversial matters and memorizing noncontroversial matters. One example of controversial knowledge we presented was the question that so excited Sue's students: the causes of the extinction of dinosaurs. The other was the question of whether the educational goals outlined by Booker T. Washington or those articulated by W. E. B. DuBois were more appropriate for African-Americans. (Washington emphasized the technical–vocational function of education, and DuBois emphasized its liberating function.)[1] The noncontroversial matters we presented were the names and sizes of dinosaurs and the dates when Washington and DuBois lived and the places they lived. These topics were introduced and discussed with each student, with books and photographs to illustrate the different types of knowledge, before we asked our questions.

These students expected that those who studied controversial topics would be more likely to find school exciting, more able to decide what they would like to become when they grew up, more committed to school learning, better able to judge what they should do in school, and more inclined to act with initiative and collaborative spirit in school as well as in later life. Overall, they favored an emphasis on controversial topics over noncontroversial ones.

We also spoke with students from first through eighth grade about the fairness of teaching that emphasized collaborative inquiry about controversial matters over individual study of noncontroversial matters. First-grade students did not show a strong preference, but by the eighth grade there was a marked tendency to see collaborative inquiry about controversial matters as fairer. Older students, unlike younger ones, assigned relatively little importance to memorization of facts and more importance to being excited about learning and becoming able to define one's direction in life.

Most of the students we interviewed appeared ready for W. E. B. DuBois' (1903/1990) suggestion that education should not be narrowly conceived but should involve "a loftier respect for the sovereign human soul that seeks to know itself and the world about it; that seeks a freedom for expansion and self-development" (p. 81). Especially as they became older, they adopted a view like that of Carter G. Woodson, who, in *The Mis-education of the Negro* (1933/1990), wrote, "The mere imparting of information is not education. Above all things it must result in making a man think and do for himself" (p. x). They did not reject simple noncontroversial knowledge, but emphasized inquiry about controversial topics and expected this to make them more inclined to think and do for themselves as well as more communal.

To gain controversial knowledge is to adopt positions that others, including some who are experts, will not agree with. We define our ideas and values by engaging those of others, and in gaining controversial knowledge we define or constitute ourselves. A historian's interpretation of the consequences of the Civil War and an educator's beliefs about how mathematics is best taught, for example, help define their identity. On noncontroversial questions, such as the locations of various battles of the Civil War or the product of 63.90 and 2.77, one's position normally indicates correctness or error and, perhaps, competence or incompetence, not one's values or one's identity. Noncontroversial knowledge offers little scope for what Woodson called thinking and doing for oneself.

Controversies are not storms before calms; they are integral to all disciplines and to contemporary society. When controversies are resolved, it is to be replaced by new controversies, not by perfect peace. The stomach for participation in intellectual and ethical controversy is the basis of cultural literacy in an adventurous, democratic society.[2]

Many students who have seen little democratic life will go some way with these arguments. But some will object more consistently than the mercurial Peter. In our interviews, we focused on motivation, asking students how motivation might be affected. If we had focused their attention on test scores, the accumulation of noncontroversial information might have seemed more important. Students' experience must also affect them. In another study, low-income city students were asked how much testing was fair. Answers depended on the type of school they attended. In a type of school common in inner cities, where there is palpable pressure to raise test scores and where there is almost no collaborative inquiry about controversial topics, most students said that the more tests they were given, the better. Tests, they said, would make sure they learned. A different vision emerged in a school that gave almost no tests and promoted student collaboration, writing, and research. Here students were more likely to declare that tests interfered with learning and were not needed to motivate them. They were more ready to think and do for themselves than were students from more traditional schools (Thorkildsen & Schmahl, 1991). Students from schools that more clearly reflected the current obsession with test scores and noncontroversial knowledge were more inclined to accept that form of education.

A fifth-grade teacher, Ada Harris, and her principal, Cathy Busch (1992), recently took the need for educational reform to heart and presented the problem to their low-income African-American students. The plan was to end the memorizing of standard steps for mathematical problems, a procedure the students were accustomed to. Harris and Busch sought to make mathematics less cut and dried and more controversial by using devices such as giving students answers to problems, asking them to think of ways to explain to others how to find the answers, and discussing whether some of these ways were better than others.[3]

They began by asking students what they thought of mathematics—a question teachers rarely risk asking. At first the class was tense. Then, sensing they could speak their minds, they erupted in conversation. First to speak was one of the top scorers in mathematics. "I think it's stupid," she said. Another called it "important but boring." They conveyed a real respect for "Mrs. Harris," but there was clearly something wrong with school mathematics. Yet, when Ada Harris proposed the new approach, they objected, feeding her back the very utilitarian reasons teachers had long given them for learning mathematics: "I'd feel like I was cheated every time I bought something at the store," said one. "I would probably get a bad grade," said another.

The class proceeded, nevertheless, with the new plan, and Ada Harris and Cathy Busch kept them talking about its value. Articulate and assertive, the student who had been the first to object to the old system kept demanding that Harris tell them exactly what to do and how to do it. Yet others, many of them previously silent and unacquainted with success, became devoted to mathematics, working on after formal sessions ended and dragging family members into negotiation of solutions to homework problems. These students eventually spoke up and carried the day for the approach they had initially feared.

At the end of the year, Harris reflected on Lisa Delpit's (1988) suggestion that black teachers might often see romantic educational ideas as culturally inappropriate.

> We do tell black students what to do. . . . It was part of the slave culture and they had to do it. . . . But let's go back to the slaves that did not take directives, those who were not obedient. . . . I'm sure no one said to [George Washington] Carver, 'Take this peanut and invent something.' Instead, he was thinking, 'What if . . .?' Just because . . . certain things are part of our culture does not mean they should remain. [Delpit] mentioned black teachers. Well, as black teachers we have learned that there are other ways to reach our students. Let them think for themselves. You'll be surprised what they come up with. (Busch, 1992, pp. 36–37)

Ada Harris and Cathy Busch did more than *let* the students think. They *provoked* them to think mathematically and to think about the value of that thinking. The students will not all see it Mrs. Harris's way, but should they never get the chance?

*   *   *

In the popular media and on billboards, figures such as Michael Jordan, Spike Lee, and Ice Cube exhort youth to "do the right thing," stay in school, and "listen to your teachers." If the right thing were a more exciting thing, there might be less need to exhort students to do it. Students might be more involved if we engaged them in the formation of the purposes that govern their activities. But the reason students should confront controversy and negotiate the means and ends of their education is so that they will become citizens of their school and society—robust, rigorous, and adventurous philosophers and practitioners of educative living.

This must mean living through times of discontent as well as times of excitement. Students who continually express themselves and want learning to be fun are missing something. One cannot confront the questions of what knowledge is worthwhile, what sort of person one is to become, or what sort of society one is to construct without confronting controversy and venturing into uncertainty. Respectful disagreement and confrontation of controversial topics involve strains that mere self-expression, ignoring others, or shouting them down does not. The angst occasioned by the task of filling a blank page is not to be compared to the narrow anxiety worksheet questions can provoke. But the page of life is neither blank nor a series of worksheet-like assignments. It is covered with the graffiti of the ages. The challenge of gaining personal strength while contributing to the polyglot conversational graffiti is the challenge of maintaining liberty and community. Full membership means becoming a theorist who reflects on the nature, direction, and details of the conversation. We might develop more skill at provoking our students to join.

Twenty years ago, when I began teaching in a public school, it was my naive hope that I might begin a year of intellectual excitement by asking my students to write how they would redesign school if they could start from scratch. These veterans of seven years' schooling thought my question weird and foolish. School made little sense to most of them, but to write about how it might be made better struck them as sillier than most class assignments. If they were eager to join a conversation about the means and ends of schooling, they weren't revealing that to me. I was confused by their reluctance to liberate themselves and blundered around looking for other ways to ignite intellectual fires.

Years later, my then 12-year-old son presented me his school mathematics text and asked, "Why do we have to do this stuff?" Looking at the book, I wondered, "Why indeed?" The stuff was dismal. But I wasn't about to give him an excuse for avoiding it. I reminded him of his long-standing interest in astronomy and pointed out that astronomers use a lot of mathematics. I began to wax lyrical. I was close to declaring the book of the cosmos to be written in the language of mathematics when his expression convinced me that, regardless of the merits of my argument, I was not giving him a reason for doing that stuff in his text. My immediate and obvious accomplishment was to dampen his interest in astronomy. Much later I realized I had squashed a legitimate critique of schoolwork. I should have confronted his question more squarely.

A friend gave up teaching high school mathematics because she could not answer, to her own satisfaction, the students who asked, "Why do we gotta do this stuff?" Do we have to choose between giving up mathematics and selling it with lame appeals to later occupations or the need to balance a checkbook? Why is it so hard to take this question seriously and negotiate new curricula with students?

My son provoked me to take seriously the theme of students as educational critics and curriculum theorists. I began by interviewing junior high students. I described to them four hypothetical high school students, each with ambitions to attend university to become a medical doctor. One wanted to become a doctor to gain wealth, a second sought the high social status of the role, a third sought knowledge of how the human body functions, and the fourth sought to improve people's health. I asked whether these students would differ in how interested and involved they would be in their high school studies. Students had no doubt that the latter two would be more interested and engaged in their high school studies. "But wouldn't it be strange," I would say, "if the [first] ones, who are sort of selfish, who are trying to get more for themselves, didn't enjoy what they were doing as much as the others?" Nevertheless, the students were confident that those who wanted to help others or to understand more about the world would find schoolwork more engaging.

As I began one of these interviews in a teachers' lounge, a school counselor came in and sat behind us in the far corner, munching his lunch. When the student left, the counselor surprised me with his own surprise. He had trouble believing the student was typical. This was not one of the adolescents he saw each day, who must have the right, expensive brand of jeans and all that went with them. Wealth, status, and self seemed the abiding preoccupations. The student in the interview was real and compelling but a stranger to the counselor. Strange also is the fact that adults so rarely confront students with more than the financial consequences of their commitments. We threaten students with poverty and low status when they declare school to be foolish, but we neglect the desire for socially useful knowledge. Perhaps the real problem with the nation's students and schools is that the adults have gotten what they wanted.

I subsequently did a study that seemed to confirm the wisdom of the junior high students I had interviewed. The desires for wealth and status were not linked to satisfaction with school or plans to continue schooling, whereas the desires to contribute to the lives of others and to comprehend the world were (Nicholls, 1989, chap. 12). Conducting this study, I relearned a lesson. I had planned to use the time after presenting questionnaires to discuss with students the actual or ideal purpose of school. Most of them were bound for high-status colleges. They were articulate and confident. They answered the questionnaire happily. When asked to discuss the purpose of school, however, they became strangely uncomfortable and inarticulate. They were obviously unaccustomed to conversation about the purpose of the institution where they spent so much of their time.

Why do students accept that school makes little sense but believe that it makes even less sense to talk about how school might make more sense? Why is the academic life both unpopular and unexamined? If adults are as inept and dishonest as I was with my son, we can hardly blame the children. Much of what we teach is hard to justify, and we might expose ourselves to the challenge of justifying it to our students and changing it when reason demands this.

Recall Dan's objection to the idea that teachers be told what to teach and Peter's insistence that scientists choose, as children should, the questions they grapple with. Dan wanted to be more active. Peter wanted to be in the world finding things, going to *his* sources, not *their* sources. Vicki and Joan wanted to explore and decide like scientists. As they declared on the first day, everyone in the class came wanting to learn. If adults spent more energy provoking children to think about what knowledge is worthwhile and less energy trying to hold their noses to the grindstones assigned by test and textbook selection committees, everyone might have more energy.

An observer (in another school) noted that parents of kinder-garten students commonly ask, "'When will my child learn to read?' She never heard a parent ask, 'What will my child read?' or 'How will the curriculum materials . . . affect how my child feels about him-self/herself?'" (Best, 1983, p. 59). Parents also don't ask, "How will schooling affect my child's ability to inquire about what knowledge is worthwhile?" Early in the year, Sue heard from parents such things as "I hope Elizabeth will be challenged this year." Challenge is code for "move ahead on the pre-assigned path to elite colleges as quickly as possible." It does not mean, "I hope Elizabeth will be challenged to examine and justify, to herself, her peers, and us, the value of the activities she engages in." Yet parents who did not think to ask Sue for this sort of challenge come to see its value. Joan's spirited defense of class discussions delighted her mother, who sensed that these conversations had something to do with the fact that she had gained her daughter back.

Researchers and educators of many persuasions assert that stu-dents are active learners. Active learner generally means someone who is busy, who chooses, or who makes meaning of the tasks the teacher presents. It almost never means someone who is an educational theo-rist ready and able to negotiate the purposes that govern learning. Consider the recent (1992) *Handbook of Research on Curriculum*. This volume, which is almost more than one hand can hold, contains a chapter on conceptions of knowledge, but not on students' concep-tions of knowledge. It has a chapter on teachers as curriculum-mak-ers, but not on the contributions students might make. There is a chapter on students' experience of the curriculum, but it falls under the heading of "The curriculum as a shaping force." The authors of that chapter observe that "The absence of student experience from current educational discourse seems to be a consequence of system-atic silencing of the students' voice" (Erickson & Shultz, 1992, p. 481). Perhaps future volumes will deal with students' contributions to the curriculum. How free and how brave is a people that does not pro-voke its children to participate in the formation of the purposes that govern their activities—that does not celebrate the vigorous exami-nation of life?

*   *   *

In general, teachers and children are not trusted to set about this sort of negotiation. Educational researchers, whose assignment is to diagnose and recommend, almost never consider students as critics of education or potential collaborators in curriculum construction. They also tend not to cast teachers in a favorable light. In an influential and more that usually sympathetic study of classroom life, Philip Jackson (1968) briefly lost his tune when he noted the here-and-nowness of teachers' talk about their work. He described their talk as marked by "conceptual simplicity . . . an uncomplicated view of causality [and] an intuitive, rather than rational approach to classroom events" (p. 144). This view of teachers is endemic.

Rationality, however, takes different forms at different times and places. What is rational depends on what one is trying to do (Feyerabend, 1987; MacIntyre, 1988). To call teachers' thinking conceptually simple and intuitive rather than rational is to embrace one conception of rationality while shunning others. The conception of rationality that makes teachers look irrational is that of the world of the seventeenth-century physicist: a Cartesian kingdom in which the province of timeless, abstract reason is divided from the land of fickle, personal emotion—a world that exalts the abstract, impersonal language of mathematics over the specific and personal stories of teachers. As Jackson (1968), recovering his tune, went on to argue, the qualities that make teachers appear conceptually simple-minded might be the very ones necessary for constructive work in blooming, buzzing, idiosyncratic classrooms. It does not follow that the teacher's disposition is not rational. A lofty, abstract stance will not get one through the day with 20 second graders. It is of uncertain value even in the daily work of scientists:

> Successful research does not obey general standards; it relies now on one trick, now on another, and the moves that advance it are not always known to the movers. A theory of science that devises standards and structural elements of *all* scientific activities and authorizes them by reference to some rationality-theory may impress outsiders—but it is much too crude an instrument for the people on the spot, that is, for scientists facing some concrete research problem. The most we can do for them from afar is to enumerate rules of thumb, give historical examples, present case studies containing diverging procedures, demonstrate the inherent complexity of research and so prepare them for the morass they are about to enter. Listening to our tale, scientists will get a feeling for the richness of the historical process they want to transform, they will be encouraged to leave behind childish things such as logical rules and epistemological principles and to start thinking in more complex ways—and this is all we can do *because of the nature of the material*. (Feyerabend, 1987, p. 281)

For the psychologist or philosopher seeking abstract and general theories, particular people are but means to larger ends.

> Those who hate gardening need a theory. Not to garden without a theory is a shallow, unworthy way of life.
> A theory must be convincing and scientific. Yet to various people, various theories are convincing and scientific. Therefore we need a number of theories.
> The alternative to not-gardening without a theory is to garden. However it is much easier to have a theory than actually to garden. (Kolakowski, 1990, p. 240)

To a teacher who fosters children's lives, the pursuit of abstract, impersonal truths about education would be irrational. Dan's problem was unlike any other Sue had encountered. She could not guess its nature, but Dan trusted her and the others enough to reveal and face it. He thereby contributed to the stuff of educative conversations about authority, responsibility, competition, and dominance. The dialogue took shapes that could not have been predicted and which there is no real need to predict. These dialogues helped define the unique community of the class and return Dan to that community. Such accomplishments, not the formulation of general statements about motivation, discipline, or moral growth, are, for Sue and teachers like her, the bottom line.[4]

Teachers are hindered by visions of abstract and impersonal truth. Like many teachers asked to write about their classroom experiences, Sue began in an impersonal style that bore no resemblance to the way she normally talked about her work. She even referred to herself as "the teacher." Somewhere, presumably not in their own classrooms, teachers learn that writing about teaching must be objective in the sense of "not personal." "I" cannot do research.

Sue was pleased with the way early drafts of the first chapters of this book captured the feel of her class and the evolving personalities of individual children. At the same time she was slightly worried, commenting that the account was "not very objective." Thus does the predominant notion of legitimate research separate teachers from their students and their own experience.[5] This explains why Sue could accept, even if only provisionally, the Assertive Discipline program. It did not fit her ways. It stifled her wit and cut her off from the children she communicates with so well. But its claims of having a scientific basis (which many researchers would regard as spurious) and the stamp of approval of the school district and a number of universities ease its acceptance. Readers and workbooks are also sold to teachers with the stamp of approval of researchers. It is easy for teachers to agree to use materials prescribed by publishers as scientifically grounded, correct teaching.[6] Parental concerns and a sense of responsibility to the system of choosing textbooks, which has some of the trappings of democracy, also make it hard to discard them entirely. But these "aids" undermine the teacher's ability to see students' needs and to negotiate purposes and practices with them.

The ideal of collaboration between researchers and teachers appears to be gaining allegiance and may signal an end to the tendency to exalt abstract knowledge that does not smell of any particular classroom, teacher, or student. But the signs are mixed. One of the many symposia at a recent conference of the American Educational Research Association concerned collaborative research on motivation. Among the speakers was a teacher who had been collaborating with researchers from a prestigious university. She told how valuable the experience had been and capped off her presentation with the observation that the collaboration had enabled her to meet some "very important people," meaning professors she had worked with. Education is not helped by the idea that the important people and the criteria of truth reside far from elementary school classrooms.

As Deborah Meier (1991) argues, good schools are "the creation of powerful communities of people who know one another well and take one another seriously (which involves quarreling)" (p. 340). Because it is constituted in vigorous conversation, "A good school [or a good class] is always particular" (p. 339). Its particularity "grows out of the fact that the school is the hard-won and carefully crafted creation of a particular group of people" (p. 339).

✳   ✳   ✳

Sue reflects:

Teaching the same grade for 20 years would be boring if my focus were not on the learner. I would simply give the same lesson with the same test questions in the same fashion from year to year. Bulletin boards, learning centers, and lesson plans would never change.

After 12 years of teaching, I had a principal and superintendent who wanted me to teach this way. They wanted the adopted texts followed, chapter by chapter, and completed by predetermined times. There I was in December with chapter four of a science text that specified planting of seeds and transplanting of seedlings. There were ice storms and snow and a vacation just ahead. Only God's intervention could make this lesson unfold the way the authors of the text must have intended.

When a parent complained that my class was not at the same point in the math text as another class, the superintendent and the principal supported her. They insisted that I stick to texts that were out of reach for this class. In effect, they insisted that I stop listening to my students.

I felt undermined. My judgment was not valued. I could not even close my classroom door on this. Teaching became boring as well as stressful. After many sleepless nights, I consulted career counselors, took aptitude tests, and interviewed for 9-to-5 work away from children. But no other role offered the daily challenge I found in teaching, even under the conditions I wanted to escape. The next year, with a new principal, I could return to using texts to provoke learning rather than to define it. I could return to dialogue rather than dictation—the real challenge of teaching. What a relief!

But teaching is rarely smooth sailing. There are always tests or some outsider's pet project to interrupt the flow of learning: a contest on this, a display of that, a composition about something else to be completed in a week's time, a day's time, or immediately. It is easy to give in and push children toward other people's outcomes—to kill trust and dampen the excitement of learning.

These pressures were easier to resist with John in the classroom. It was reassuring to see him become increasingly fascinated with the individuality of each child and to see his growing interest in the power of classroom conversations. This encouraged me to prod and challenge the children toward deeper and more vigorous discussions. These were the moments we relished most.

John talked more and more about how important it was becoming for him to catch the unique moods and personalities of individual students. Generalizations became less important. He enjoyed struggling to capture in words what I would call intuitions about the children. This was something new for him—trying to describe children the way I was most comfortable viewing them. This was not, I thought, the way researchers analyzed the process of education. Accepting it meant accepting my own ways more fully than I had. As time progressed I became acutely aware that I am a researcher on a daily basis. I am always in the midst of "collecting and analyzing data, testing hypotheses and revising theories." I can now find comfort with those once cold terms.

Like many teachers, I thought my personal intuitions and practical classroom experience were my best guide. I felt I had first learned respect for others from my parents. I also knew I had learned about teaching from my college courses. I knew I had learned from reports on research. I was and am grateful to a number of professors who confirmed the importance of respect and helped me find ways to become the sort of teacher I am.[7] Still, I felt separate from the world of research and professors and sheltered my personal experience as my source of teaching wisdom.

Looking back, I see more clearly that my intuitions and common sense did not spring fully formed from practical experience. It is easier to acknowledge that my practice was partially formed by the work of many others whose ideas I encountered in diverse places. I am now less separate from the world of research, more part of a wider conversation, an authority among authorities. I can give as well as receive. But my authority depends greatly on listening, not only to other adults, but to the children. They provide the most immediate and compelling evidence about the worth of my teaching. With my focus more firmly on them, I am more able to listen to others without being overwhelmed, to take from them without losing my own direction, and to speak back when necessary.

Teachers' stories and books like this one do not seem sufficiently objective to some researchers or, sometimes, to teachers. These accounts, one hears, may not be typical of classrooms and so do not count for much more than hypotheses that must be tested more rigorously. Stories like ours don't tell how representative the participants or their practices are. But, as no one is the typical teacher with the typical class, for whom is all this hard-won information about the typical situation intended?

Statements about "what works" in general, derived from positivist research conducted across many classrooms, can carry considerable weight with audiences of higher-level decision makers. . . .

Such statements . . . serve to support belief in the fundamental uniformity of practice in teaching. Such belief is functional for decision makers [remote from classrooms], since it justifies uniform treatment by general policy mandates that are created by centralized decision making and implemented in "top-down" fashion. (Erickson, 1990, p. 186)

The possibility that accounts such as ours might be fiction is also a common concern among researchers. If this were a work of fiction, and if only at this point did we reveal it as such, should you (if you could recover from the discovery having been thus deceived) then discount anything new you might have been contemplating about education? A well-imagined piece of fiction is no mere figment. As Geertz (1988) suggests, we should not confuse "the fictional with the false" (p. 140). Perhaps it would not be wholly bad to claim this book, and other books on education, to be fiction. Then teachers might themselves set out to test the validity of the suggestions on their students, rather than being bound by "scientifically established" practices, or (the other side of the same bad penny) rejecting suggestions simply because they appear to be established by remote researchers. In the end, teachers must negotiate life and work with the particular students they face. There, not far away, is the place where the curriculum question "What knowledge is most worthwhile and how shall we gain it?" must be framed and answered.

We need all we can get in the way of diverse perspectives on education. We do not need researchers or other authorities who circumvent conversation about the ends and means of education by assigning destinations and specifying travel schedules.[8] Rather than trying only to discern whether authorities are speaking *truths* about education, we could put their suggestions to a different test: Do they promote fruitful conversation? Paraphrasing Geertz, whatever use studies like ours will have in the future, if in fact they actually have any, it will involve enabling conversation on education across lines of ethnicity, religion, class, gender, and, especially in this case, age.[9]

*   *   *

A journey can have its end defined before it begins: The traveler moves toward an anticipated destination. Other travelers begin in the hope of arriving at locations they could not have fully anticipated, and expanding their horizons. When state and national legislators and others assign teachers and students destinations in the form of national standards and scores on tests constructed by unknown people in remote places, they define the nature of the journey through school. More locally, text and workbook adoption policies constrain the journey further, undermining the participation of teachers and students in the formation of the purposes that guide learning. When students, their parents, and their teachers become preoccupied with narrowly defined destinations, they become collaborators in the narrowing of education, life, and culture.

When, thinking of the third grade and the race ahead, Peter disparaged conversation, he was not the boy who, a moment before, had declared he would remember "the friends and the teacher." When concerned about getting ahead in the preordained journey, he forgets his own claim that he, like scientists, should ask his own questions. He forgets his own enthusiastic contributions to classroom conversations and the robust virtues of conversation:

> Conversational talk . . . is 'not an enterprise designed to yield an extrinsic profit,' neither a 'contest where a winner gets a prize,' . . . but only 'an unrehearsed intellectual adventure.' . . . [Conversation] need not be . . . clear and precise. . . . Such precision may even be a handicap. 'Look for precision in each class of things only in as far as the nature of the subject permits,' suggested the canny Aristotle. And John Locke . . . was careful to distinguish 'civil communication by words' from 'philosophical communication by words.' He insists not only that 'these two uses are very distinct' but that a 'great deal less exactness will serve in the one [the civil], than in the other.' Because conversation responds to the endless variety of human experience and respects the initial legitimacy of every human perspective, it is served by many voices rather than by one and achieves a rich ambiguity rather than a narrow clarity. It aims at creating a sense of commonality, not of unity, and the mutualism it aspires to weaves into one carpet the threads of a hundred viewpoints. . . . All it can hope to attain is a dynamic of interaction that permits transient convergences as well as ongoing differences and that makes moments of shared vision desirable oases in a never-ending conversational journey. (Barber, 1984, pp. 184–185)[10]

We need more conversation across the lines between students and teachers and through the walls that divide them from academic researchers, administrators, legislators, and parents. In the shadow of the quest for certainty, of generalizations about education, and of state and national testing programs, conversation may appear mundane and weak. As Dewey argued, however, the only solution to the problems of education is education: that form of conjoint communicated experience which enables us to extract meaning from experience and promotes the desire for more such experience. That, in the end, is democracy: a rich, adventurous conversation. This is the point and the process of education.

During a "McNeil-Lehrer News Hour" discussion, H. Ross Perot declared education a national priority. There was, he argued, much to be done. Not exciting work, he said; more like cleaning out the stable. But the stable, if that is what we are in, is fouled by the idea that democracy and education are not exciting. If parents, educators, and legislators engage children in conversation about school, the children will join in with wit and will, and education might yet become a strenuous, invigorating, and often hilarious journey.

Notes

Preface (pp. ix–xii)

1. In ethnography, "The pretense of looking at the world directly, as through a one-way screen, seeing others as they really are when only God is looking, is indeed quite widespread. But that is itself a rhetorical strategy, a mode of persuasion" (Geertz, 1988, p. 141). James Clifford (1988) writes that "neither the experience nor the interpretive activity of the scientific researcher can be considered innocent. It becomes necessary to conceive of [observation] . . . as a constructive negotiation involving at least two, and usually more, conscious, politically significant subjects" (p. 41). Action research can be seen as going beyond merely accepting that observers are inevitably involved in political dialogues and influence and are influenced, to the open attempt to be influenced and to influence and to tell stories of these attempts (Reason, 1988). That, we think, is our game.

As Clifford points out, recognition of the polyphonic nature of participant observation creates problems for writing about such observation. We tried not to write in the first person—not to write as if this were John's story in which Sue played a role. "I saw this and Sue did that" seemed awkward and inappropriate. Referring to ourselves as "Sue," "John," and "we" more accurately reflected the relationship that seemed to be emerging. This, however, made us appear as actors in a story written by God or a somewhat literate fly on the wall. Furthermore, as John did the bulk of the writing, for him to refer to himself as John was artificial. Ambivalently, we deliver what you now see.

As one reader suggested, one might think a collaboration such as ours not genuine if the researcher rather than the teacher does most of the writing. Reciprocity, however, would have required me to teach, which would have left Sue little of virtue to write about. A more serious problem with this criticism is the lurking assumption that writing is more important than teaching.

When Sue reads my first hasty draft account of the early days, she is relieved to see confirmed, now on paper, that the themes she values have been recognized. Soon we have lunch together almost every day, analyzing what has happened, how it might be reported, and what to do next. The idea of trying to disentangle who is responsible for which aspects of the story is, given our purpose, as inappropriate as it is impossible. The guiding question becomes: Where might this journey next take us and the children? Our roles become not easier but more satisfying and meaningful, not more obvious or certain but more exciting.

We have some different preoccupations. I, more than Sue, wonder how the emerging story will read in Peoria and in colleges of education, and wake up at night wondering which of the welter of mundane, electrifying, and paradoxical events I should try to entrap and how to trade them for words that will suggest their meanings. Sue thinks of the parents (what do they make of the children's stories of the second grade?) and of the colleagues she must live with when I am gone. Will she move away from what they can accept? If a book ever comes of this, how will it affect her life?

What use are details on method? As Geertz (1988) says, "Like poems and hypotheses, ethnographies can only be judged *ex post*, after someone has brought them into being" (p. 147). The way one ethnography comes into being is an uncertain guide for new ones. Some details of this one are part of the story. I was in the class almost all the time for the first three weeks and became fast at taking field notes, which I then fleshed out, usually the same day. Walking into new classrooms now, I feel lost and am reminded how long it takes for individuals, actions, and useful questions to become vivid, to fix easily in the mind. As this class became more vivid to me, its people, themes, and questions more obvious, and Sue and I better at communicating, I gradually began to attend more selectively—to follow the dinosaur story, for example.

Chapter 1 (pp. 3–8)

1. The idea that "delinquent" behavior can reflect a search for excitement is not new. Homer Lane was, early in this century, superintendent of playgrounds in Detroit. "He discovered that it was the playgrounds with the most adult supervision in which the rate of juvenile crime increased: Crime, he concluded, was essentially a form of play" (Croall, 1983, p. 82).

2. Authorities whose criticisms of conventional schooling resonate with descriptions of "lads" such as those Willis described include Dewey (1938), Goodlad (1983), Jackson (1968), and Sarason (1990). "Schools are uninteresting places in which the interests and questions of children have no relevance to what they are required to learn" (Sarason, 1990, p. *xiv*).

Chapter 2 (pp. 9–24)

1. The importance of the early days of the school year is suggested by Emmer, Evertson, and Anderson (1980), who found early practices predic-

tive of attainment later in the year. Daily beginnings can also reveal the ethical assumptions students and teachers share (Hansen, 1989).

2. The example is Mrs. Hunt, from Bossert's (1979) description of four very different teachers in one school. A similarly useful contrast of "telling" with more subtle teaching is given by Sarason, Davidson, and Blatt (1962, chap. 3), who hold that the teacher "must be viewed as a kind of psychological observer and tactician in an increasingly independent, curiosity-satisfying productive attack on the world of ideas and problems. To the extent that the teacher perceives [his or] her role as involving the input of knowledge, with little or no attention to the covert processes of learning, she [or he] is performing as a technician" (p. 73).

3. Willis argues that teachers cannot rely on their personal moral authority (or mere power) to maintain order in school, but must appeal to socially negotiated teaching paradigms, agreements about the mutual obligations of students and teachers—what fair exchanges school should involve. In a common paradigm, teachers provide knowledge that will help students secure well-paying employment in return for student conformity. Different academic subjects can favor different mini-paradigms. As we will see, Sue's students presume that reading and science offer different goods or types of knowledge and require different teaching practices. Worksheets and workbooks often precipitate the negotiation of a different paradigm.

Chapter 3 (pp. 27–39)

1. Jodie's "That's you," including me in the picture, evokes Clifford's (1988) discussion of the frontispiece of Malinowski's *Argonauts of the Western Pacific*, which shows a line of Trobriand Islanders ceremoniously offering necklaces of shell to a chief. The men face the chief, who returns their gaze. The camera captures the participants in profile, its position suggesting the supposedly detached perspective of the researcher. But the islander standing furthest from the chief does not play along; he looks directly into the camera. Like Trobriand Islanders and teachers, second graders observe those who observe them. Thus the observer's splendid isolation is gone; but it was never very isolated or splendid.

2. Holt (1964) and McDermott and Hood (1982), for example, emphasize the pervasiveness of attempts by teachers and students to manage displays of competence so as to avoid putting people on the spot. "Dumbing down" work can be seen as one way of avoiding displays of incompetence—as suggested in our Chapters 6 and 7.

3. The development of students' conceptions of the nature of competence is reviewed in Nicholls (1989). Bossert (1979) describes classrooms with strict pecking orders based on relative competence and others with almost none.

4. Thorkildsen (1991) shows that many first- and second-grade students do not fully comprehend why adults might see helping on tests as illegitimate.

5. Similar strategies employed by another second-grade teacher as she seeks to establish an emphasis on inquiry rather than on individual differences in ability are described by Cobb, Yackel, and Wood (1988).

Chapter 4 (pp. 40–52)

1. Thorkildsen (1989a; 1989b; 1991) finds age variation in understanding of tests, contests, and learning situations, but even first graders see the three as demanding different practices if they are to be fair and effective.

2. Here we emphasize effects, inside the class, of the test. Consider also the substantial time and expense involved in testing sessions. Where might we be if more of this time, money, and energy were spent improving teaching instead of evaluating one aspect of its outcomes? Teaching methods that increase test scores can also decrease interest in learning (Helmke, Schneider, & Weinert, 1986; Pascarella, Walberg, Junker, & Haertel, 1981). The long-term effects of the preoccupation with tests might be quite negative.

3. Gjesme (1974) compared performance when problems were said to be a test to performance when they were said to be a type of problem students would be tested on a year later. The "pretest" led to better scores for students who were prone to worry about failing.

4. Hill (1984) advocates less testlike testing conditions and summarizes evidence that the performance of test-anxious students is less impaired in such circumstances. Illegitimate test administration practices have been observed by Wodke, Harper, Schommer, and Brunelli (1989) and Nolen, Haladyna, and Haas (1992).

5. Lambert (1980-1981) reports on legislators' and deans' attitudes toward teachers' attitudes and agrees with the legislators that teachers should be more accepting of tests.

6. Deci, Spiegel, Ryan, Koestner, and Kauffman (1982) found that holding an instructor "responsible" for a student's scores increased rigid, coercive behavior. This inhibiting effect is most likely to be felt in schools serving the urban poor, who are thereby doubly disadvantaged. Waller (1932) points out how the task of impersonal testing undermines the personal task of teaching, which is that of stimulating growth.

7. First graders see tests as different from learning situations (Thorkildsen, 1989b). Not until about age 11, however, do most students gain a wholly adultlike understanding of why, in our society, helping someone during a test is unfair and an ineffective method of conducting a test (Thorkildsen, 1991).

8. Power, Higgins, and Kohlberg's (1989) account of just community schools shows the focus of meetings to be on those aspects of conduct, such as stealing, loyalty to the group, and drug use, encompassed by Kohlberg's account of the development of moral reasoning. The narrowness of the definition of the field of morality is a problem.

9. Bowles and Gintis (1976) distinguish the autocratic economic life from the somewhat more democratic political life of the United States and

make a classic statement of the parallel between the undemocratic nature of economic life and the undemocratic nature of the conduct of schoolwork.

10. Children of different ages give different reasons for favoring peer tutoring. Only toward the end of high school do students clearly see it as fair that some should develop faster than others, but many older students favor peer tutoring, partly on the ground that it fosters learning in both tutor and tutee (Thorkildsen, 1989a).

11. The centrality of the communal impulse in Dewey's thought is clearly brought out by Westbrook (1991).

Chapter 5 (pp. 53–70)

1. One text on classroom discipline (Charles, 1989, p. 116) concludes a brief critique of the Canter approach thus: "All in all, however, the widespread popularity of assertive discipline speaks for itself." But what does it say?

2. Canter does recommend recognition of the fact that different treatments are needed for different students—an assertion in contradiction with his directive to make the consequences of misbehavior explicit in advance and to make application of those consequences virtually automatic. Sue's approach is more compatible with that of Dreikurs, Grunwald, and Pepper (1982), another "popular" perspective on discipline, which holds that reactions to troublesome action should be based on its causes—on changing, often by negotiation, the student's reasons for action.

3. Numerous studies in various cultures show that children regard gratuitous killing as wrong (Turiel, 1983). They maintain that it would be wrong even if God ordered it (Nucci, 1985). On the other hand, they readily concede that some religious rules, such as honoring the Sabbath, can be changed by religious or secular authorities or groups.

4. In this passage, Greene explicates Noddings's (1983) vision of connected teaching. It is contrasted with the Kohlbergian vision of analytical Socratic dialogues about abstract principles remote from the intimate, gritty, and perhaps banal details of daily life. The distinction is important, though it is not clear that the charges against Kohlberg are wholly warranted (Power, Higgins, & Kohlberg, 1989). Students in his just community schools are, for example, encouraged to discuss dilemmas that arise in the school community and to act on the basis of their deliberations. There is, nevertheless, a difference in flavor between Noddings's and Kohlberg's proposals.

5. These discussions can be read in two ways: (1) They can be viewed in terms of a Piagetian sequence of increasingly complex, differentiated conceptions. Children with more advanced conceptions are, in this view, likely to see weaknesses in less sophisticated reasoning. Thus Peter raises objections to Paul's power-oriented conception of authority, which he is hardly likely to be persuaded to adopt, as his thinking has already progressed beyond it. Paul will not see Peter's more complex points immediately but

might be stimulated to puzzle them out. Development is not easy but it is unlikely to go backward. Evidence on the stimulating effect of discussion is reviewed by Berkowitz (1985). (2) Alternatively, these dialogues might involve the meeting of incommensurable theories (larger than concepts and incorporating a variety of concepts) about how to define situations, what is important, or what goods are at stake. Peter might be arguing that the situation should be defined as one where norms are jointly determined, whereas Ann argues for a situation closer to that of the military. They might be defining two different types of situations rather than differing in how well they understand a given type of situation. In the case of the class discussion of authority, there appears to be no direct evidence to suggest whether one perspective is more apt or whether both apply. But this distinction between concepts and theories (or understandings of a particular well-defined type of situation—such as a test—versus the particular ways people define ambiguous situations) has been explicated in children's reasoning about the fairness of school practices (Thorkildsen, 1989b) and causes of academic success (Nicholls, 1989, 1992).

6. Joan's objection to "the rules" echoes the ruminations of A. S. Neill, who later founded the famous "free" school, Summerhill. Teaching in Scotland during World War I, in conflict with parents who believed in traditional ways of training and punishing, he wrote, "Many a night I feel disheartened. I find that I am on the side of the bairns [children]. I am against law and discipline; I am all for freedom of action" (Croall, 1983, p. 71).

Chapter 6 (pp. 71–86)

1. Consistent with Dewey School notions, Sue's approach to writing derives much from the whole-language movement (e.g., Calkins, 1983, 1986; Goodman, 1987; Graves, 1983; Willinsky, 1990), which has considerable grass-roots support among teachers. The emphasis on learning skills in the context of larger acts of meaning-making and on students as collaborators, audience, and critics highlights the role of language in the personal and social life.

2. Stevens, Madden, Slavin, and Farnish (1987) review evidence on deficiencies in follow-up activities commonly prescribed for students and describe one response to this problem.

3. The ambiguity of workbook instructions and formats is sometimes a matter of cultural variation in conventions of communication (Heath, 1983). However, in some cases it seems more a matter of failure to follow any convention consistently. Problems with the reductionist approach to learning implicit in the usual workbooks and worksheets have been highlighted by advocates of whole-language approaches (e.g., Goodman, 1987) as well as opponents of those approaches.

4. Nehring (1989) and McNeil (1986) are among those who discuss the challenge of avoiding a dichotomy between personal and school knowledge.

5. Calkins (1983), Goodman (1987), Graves (1983), Harste (1989), Heath (1983), and Manning and Manning (1989) are whole-language advocates. Willinsky (1990) presents a sympathetic but searching critique of these "new literacy" approaches.

Chapter 7 (pp. 89–103)

1. Exceptions to the lack of interest in students as curriculum theorists include studies by Schubert and Lopez Schubert (1981), and Sosniak and Perlman (1990), as well as others reviewed by Erickson and Shultz (1992).

2. McNeil (1986) describes a sort of implicit contract that exists in many high schools, wherein teachers assign unchallenging workbook-like tasks and students reciprocate with acquiescence. See also Willis (1977).

3. The identification of Dewey's progressive education with the hands-off, child-centered romantic tradition in progressive education continues to this day. E. D. Hirsch (1988), for example, makes this error. Sidney Hook's (1973) essay "John Dewey and His Betrayers" deserves to be resurrected. On the social and dialectical nature or "foundations" of freedom and on Dewey's and others' contributions to the question, see Greene (1988) and Westbrook (1991). Though Kallen (1940) described Dewey as "the prophet of intelligence as an adventure," he did not represent Dewey as explicitly calling for students to examine the nature and purpose of intellectual disciplines. Despite the quotation that begins our book, Dewey seems not to have elaborated the ways that students should help construct the purposes governing their learning.

4. Korn (1991) discusses contemporary schools offering choice. Psychological conceptions of choice, control, and freedom also emphasize freedom from constraint rather than the process of constructing purposes in negotiation with others (Deci & Ryan, 1985). These traditions have, nevertheless, made sterling contributions by specifying constricting effects of exogenous incentives and coercion.

Chapter 8 (pp. 104–127)

1. Dan illustrated Kohl's (1991) point that students often choose not to learn for reasons of identity or morality. Questionnaire studies also indicate that different types of academic motivation are associated with different ethical and political stances on the purpose of school. This bolsters the notion that attempts to change student motivation should be seen as involving the negotiation of ethical and political stances rather than (as is often the case) ethically neutral manipulations of student self-perceptions (Nicholls, 1989). Willis (1977) addresses this question in his chapter "Monday Morning and the Millennium."

2. Paradoxically, when preoccupation with one's ability increases, both the probability of unrealistically high aspirations and that of low aspirations increase, particularly in those who doubt their abilities (Nicholls, 1989).

3. Whole-language approaches often imply that students should be seen as theorists (Willinsky, 1990).

4. Dewey's theory of experience, which is also a theory of motivation, is presented in various places, including *Democracy and Education*. As with his theory of experience (or motivation), he centered his ethical theory around the "pursuit of ends harmonious with all the capacities and desires of the self and which expanded them into a cooperative whole" (Westbrook, 1991, p. 157). He also stressed the social nature of experience, of motivation, and of the good. Dewey's work is like a hologram: Each part contains the form of the whole. Britton (1982) emphasizes writing as discovery and the importance of expressive, personal, imaginative writing. There is some evidence (Durst & Newell, 1989) that poetic and expressive writing is more engaging for students than writing concerned with more "factual" matters. For college students, commitment to poetic or aesthetic writing goals and to using writing to clarify or develop one's values has been found to be associated with the experience of writing as inherently valuable. The use of writing to learn academic subjects was less so (Silva & Nicholls, in press). The contrast between Jill and Peter parallels these findings. Current emphases on making the writing process meaningful, personal, and social (e.g., Calkins, 1983; Goodman, 1987) have appreciable affinity with Dewey's notions about educative experience, though they tend toward what Dewey would see as romantic excess (Hook, 1973; Willinsky, 1990).

5. Willinsky (1990) reviews studies that can be seen as casting students as literacy theorists, including some who make choices like Peter's (p. 167).

Chapter 9 (pp. 128–147)

1. Education most consistent with Piagetian constructivism would have students collaboratively identify conceptual problems and solve them, with a successful solution being one that makes sense to students (Duckworth, 1987; Kamii, 1985; Kohlberg & Mayer, 1972). Kohlberg and Mayer are explicit about the importance of social process; they use the metaphor of dialogue to characterize their Piagetian progressivism. In some versions of this dialogue, a central role for the teacher is to help establish an ethic whereby students listen and respond to one another's arguments and avoid egoistical concerns about who is abler (Cobb, Yackel, & Wood, 1988). The Piagetian framework, however, has no obvious place for dialogue about what question should be asked or what paradigm, in the Kuhnian sense of world view, one should try out. Piaget's is a psychology of puzzle-solving rather than of paradigm-choosing (in the Kuhnian sense of puzzles as problems defined within world views or paradigms). The later Piaget, if not the early one, always knew what question he wanted to put to children and framed his questions to ensure that they answered his questions rather than others they might have been more disposed to ask. Here lies the key to the power of his work as well as to its limitations.

2. To be on the safe side, Sue calls Jack's parents to discuss this discussion. Already assured about Jack's adjustment and progress, they are not alarmed. Given Jack's assurance throughout the episode, there is no reason they should be. It is easy to see why teachers avoid controversial issues in the classroom. Yet, without taking the risk—averting problems when possible and facing them when necessary (Zola, 1990)—teachers avoid the very matters that give life meaning, direction, and substance. Important questions are controversial. If a question is not controversial, it is settled. If it is settled, there is nothing to talk about—no question.

3. Lave (1988) presents this preoccupation with "well-formed" problems as a common and limiting feature of research on cognition in schools. In the common genre of research on transfer of learning, "'problems' are small-scale demands for an acquiescent problem solver to operate on the information given by a problem giver using algorithms or formal inferential reasoning to match a correct or ideal answer" (p. 35).

4. The research of Piaget (1972) on the development of formal operational thought, as well as subsequent work, indicates that understanding the need to control other variables while examining the effect of a given one comes approximately between ages 11 and 14, though the timing varies greatly with the topic.

5. Thomas emphasizes the pluralistic, problem-raising, controversial nature of scientific thought, not just the puzzle-solving activities of normal science in T. S. Kuhn's sense. So do Siegel (1988) and, in mathematics, Resnick (1988). Duckworth's (1991) emphasis on keeping science complex, which also represents science as exploration, appears more an emphasis on puzzle-solving. Controversial matters are not to be confused with complex matters. Children often encounter complex matters for which they know there is but one acceptable answer. For the second graders inquiring into the effects of immersing objects in a glass of water, the distinction might be slight. Keeping it slight appears to be Duckworth's aim.

Chapter 10 (pp. 148–159)

1. E.g., Haggerty (1966); Kohl (1988); Wagner (1976).

2. Among the various justifications for drama is the role of drama in promoting intellectual development, narrowly conceived. But, in the light of these children's productions, this seems a thin justification. Of what value is intelligence that does not enhance life?

Chapter 11 (pp. 163–177)

1. This discussion engages children's conceptions of ability and the fairness of testing practices (Thorkildsen, 1991). Peter's and Joan's conceptions appear more advanced than most. However, Joan is more concerned about the feelings of low scorers than is Peter—a difference in priorities or

theories about what school should be for, rather than in conceptions of abilities or tests.

2. Coming to terms with inequality of learning ability is cognitively difficult, even for high school students. The belief that all cannot learn at the same rate and that, thus, it would be unfair to expect abler students not to achieve more than less able students is not usually strongly established until about age 18 (Thorkildsen, 1989a).

3. For a discussion of obstacles to education as adventure see Cohen (1988) and Sarason (1971). Cohen notes that adventurous instruction requires teachers to "depend on their students . . . for if students are to become inquirers . . . they must take a large responsibility in producing instruction" (p. 76). If no one depends on teachers, are they likely to take the risk of depending on students?

4. In contexts where comparison of student performance is emphasized, the disposition to make sense of the world does not predict intrinsic satisfaction with learning. It does, however, do so in less evaluative contexts (Nicholls, 1989). In evaluative contexts, satisfaction is predicted by perceived ability. Thus, Tim's chances of satisfaction and absorption decrease as the emphasis on his standing on tests increases.

Chapter 12 (pp. 178–193)

1. We inevitably simplified the contrast between the views of DuBois and Washington. DuBois argued, "The aim of the higher training of the college is the . . . training of a self whose balanced assertion will mean as much as possible for the great ends of civilization. The aim of technical training on the other hand is to enable the student to master the present methods of earning a living in some particular way" (DuBois, 1973, pp. 13–14). This might not do full justice to Washington's vision of an education of "hand, head, and heart," which was, more than DuBois' vision, worked out in action (Franklin, 1990).

2. E. D. Hirsch (1988) has produced dictionaries of the noncontroversial knowledge he suggests children should know. Graff (1990) points out that such prescriptive efforts themselves provoke controversy and that we should accept and teach controversy. McNeil (1986) and Page (1991) suggest the alienating effects of an emphasis on simple, noncontroversial knowledge in high schools.

3. Busch (1992). The reforms were based in part on the approach of Cobb, Yackel, and Wood (1988).

4. Rorty (1983) describes a similar contrast—that between the Kantian search for principles of justice and the Deweyian "search for human perfection, as something distinct from justice" (p. 174). For Dewey, justice is simply taken for granted and any general definition of justice is "too abstract to do the moral agent or the policy maker much good. . . . [Dewey's] real concern is with the possible forms of human relationships that might come

to exist if we changed ourselves and our societies . . . [and] the search for principle is [seen as] a primitive stage of moral development. What counts as moral sophistication is the ability to wield sensitive moral vocabularies, and thereby to create moral relevance" (p. 174). Noddings puts it slightly differently, "We need to talk to the participants, to see their eyes and facial expressions, to receive what they are feeling" (1983, pp. 2–3).

5. Geertz (1983) presents common-sense, everyday thought as a cultural system, "a relatively organized body of considered thought, rather than just what anyone clothed and in his right mind knows. . . . [This view of common sense] should lead on to some useful conclusions; but perhaps the most important is that it is an inherent characteristic of common-sense thought precisely to deny this and to affirm that its tenets are immediate deliverances of experience, not deliberated reflections upon it" (p. 75). This misleading common-sense reading of common sense as the immediate deliverance of experience leaves common sense hard to defend against forms of thought that claim the systematic nature that common sense denies itself. An example is given by Lave (1988), who describes everyday forms of mathematics that enable people to solve everyday problems effectively. The users deny that their everyday numerical reasoning is real mathematics, reserving that term for school mathematics, which they revere more than the mathematics that enables them to conduct their lives. Thus are people divided against themselves as they accept the "uplifting," "superior" value of school knowledge.

6. Shannon (1983) found that teachers accepted commercially prepared reading materials (of the type Peter attacked) as based on scientific research and presumed that "application" of these materials would lead to learning. Thus the teachers were alienated from their work. Pressures to accept publishers' materials can also be immediate: Hawkins (1990, p. 138) describes an elementary school teacher who stocked her room with science equipment including a water table. "Seeing this, her principal spoke to her nervously: 'You know, Mrs. ——, our school has a strong *academic* emphasis.' 'Oh yes,' she replied, 'I couldn't teach *physics* without this equipment.' She later found piles of fill-in-the-blank workbooks in her closet. Asking if she would be required to use them, she was told that indeed she must. 'So,' she said, 'We used them. We weighed them singly and by twos and by threes. We weighed them dry and we weighed them wet." Not all are so courageous.

7. I am especially grateful to Al DeVito, Don Ferris, Gerry Krockover, and Pose Lamb.

8. One currently popular idea is that, because teaching is driven by (toward) tests, development of more intelligent tests is a key reform: If we get the right tests, we will produce independent, creative thinkers. This smacks of a torturer threatening prisoners: "We have ways of making you think." The problem of promoting independence in such ways was recognized by the Monty Python crew (in their film *The Life of Brian*), who showed

us a crowd seeking guidance from Brian, whom they took for the Messiah. "You don't need to follow anyone!" calls the besieged Brian. "You've got to think for yourselves! You are all individuals!" "Yes!" intones the crowd in unison. "We are all individuals!" "You are all different!" cries Brian. "We are all different!" echoes the crowd. "I'm not different!" says one. "Shhh!" says the crowd.

9. Geertz (1988, p. 147) does not refer to the complex boundaries between the young and the "mature" of any culture.

10. Barber's account of democracy is in the Deweyian tradition. Others in this tradition are discussed by Westbrook (1991).

References

Ashton-Warner, S. (1958). *Spinster.* London: Martin, Secker & Warberg.

Barber, B. (1984). *Strong democracy: Participatory politics for a new age.* Berkeley: University of California Press.

Berkowitz, M. W. (1985). The role of discussion in moral reasoning. In M. W. Berkowitz (Ed.), *Moral education: Theory and practice* (pp. 196–218). Hillsdale, NJ: Erlbaum.

Best, R. (1983). *We've all got scars: What boys and girls learn in elementary school.* Bloomington: Indiana University Press.

Bossert, S. T. (1979). *Tasks and social relationships in classrooms: A study of instructional organization and its consequences.* New York: Cambridge University Press.

Bowles, S., & Gintis, H. (1976). *Schooling in capitalist America.* New York: Basic Books.

Britton, J. (1982). *Retrospect and prospect: Selected essays.* Upper Montclair, NJ: Boynton/Cook.

Busch, C. L. (1992). *The desire for meaning and the fear of freedom.* Unpublished paper, University of Illinois, Chicago.

Calkins, L. M. (1983). *Lessons from a child.* Portsmouth, NH: Heinemann.

Calkins, L. M. (1986). *The art of teaching writing.* Portsmouth, NH: Heinemann.

Canter, L. (1989). *Beyond assertive discipline.* Santa Monica, CA: Lee Canter & Associates.

Charles, C. M. (1989). *Building classroom discipline* (3rd ed.). New York: Longman.

Cleary, B. (1955). *Beezus and Ramona.* New York: Scholastic.

Cleary, B. (1968). *Ramona the pest.* New York: Morrow.

Clifford, J. (1988). *The predicament of culture: Twentieth-century ethnography, literature, and art.* Cambridge, MA: Harvard University Press.

Cobb, P., Yackel, E., & Wood, T. (1988). Young children's emotional acts while doing mathematical problem solving. In D. B. McLeod & V. M. Adams (Eds.), *Affect and problem solving: A new perspective* (pp. 117–148). New York: Springer-Verlag.

Cohen, D. K. (1988). Teaching practice: Plus que ça change ... In P. W. Jackson (Ed.), *Contributions to educational change* (pp. 27–84). Berkeley, CA: McCutchan.

Croall, J. (1983). *Neill of Summerhill: The permanent rebel*. New York: Pantheon.

Damon, W. (1977). *The social world of the child*. San Francisco: Jossey-Bass.

Deci, E. L., & Ryan, R. M. (1985). *Intrinsic motivation and self-determination in human behavior*. New York: Plenum.

Deci, E. L., Spiegel, N. H., Ryan, R. M., Koestner, R., & Kauffman, M. (1982). The effects of performance standards on controlling teachers. *Journal of Educational Psychology, 74*, 852–859.

Delpit, L. D. (1988). The silenced dialogue: Power and pedagogy in educating other people's children. *Harvard Educational Review, 58*, 280–298.

Dewey, J. (1938). *Experience and education*. New York: Macmillan.

Dewey, J. (1940). Creative democracy—the task before us. In *The philosopher of the common man: Essays in honor of John Dewey to celebrate his eightieth birthday* (pp. 220–228). New York: Putnam.

Dewey, J. (1988). *The quest for certainty*. (John Dewey: The later works, 1925–1953, Volume 4: 1929.) Carbondale: Southern Illinois University Press.

Dewey, J., & Dewey, E. (1915). *Schools of tomorrow*. New York: Dutton.

Dreikurs, R., Grunwald, B., & Pepper, F. (1982). *Maintaining sanity in the classroom*. New York: Harper & Row.

Driver, R. (1983). *The pupil as scientist*. Milton Keynes, England: Open University Press.

DuBois, W. E. B. (1973). *The education of black people: Ten critiques, 1906–1960* (H. Aptheker, Ed.). New York: Monthly Review Press.

DuBois, W. E. B. (1990). *The souls of black folk*. New York: Vintage. (Original work published 1903)

Duckworth, E. (1987). *"The having of wonderful ideas" and other essays on teaching and learning*. New York: Teachers College Press.

Duckworth, E. (1991). Twenty-four, forty-two, and I love you: Keeping it complex. *Harvard Educational Review, 61*, 1–24.

Durst, R. K., & Newell, G. E. (1989). The uses of function: James Britton's category system and research on writing. *Review of Educational Research, 59*, 375–394.

Edwards, D., & Mercer, N. (1987). *Common knowledge*. New York: Methuen.

Edwards, J. (1974). *The last of the really great whangdoodles*. New York: Harper & Row.

Emmer, E. T., Evertson, C. M., & Anderson, L. M. (1980). Effective classroom management at the beginning of the school year. *Elementary School Journal, 80*, 219–231.

Erickson, F. (1990). Qualitative methods. In *Research on teaching and learning* (Vol. 2, pp. 75–194). A project of the American Educational Research Association. New York: Macmillan.

Erickson, F., & Shultz, J. (1992). Students' experience of the curriculum. In P. W. Jackson (Ed.), *Handbook of research on curriculum* (pp. 465–485). New York: Macmillan.

Eylon, B-S., & Linn, M. C. (1988). Learning and instruction: An examination of four research perspectives in science education. *Review of Educational Research, 58,* 251–301.

Feyerabend, P. (1987). *Farewell to reason.* New York: Verso.

Franklin, R. M. (1990). *Liberating visions: Human fulfillment and social justice in African-American thought.* Minneapolis: Fortress Press.

Gardner, J. (1978). *On moral fiction.* New York: Basic Books.

Geertz, C. (1983). *Local knowledge: Further essays in interpretive anthropology.* New York: Basic Books.

Geertz, C. (1988). *Works and lives: The anthropologist as author.* Stanford, CA: Stanford University Press.

Gjesme, T. (1974). Goal distance in time and its effects on the relations between achievement motives and performance. *Journal of Research in Personality, 8,* 161–171.

Goodlad, J. I. (1983). *A place called school: Prospects for the future.* New York: McGraw-Hill.

Goodman, K. (1987). *What's whole in whole language.* Portsmouth, NH: Heinemann.

Graff, G. (1990). How to deal with the humanities crisis: Organize it. *ADE Bulletin, 95,* 4–10.

Graves, D. H. (1983). *Writing: Teachers and children at work.* Portsmouth, NH: Heinemann.

Gray, P., & Chanoff, D. (1986). Democratic schooling: What happens to young people who have charge of their own education? *American Journal of Education, 94,* 182–213.

Greenberg, D. (1973). *"Announcing a new school . . ." A personal account of the beginnings of the Sudbury Valley School.* Framingham, MA: The Sudbury Valley School Press. (Winch Street, Framingham, MA 01701)

Greene, M. (1988). *The dialectic of freedom.* New York: Teachers College Press.

Haggerty, J. (1966). *Please, Miss, can I play God?* London: Methuen.

Hansen, D. T. (1989). Getting down to business: The moral significance of classroom beginnings. *Anthropology and Education Quarterly, 20,* 259–274.

Harste, J. C. (1989). *New policy guidelines for reading: Connecting research and practice.* Urbana, IL: National Council of Teachers of English.

Hawkins, D. (1990). Defining and bridging the gap. In E. Duckworth, J. Easley, D. Hawkins, & A. Henriques (Eds.), *Science education: A minds on approach for the elementary years* (pp. 97–139). Hillsdale, NJ: Erlbaum.

Heath, S. B. (1983). *Ways with words: Language, life, and work in communities and classrooms.* Cambridge, England: Cambridge University Press.

Helmke, A., Schneider, W., & Weinert, F. E. (1986). Quality of instruction and classroom learning outcomes: The German contribution to the IEA classroom environment study. *Teaching and Teacher Education, 62,* 1–18.

Hill, K. T. (1984). Debilitating motivation and testing: A major educational problem—possible solutions and policy applications. In R. Ames & C. Ames (Eds.), *Research on motivation in education* (Vol. 1, pp. 245–274). New York: Academic Press.

Hirsch, E. D., Jr. (1988). *Cultural literacy.* New York: Vintage.

Holt, J. (1964). *How children fail.* New York: Dell.

Hook, S. (1973). John Dewey and his betrayers. In S. Hook, *Education and the taming of power* (pp. 89–107). La Salle, IL: Open Court.

Jackson, P. W. (1968). *Life in classrooms.* New York: Holt, Rinehart & Winston.

James, W. (1907). *Pragmatism: A new name for some old ways of thinking.* New York: Longman.

Jonas, A. (1983). *Round trip.* New York: Greenwillow.

Kallen, H. M. (1940). Freedom and education. In *The philosopher of the common man: Essays in honor of John Dewey to celebrate his eightieth birthday* (pp. 15–32). New York: Putnam.

Kamii, C. (1985). *Young children reinvent arithmetic: Implications of Piaget's theory.* New York: Teachers College Press.

Knapp, M. S., & Turnbull, B. J. (1990). *Better schooling for children of poverty: Alternatives to conventional wisdom.* Volume 1. Summary. Washington, DC: U.S. Department of Education, Office of Planning, Budget, and Evaluation.

Kohl, H. (1988). *Making theater: Developing plays with young people.* New York: Teachers and Writers Collaborative.

Kohl, H. (1991). *I won't learn from you!* Minneapolis: Milkweed.

Kohlberg, L., & Mayer, R. (1972). Development as the aim of education. *Harvard Educational Review, 42,* 449–496.

Kolakowski, L. (1990). *Modernity on endless trial.* Chicago: University of Chicago Press.

Korn, C. V. (1991). *Alternative American schools.* Albany: State University of New York Press.

Kurfiss, J. (1977). Sequentiality and structure in a cognitive model of college student development. *Developmental Psychology, 13,* 565–571.

Lambert, R. E. (1980–1981). Teacher attitudes on testing: A multiple perspective. *College Board Review, 118,* 13, 14, 29, 30.

Lave, J. (1988). *Cognition in practice: Mind, mathematics and culture in everyday life.* New York: Cambridge University Press.

Lazarus, K. F. (1970). *The Gismo.* Chicago: Follett.

Lipman, M. (1988). *Philosophy goes to school.* Philadelphia: Temple University Press.

MacIntyre, A. (1988). *Whose justice? Which rationality?* Notre Dame, IN: University of Notre Dame Press.

Manning, G., & Manning, M. (1989). *Whole language: Beliefs and practices K-8.* Washington, DC: NEA.

Martin, G. (1987). A letter to Breadloaf. In D. Goswami & G. S. Stillman

(Eds.), *Reclaiming the classroom: Teacher research as an agency for change.* Upper Montclair, NJ: Boynton/Cook.

Mayhew, K. C., & Edwards, A. C. (1965). *The Dewey school: The Laboratory School of the University of Chicago.* New York: Atherton. (Original work published 1936)

McDermott, R. P., & Hood, L. (1982). Institutionalized psychology and the ethnography of schooling. In P. Gilmore & A. A. Galtthorn (Eds.), *Children in and out of school: Ethnography and education* (pp. 232–249). Washington, DC: Center for Applied Linguistics.

McNeil, L. M. (1986). *Contradictions of control: School structure and school knowledge.* New York: Routledge & Kegan Paul.

Meier, D. W. (1991, September 23). The little schools that could. *The Nation*, pp. 338–340.

National Assessment of Educational Progress. (1979). *Attitudes toward science: A summary of results from the 1976-77 national assessment of science* (Report No. 08-S-02). Denver, CO: Education Commission of the States.

Nehring, J. (1989). *"Why do we gotta do this stuff, Mr. Nehring?"* New York: Ballantine.

Newman, D., Griffin, P., & Cole, M. (1989). *The construction zone: Working for cognitive change in school.* New York: Cambridge University Press.

Nicholls, J. G. (1989). *The competitive ethos and democratic education.* Cambridge, MA: Harvard University Press.

Nicholls, J. G. (1992). The general and the specific in the development and expression of achievement motivation. In G. C. Roberts (Ed.), *Motivation in sport and exercise* (pp. 31–56). Champaign, IL: Human Kinetics Press.

Nicholls, J. G., & Nelson, J. R. (1992). Students' conceptions of controversial knowledge. *Journal of Educational Psychology, 84*, 224–230.

Nicholls, J. G., Nelson, J. R., & Gleaves, K. (1992). *Students' perceptions of the consequences of studying controversial versus noncontroversial matters.* Unpublished manuscript.

Nicholls, J. G., & Thorkildsen, T. A. (1988). Children's distinctions among matters of intellectual convention, logic, fact, and personal preference. *Child Development, 59*, 939–949.

Nicholls, J. G., & Thorkildsen, T. A. (1989). Intellectual conventions versus matters of substance: Elementary school students as curriculum theorists. *American Educational Research Journal, 26*, 533–544.

Noddings, N. (1983). *Caring: A feminine approach to ethics and moral education.* Berkeley: University of California Press.

Nolen, S. B., Haladyna, T. M., & Haas, N. S. (1992). Uses and abuses of standardized achievement test scores. *Educational Measurement: Issues and Practices, 11*, 9–15.

Nucci, L. P. (1985). Children's conceptions of morality, societal convention, and religious prescription. In C. G. Harding (Ed.), *Moral dilemmas* (pp. 137–174). Chicago: Precedent.

Osborn, J. (1984). Workbooks that accompany basal reading programs. In G. R. Duffy, L. R. Roehler, & J. Mason (Eds.), *Comprehension instruction: Perspectives and suggestions* (pp. 163–186). New York: Longman.

Page, R. N. (1991). *Lower-track classrooms: Curricular and cultural perspective.* New York: Teachers College Press.

Pascarella, E. T., Walberg, H. J., Junker, L. K., & Haertel, G. D. (1981). Continuing motivation in science for early and late adolescents. *American Educational Research Journal, 18,* 439–452.

Perry, W. G., Jr. (1970). *Forms of intellectual and ethical development in the college years.* New York: Holt, Rinehart & Winston.

Piaget, J. (1972). Intellectual evolution from adolescence to adulthood. *Human Development, 15,* 1–12.

Power, F. C., Higgins, A., & Kohlberg, L. (1989). *Lawrence Kohlberg's approach to moral education.* New York: Columbia University Press.

Reason, P. (1988). *Human inquiry in action: Developments in new paradigm research.* London: Sage.

Resnick, L. B. (1988). Teaching mathematics as an ill-structured discipline. In R. I. Charles & E. A. Silver (Eds.), *The teaching and assessing of mathematical problem solving* (pp. 32–60). Hillsdale, NJ: Erlbaum.

Rorty, R. (1983). Method and morality. In N. Haan, R. N. Bellah, P. Rabinow, & W. M. Sullivan (Eds.), *Social science as moral inquiry* (pp. 155–176). New York: Columbia University Press.

Rousseau, J-J. (1911). *Emile, or education* (B. Foxley, Trans.). London: J. M. Dent. (Original work published 1762)

Sarason, S. B. (1971). *The culture of the school and the problem of change.* Boston: Allyn & Bacon.

Sarason, S. B. (1990). *The predictable failure of school reform: Can we change course before it's too late?* San Francisco: Jossey-Bass.

Sarason, S. B., Davidson, K., & Blatt, B. (1962). *The preparation of teachers: An unstudied problem.* New York: Wiley.

Schubert, W. H., & Lopez Schubert, A. L. (1981). Toward curricula that are of, by, and therefore for students. *Journal of Curriculum Theorizing, 3,* 239–251.

Shannon, P. (1983). The use of commercial reading materials in American elementary schools. *Reading Research Quarterly, 19,* 68–85.

Siegel, H. (1988). *Educating reason: Rationality critical thinking and education.* New York: Routledge.

Silva, T., & Nicholls, J. G. (in press). College students as writing theorists, *Contemporary Educational Psychology.*

Sosniak, L. A., & Perlman, C. L. (1990). Secondary education by the book. *Journal of Curriculum Studies, 22,* 427–442.

Stevens, R. J., Madden, N. A., Slavin, R. E., & Farnish, A. M. (1987). Cooperative integrated reading and composition: Two field experiments. *Reading Research Quarterly, 22,* 433–454.

Thomas, L. (1974). *The lives of a cell: Notes of a biology watcher.* New York: Viking.

Thomas, L. (1982, March 14). The art of teaching science. *New York Times Magazine*, pp. 89–93.

Thorkildsen, T. A. (1989a). Justice in the classroom: The student's view. *Child Development, 60*, 427–442.

Thorkildsen, T. A. (1989b). Pluralism in children's reasoning about social justice. *Child Development, 60*, 965–972.

Thorkildsen, T. A. (1991). Defining social goods and distributing them fairly: The development of conceptions of fair testing practices. *Child Development, 62*, 852–862.

Thorkildsen, T. A., & Schmahl, C. (1991, April). *Urban students' conceptions of fair testing practices*. Paper presented at the meeting of the American Educational Research Association, Chicago.

Toulmin, S. (1990). *Cosmopolis: The hidden agenda of modernity*. New York: The Free Press.

Turiel, E. (1983). *The development of social knowledge: Morality and convention*. New York: Cambridge University Press.

Wagner, B. J. (1976). *Dorothy Heathcote: Drama as a learning medium*. Washington, DC: National Educational Association.

Waller, W. (1932). *The sociology of teaching*. New York: Wiley.

Weiner, B. (1979). A theory of motivation for some classroom experiences. *Journal of Educational Psychology, 71*, 3–25.

Westbrook, R. B. (1991). *John Dewey and American democracy*. Ithaca, NY: Cornell University Press.

Willinsky, J. (1990). *The new literacy: Redefining reading and writing in the schools*. New York: Routledge.

Willis, P. (1977). *Learning to labor: How working class kids get working class jobs*. New York: Columbia University Press.

Wodke, K. H., Harper, F., Schommer, M., & Brunelli, P. (1989). How standardized is school testing? An exploratory observational study of standardized group testing in kindergarten. *Educational Evaluation and Policy Analysis, 11*, 223–235.

Woodson, C. G. (1990). *The mis-education of the Negro*. Trenton, NJ: Africa World Press. (Original work published 1933)

Zola, J. (1990). Be prepared: Using controversial topics or methods in the classroom. *ESR Journal: Educating for Social Responsibility, 1*, 101–106.

Zorn, E. (1987, October 11). Pupils in Naperville are going through a rough spell. *Chicago Tribune*, pp. 7–8.

Index

Active learning, 185
African-American students, approach to
knowledge and, 178–182
Alternative schools, 101–103
American Educational Research Associa-
tion, 188
Anderson, L. M., 196n1
Ashton-Warner, Sylvia, 111
Assertive Discipline program, 53–63
described, 53–56
punishment in, 54, 57, 59
teacher adaptation to, 59–63, 187–188
Attribution theory, 18–19
Authority. *See* Social authority

Barber, B., 192, 206n10
Bennett, William, 41
Berkowitz, M., 200n5
Best, R., 185
Bingo game, 15–17
Blatt, B., 197n2
Bloom, Benjamin, 86
Bossert, S. T., 197n2–3
Bowles, S., 198n9
Brainstorming, 72
Britton, J., 115, 202n4
Brunelli, P., 198n4
Busch, Cathy L., 180–182, 204n3

Calkins, L. M., x, 200n1, 201n5, 202n4
Canter, Lee, 55, 63, 199n1–2
Chanoff, D., 103
Charles, C. M., 199n1
Cheating, 32–34, 37
collaborative learning vs., 44–46, 48–50,
51
competence and, 32–34, 37
copying as, 22, 32–34, 37, 44–45

discussion of, 46–47
tests and, 40, 42, 44–50
Checkers, 47
Cleary, Beverly, 104
Clifford, James, 195n1, 197n1
Cobb, P., 198n5, 202n1, 204n3
Cognitive development
concept of authority and, 66–67
scientific exploration and, 130
Cohen, D. K., 204n3
Cole, M., x
Collaborative learning, 8, 18
cheating vs., 44–46, 48–50, 51
curriculum theory and, 91, 100–103
opportunities for, 50–51
in science, 94–96
student attitudes toward, 47–48, 50–51
tests vs., 44–51
College
student attitudes toward education and,
184
student attitudes toward knowledge
and, 172–173
Commission on Excellence in Education
(1983), 41
Communication
drama and, 148–159
of experience, 108–109, 111
language and symbols in, 89–91
Comparison, social, 19–20, 31–32, 164–
170, 175
Competence, 17, 27–39, 163–177
cheating and, 32–34, 37
class hierarchy and, 4, 6, 29, 30–32, 75–79
cooperation and, 30, 44–45
egotism and, 166, 169, 174–175
evaluation of, 29–30
grades and, 38–39, 77, 163–164, 174–175

About the Authors

John Nicholls grew up in New Zealand. He obtained teacher certification from Wellington Teachers College and his Ph.D. from Victoria University of Wellington. He has been a public school and university teacher in New Zealand. In the United States, he has taught educational psychology at the University of Illinois at Champaign-Urbana, Purdue University, and the University of Illinois at Chicago, where he presently teaches. He used to gain a sense of adventure from finding new ways up New Zealand's mountains with friends. Working on this book has proven a more than satisfactory substitute.

Susan Hazzard grew up in Pittsburgh. Her bachelor's and master's degrees in education are from Purdue University. She has taught second and third grades since 1968 in West Lafayette, Indiana. She taught a process approach to science at Purdue in 1973 and has conducted various teacher workshops. Her commitment to teaching includes participation in local branches of teachers' organizations. She has especially enjoyed working with children from many nations, even though—as with the class described in this book—often three quarters of the students leave the school district in the course of three years.